Voluntary Organizations and Public Service Delivery

Routledge Studies in the Management of Voluntary and Non-Profit Organizations

SERIES EDITOR: STEPHEN P. OSBORNE (UNIVERSITY OF EDINBURGH, UK)

This series presents innovative work grounded in new realities, addressing issues crucial to an understanding of the contemporary world. This is the world of organised societies, where boundaries between formal and informal, public and private, local and global organizations have been displaced or have vanished, along with other nineteenth century dichotomies and oppositions. Management, apart from becoming a specialized profession for a growing number of people, is an everyday activity for most members of modern societies.

Similarly, at the level of enquiry, culture and technology, and literature and economics, can no longer be conceived as isolated intellectual fields; conventional canons and established mainstreams are contested. Management, Organization and Society addresses these contemporary dynamics of transformation in a manner that transcends disciplinary boundaries, with books that will appeal to researchers, student and practitioners alike.

Voluntary Organisations and Public Service Delivery

Edited by Ian Cunningham
and Philip James

Routledge
Taylor & Francis Group
New York   London

First published 2011
by Routledge
270 Madison Ave, New York, NY 10016

Simultaneously published in the UK
by Routledge
2 Park Square, Milton Park, Abingdon, Oxon OX14 4RN

Routledge is an imprint of the Taylor & Francis Group, an informa business

© 2011 Taylor & Francis

Typeset in Sabon by IBT Global.
Printed and bound in the United States of America on acid-free paper by IBT Global.

Library of Congress Cataloging-in-Publication Data
Voluntary organizations and public service delivery / edited by Ian Cunningham and
    Philip James.
      p. cm. — (Routledge studies in the management of voluntary and non-profit
organizations ; 14)
    Includes bibliographical references and index.
    ISBN 978-0-415-87473-1
      1. Social service—Contracting out. 2. Public welfare—Contracting out. 3. Volunteer
workers in social service.   4. Nonprofit organizations—Management.   I. Cunningham,
Ian, 1964–   II. James, Philip.
    HV41.V65 2011
    658.4'058—dc22
    2010037995

ISBN13: 978-0-415-87473-1 (hbk)
ISBN13: 978-0-203-82928-8 (ebk)

Contents

PART IV
Work Experiences in an Era of Outsourcing

PART V
Conclusions

Tables

Part I

Introduction

1 Outsourcing and Voluntary Sector Employment

Understanding the Connections

Ian Cunningham and Philip James

INTRODUCTION

The outsourcing of the delivery of public services has formed a significant element of government policy in Britain with regard to public sector reform over the last three decades. Commencing under the post-1979 Conservative governments, it continued to be pursued enthusiastically by Labour Governments during the period from 1997, while also being adopted more widely internationally, most notably in Anglo-Saxon countries.

This focus on outsourcing has come to encompass a considerable emphasis, again both domestically and internationally, on the use of voluntary sector organisations to deliver services, particularly, but not exclusively, in the broad area of social care (Banting, 2000; Evans, Richmond, and Sheilds, 2005). An emphasis which has reflected the alleged virtues of such organisations, relative to their public sector counterparts, and a perception that their usage in this way is more politically acceptable than the transference of service provision to private, for-profit, ones (Davies, 2007).

Inevitably, this policy of outsourcing to the voluntary sector has attracted much debate. Its desirability in terms of both the efficiency and quality of service delivery has, for example, received a good deal of attention, as has the nature of the market-based relations that it has served to generate (Cunningham, 2008). The same is true of the implications it has for the independence of voluntary organisations and hence their capacity to act as lobbyists and advocates and as a source of innovative ideas and practices (Wainwright, Clark, Griffith, Jochum, and Wilding, 2006; Charities Commission, 2007).

At the same time, however, what is also apparent is that relatively little systematic attention has been paid in these debates to the implications that outsourcing has for the employment policies and practices of voluntary organisations and the work experiences of those working in them. This lack of attention can be viewed as both surprising and problematic given the labour-intensive nature of public service work since this feature means that the capacity of organisations, whether public, private, or voluntary, to deliver services effectively is intimately connected to such factors as their ability to recruit and retain staff with appropriate skills and qualifications and the degree to which they are able to provide terms and conditions and employment relationships more generally, that support adequate levels of staff commitment, satisfaction, and motivation.

The present volume is therefore centrally concerned with addressing this lack of attention to the employment implications of the current policy thrust toward the outsourcing of the delivery of public services to voluntary organisations. More specifically, it centres attention on the following two key issues:

a) How the process of outsourcing is affecting the internal and external labour markets of voluntary organisations; and
b) The way in which employers, employees, and their representatives in the voluntary sector are dealing with, and responding to, the employment-related challenges posed by the sector's growing involvement in market-based outsourcing.

ORIGINS AND STRUCTURE OF THE VOLUME

As a first stage in the production of the volume, a range of potential contributors were invited to contribute papers to a colloquium held at the University of Strathclyde in April 2008. This invitation received a positive response, and a number of the contributions which follow are, in fact, revised versions of the papers given at this event, namely those by the editors, Short, Clarke and Wilding, Davies, Parry and Kelliher, and Hurrell and Greer and their colleagues.

The Strathclyde colloquium served to reinforce the value of producing an edited volume. It was, however, felt that the nature and operation of employer recruitment processes and policies merited greater attention given available evidence indicating that voluntary organisations are often facing difficulties in obtaining the staff they need. Therefore a chapter by Scholarios and Burt was commissioned to address this issue. In addition, on reflection, it was felt that the comparative element introduced by the contribution by Greer et al. via an Anglo-German comparison should be strengthened as a means of better locating British developments in a wider international context and thereby shedding greater light on how far they reflect, or differ from, those occurring in other countries. To this end, further contributions were invited from US (Smith), Canadian (Baines), and Australian (McDonald and Charlesworth) scholars.

Taken together, the contributions so assembled are seen to provide, as intended, a rich and varied collection of analyses that differ widely in their foci and modes of analysis, and which go a long way toward addressing the lack of attention that has hitherto been paid to the employment consequences of the current trend to outsource the delivery of public services to voluntary sector organisations. Although inevitably they can be seen to contain lines of analysis that overlap to a greater or lesser extent, these contributions do for the most part focus on one of the following three themes: policy and labour market contexts, employment policies and practices in the voluntary sector, and work experiences in an era of outsourcing. As a result, at the collective level, the contributions provide analyses that encompass the consideration of macro-level labour and policy issues; 'middle ground' explorations of developments relating to how organisations recruit, manage, and develop their human resources; and more micro-based examinations of how such developments have impacted voluntary sector staff.

POLICY AND LABOUR MARKET CONTEXTS

Three of the chapters, those by Davies, Clark and Wilding, and Short, can be identified as being centrally concerned with the provision of such contextual analysis.

In the first of these chapters, Davies initially examines the nature and dimensions of outsourcing to the voluntary sector, as well as the way in which these have changed. In doing so he highlights how the evolution of outsourcing has resulted in a situation in which more than 70 percent of UK social care is now provided by voluntary, or to a much lesser extent private, providers. Davies then demonstrates how this profound shift in the role that such providers play has been intimately connected to policy developments under post-1997 Labour Governments, which saw them attempt, in his words, to '*graft a neo-liberal programme of public service reform on to a social democratic tradition.*' He further shows how this attempt was informed by both 'technocratic' rationales, encompassing the propounding of a series of alleged superior attributes of voluntary sector providers, alongside a more general endorsement of the role that a combination of market choice and discipline could play in improving service delivery, and a 'marketing' rationale concerning the greater acceptability of outsourcing to the public and the Labour Party. At the same time, however, Davies notes that there is little hard evidence to support the alleged attributes of such providers or to show that their greater usage has improved service outcomes. He also, somewhat ironically, draws attention to growing concerns about the potential for these attributes, such as closeness to clients and innovativeness, to be undermined by a contracting marketplace that reduces the independence of voluntary organisations, both by increasing their dependence on contract income from public sector funders and by encompassing a tendency to marginalise smaller organisations.

Against the background of this growth in the role of the voluntary sector in delivering public services, the chapter by Clark and Wilding examines trends in the size, scope, sectoral and organisational location, and characteristics of the UK voluntary sector workforce, as well as the skills gaps and shortages that exist within it. Their data shows that the size of this work-force has increased significantly in recent years, rising by nearly a quarter in ten years, and reveals that nearly 40 percent of staff work part-time, 10 per-cent are on temporary contracts, nearly a third are employed in workplaces with fewer than ten employees, more than two-thirds are women, and more than half are employed in social work activities. Clark and Wilding further indicate that the sector experiences significant recruitment problems and skill shortages, problems and shortages, which, it is argued, *'continue to inhibit the sector's ability to deliver public services,'* and that are seen to be linked, at one level to insufficient training and development activity, and at a more general level to short-term funding mechanisms that fail to address the *'core costs associated with being a good employer.'* The authors' chap-ter ends by drawing attention to the risk that an approach centred on vol-untary organisations demonstrating their ability to deliver services more efficiently and cheaply will, in the forthcoming 'era of austerity,' create a risk of a 'race to the bottom' in terms of cost and quality.

Last, in terms of setting the policy and labour market context, Short in his chapter sheds light on the extent to which trade unions have a presence and exert an influence over the labour market positions of vol-untary sector workers and hence the employment policies and practices of voluntary sector organisations. Short focuses particularly on the case of the union he works for, UNISON. His analysis commences by draw-ing attention to how UNISON's membership has increased both rapidly and significantly in the sector against the background of the growth of employment in it. He also, however, notes that overall union membership density is estimated to stand at around only 25 percent, and that much of the growth in membership that has occurred stems not from 'organic growth' but from the transfer of members out of the public sector. In addition, unions are further noted to face a variety of challenges in seek-ing to improve this situation. These challenges include employer opposi-tion to union recognition, the problems of accessing potential members in a workforce that is often based in small organisations or work units, the difficulty of obtaining sufficient numbers of workplace stewards in the absence of adequate employer-provided facility time and/or difficulties in utilising it, and the consequent need for full-time union organisers to often devote a significant amount of their time to individual representa-tion rather than organising activities. In the case of UNISON, however, Short argues that it has developed a number of initiatives that are begin-ning to better address these challenges and thereby improve recruitment and member participation and commitment. These initiatives include the launching of campaigns focused on occupational issues and professional concerns, rather than narrower workplace ones, the employment of a growing number of organisers, the creation of national branches in some larger charities, the development of learning partnerships with employers, and the launching of 'virtual branches.'

EMPLOYMENT POLICIES AND PRACTICES

Another three chapters in the volume, those of Parry and Kelliher, Hurrell et al., and Burt and Scholarios, focus attention on the employment policies and practices of voluntary sector organisations and how these have been changing.

The chapter by Parry and Kelliher focuses on how government has acted to shape the development of human resource management within voluntary sector substance misuse providers. Drawing on evidence from a series of empirical studies, Parry and Kelliher show that new legislation and other government policies had, both directly and indirectly, prompted such providers to introduce a number of reforms to their existing human resource arrangements. Workforce standards and skills agendas, for example, were found to have not only led to a greater focus on staff development, but also encouraged employers to improve their record keeping and to develop job descriptions and specifications. Meanwhile, organisational growth, arising from both increased funding and the winning of additional contracts, and the need for enhanced levels of professionalism in order to improve competitiveness and work in partnership with the statutory sector, were also found to have led indirectly to the adoption of a more professional approach to human resource management in general and the establishment of more coherent policies and practices, often on the basis of mimicking those used by public sector organisations. Indeed, Parry and Kelliher argue that this process of reform, and the role of government in prompting it, serves to cast doubt on whether it is any longer valid to see the voluntary sector as lacking a sophisticated approach to human resource management.

The chapter by Hurrell et al. concentrates more narrowly on the recruitment policies and practices of voluntary organisations and more specifically on those relating to the recruitment of graduates. The authors start by observing that whereas outsourcing has, by increasing the need for voluntary sector employers to be more business-like, served to generate an increased demand for graduates, employers continue to confront difficulties in recruiting them, notwithstanding the increasing supply. The authors then go on to explore why this is the case. Drawing on secondary evidence, they conclude that these difficulties do not straightforwardly stem from the lower pay on offer because there are grounds for believing that many *'purist'* graduates seek employment that aligns with their own values. Rather, they conclude that the difficulties arise from *'systems'* and *'administrative'* failures. The former are seen to encompass misconceptions among graduates about the job opportunities available in the sector that reflect the failure of employers in the sector to communicate them, via such means as engaging with graduates, students, and university careers personnel. The latter failings, in contrast, are argued to be attributable to a *funding deficit*, encompassing both inadequate and uncertain funding, that acts to limit the capacity of voluntary sector organisations to fill needed graduate positions, while also damaging the sustainability and viability of intermediary bodies that could help to address the recruitment problems.

Burt and Scholarios's chapter, as already mentioned, focuses attention on the recruitment policies and processes of voluntary organisations more generally and the imperatives acting to shape them. Drawing on the findings of four comparative case studies, as well as available secondary evidence, the analysis reveals that such processes seem to embody both marked similarities and differences. The authors further point to the fact that these similarities and differences reflect the influence of a range of imperatives, arising in part from the engagement of such organisations in the delivery of public services, which serve to shape recruitment needs and the way that they are addressed. As a result, their analysis highlights how the recruitment policies and processes are intimately and dynamically connected to, although not straightforwardly determined by, the specific labour and 'product' market contexts confronting organisations.

WORK EXPERIENCES IN AN ERA OF OUTSOURCING

The remaining six chapters of the volume, the largest proportion, all concentrate centrally on examining how outsourcing has impacted the working lives of those employed in the voluntary sector. Two chapters, those by Cunningham and James, and by Cunningham, explore this issue from a domestic, British perspective. A third chapter, that by Greer and his colleagues, does so through the lens of an Anglo-German perspective. The remaining three chapters concentrate on developments in Canada, the United States, and Australia, respectively.

In their chapter, Cunningham and James draw on existing and new empirical evidence to examine how far market-based contracting, and its financial implications, has prompted organisations to reform work processes and arrangements, and the pay and other rewards offered to staff. In doing so, they focus particular attention on whether the recent, post-1997 policy context of outsourcing, and particularly the emphasis placed within it on full-cost recovery and the establishment of longer-term contractual relations, has acted to challenge the previously observed tendency for the transfer of public service work to be associated with the creation of lower levels of worker security, including with respect to pay and other conditions of employment, job roles, and vulnerability to redundancy. The findings they report point to a relatively limited uptake of either full-cost recovery or longer-term commissioning and, against this backdrop more generally provide little support for the thesis that current outsourcing is having a more benign impact on voluntary sector workers. They further suggest that in the present economic environment this situation is unlikely to change.

Cunningham, in his own chapter, effectively builds on the chapter written with James by exploring the experiences of workers transferred from one voluntary organisation to another as a result of re-tendering exercises and, in particular, examines how such transfers impact their psychological contracts. His findings reveal a significant degree of resilience in such contracts, notwithstanding the provision by employers of flawed and incomplete information regarding employment rights, and against the backloth of staff continuing to exhibit high levels of commitment to their client groups and even the new employer. In seeking to explain these findings, Cunningham argues that they are attributable to the roles played by a number of moderating factors, such as the protection offered to terms and conditions through the Transfer of Undertakings (Protection of Employment) Regulations, management actions to maintain service quality and alleviate staff concerns, and, to a lesser extent, union activity, which have served to protect key elements of worker psychological contracts. Cunningham, nevertheless, concludes that the data obtained raises concerns regarding the sustainability of this stability in psychological contracts should successive re-tendering exercises impact pay, working practices, and service quality.

The Anglo-German comparative study provided by Greer and his colleagues focuses on employment in outsourced welfare-to-work. Their analysis both highlights the potential for outsourcing to impact negatively on wages, job security, and employee well-being and draws attention to the way in which outsourcing has supported, in both Germany and Britain, the emergence of a huge diversity in terms and conditions, in part as a result of employment moving away from the coverage of public sector collective bargaining arrangements. The analysis also, however, suggests that a 'race to the bottom' among contractors is not an inevitable result. Rather, the authors argue that much depends on such factors as the performance of individual organisations, employer policies, the character of particular funding regimes, and the extent of worker representation. Indeed, and more generally, the authors argue that it is increasingly the nature of funding regimes, rather than industrial relations systems, which is determining the direction of labour-management relations within voluntary organisations involved in contracting for the delivery of public services.

Baines's chapter examines how the delivery of social care services has been changing in Canada and the implications of this change for those working for not-for-profit organisations. Her examination shows that, against the backdrop of the removal of federal government standards and funding, all of the country's provinces and territories have embraced market-orientated restructuring of service provision, while ironically legitimating it by reference to a wider human rights discourse centred on the need to develop less rigid and oppressive services. Such re-structuring, Baines argues, has resulted in a growth of managerialism and a related standardisation of front-line work, reduced staffing levels and increased work intensification, curtailment of opportunities for shared decision-making, rapid expansion in the use of cheaper, precarious forms of employment, and an increase in (both voluntary and involuntary) unpaid overtime working among a largely feminised workforce. This re-structuring has also, she notes, led to various forms of worker resistance, including social union mobilisation and various types of self-exploitation aimed at protecting clients and services and has occurred, in an echo of Greer et al.'s point about the influence exerted by the nature of funding regimes, alongside the development of wide variations in service entitlements and levels of social care provision across the country.

Developments in Australia identified by McDonald and Charlesworth in their chapter with regard to how voluntary sector care workers have been affected by market-orientated re-structuring bear many similarities with those reported by Baines. These developments are also noted by the authors to be the outcome of similar processes, notably a rise in managerialist employer strategies, cost-based contracting arrangements, and, more generally, inadequate levels of government funding. McDonald and Charlesworth, however, in echoes of parts of Baines's analysis, also highlight how the highly gendered nature of care work has contributed importantly to the existence of labour market and policy contexts that are facilitative of the undervaluing of care work and a lack of regulation of the terms and conditions under which it is carried out. They point out, for example, that not only have many of those engaged in such work been excluded from the coverage of national (and state) wage setting arrangements, but that there are good grounds for seeing this lack of institutional recognition, as well as the inadequate levels at which care services are funded, as stemming from the feminised nature of the workforce that delivers them and a related perception that 'care work' is not 'real work.' This perception is seen to be compounded by the 'deep ambivalence many community service workers have about pursuing their industrial rights.'

Finally, in the fourth part, Smith's chapter, focusing attention on the United States, reveals a range of developments which echo those of previous chapters and hence further points to the fact that a substantial degree of commonality exists internationally with regard to how current trends toward the market-based outsourcing of public services to voluntary sector organisations are impacting the work experiences of staff. More specifically, having traced the way in which government contracting with voluntary agencies has evolved (and expanded) since the 1960s, Smith highlights how this process of development has not only served to increase the number of such agencies, as well as the numbers employed by them, but has further acted to engender a variety of employment-related changes. He observes, for example, that government imposed performance management regimes and standards have promoted a process of professionalisation within voluntary agencies that has increased their demand for qualified professionals who understand programme evaluation, information technology systems, financial management and strategic planning, and has also led to important changes in the role of volunteers, the backgrounds and qualifications of chief executives, and the composition of governing boards. He further, and again in line with the analyses provided in other chapters, draws attention to the way in which this desire by service funders to ensure appropriate standards of performance and accountability on the part of agencies has acted to engender a greater standardisation of staff work roles and hence served to reduce worker discretion.

CONCLUDING COMMENTS

As can be seen from the above summaries, the analyses that follow encompass many points of similarity in terms of the evolving policy landscapes relating to the voluntary sector's engagement in the delivery of public services internationally, the ways in which employers are configuring service delivery against the background of these landscapes, and the way in which this process of re-configuration is impacting the work roles and experiences of those employed in the sector. At the same time, however, the summaries also to some extent highlight that points of dissimilarity and contradiction also exist. The summaries make clear, for example, that the outsourcing of public services cannot be seen to lead inevitably to either a reduction in employment conditions or to a deterioration in the attitudes and commitment of staff. They also indicate that trends in employment conditions may simultaneously encompass a deterioration in substantive terms and conditions and an enhancement of development opportunities to staff and the establishment more generally of improved human resource 'processes.' Indeed, it is further clear that the nature of outsourcing, and its impact on workers, can vary across different types of organisations, different subsectors, and even, within federal nations, different parts of the country.

A central task of the volume's concluding chapter is therefore both to trace these points of similarity, difference, and contradiction in more detail and to identify the dynamics underlying them. Such an analysis seems a necessary pre-condition to gaining, to return to the title of the present chapter, an adequate theoretical and empirical understanding of the connections that exist between the outsourcing of public services to voluntary sector organisations and the changing nature of employment within them. This understanding is not only needed from a purely academic perspective but because of its policy relevance to the delivery of public services, given their labour-intensive nature and the extent to which their provision, both in quantity and quality terms, is therefore crucially influenced by the ability of those providing them to secure and retain appropriately qualified and committed staff.

BIBLIOGRAPHY

Banting, K. (2000). *The nonprofit sector in Canada: Roles and relationships*. Published for the School of Policy Studies, Queen's University. Montreal: McGill-Queen's University Press.

Charities Commission. (2007). *Stand and deliver: The future for charities providing public services*. London: Charities Commission.

Cunningham, I. (2008). *Employment relations in the voluntary sector*. London: Routledge.

Davies, S. (2007). *Third sector provision of local government and health services. Unison*, May.

Evans, B., Richmond, T., and Shields, J. (2005). Structuring neoliberal governance: The nonprofit sector, emerging new modes of control, and the marketisation of service delivery. *Policy and Society*, 24 (1), 73–97.

Wainwright, S., Clark, J., Griffith, M., Jochum, V., and Wilding, K. (2006). *The UK voluntary sector almanac, 2006*. London: NCVO Publications.

Part II

Policy and Labour Market Contexts

2 Outsourcing and the Voluntary Sector

A Review of the Evolving Policy Landscape

Steve Davies

INTRODUCTION

Voluntary sector provision of public services in the UK is not a new development. What is undeniably new, however, is wholehearted government support for the shift in voluntary sector provision from a specialist niche into the mainstream. This is a key element in the latest phase of public sector reform and, as such, has been described as *'a revolution every bit as far reaching as the privatisation of nationalised industries under Margaret Thatcher'* (Mathiason, 2005). Four key differences separate the way that the state relates to the voluntary sector today, compared to the situation before 1997: the scale of funding; the range of services provided by the sector; the method of funding the sector; and the political approach of the government.

This chapter sets the current debate around outsourcing public services to the voluntary sector within the broader context of change and continuity. It examines what is new and what is not in government policy toward the sector (and how this developed and why); the response of the sector in terms of its embrace of outsourcing (and the effects); and its relationship with government. The first section discusses the nature, dimensions, and dynamics of outsourcing to the voluntary sector, including the size of the sector, the extent of government funding, and the range of services provided. The second section examines the evolution of government policy in the area and its connection to the government's wider programme of public sector reform; and the third section considers the likely impact that this growth of outsourcing will have on the quality of public services, voluntary organisations themselves, and the relationship between the sector as a whole and the state.

NATURE, DIMENSIONS AND DYNAMICS OF OUTSOURCING TO THE VOLUNTARY SECTOR

The UK voluntary sector has grown considerably in the last decade. Today, it represents a substantial and growing area of the economy, with more than 600,000 workers (The chapter by Clark and Wilding in this volume provides precise and up-to-date workforce figures) (National Council for Voluntary Organizations [NCVO], 2009a).

The NCVO (2009a) estimates that in 2006–07 there were 170,905 general charities—an increase of 6,800 over the previous year (870,000 organisations in its broader category of civil society). The general charities had a total annual income of £33 billion in 2006–07, up from £31 billion in 2005–06 (NCVO, 2009b; NCVO, 2008a). Of this earned income, £17 billion accounts for more than 50 percent of charities' income—largely a result of contracts for the provision of public services—whereas income from grants, donations, and legacies represents 41 percent of total income (NCVO, 2009b).

In recent years there has been a large increase in the funding from the public sector. Income from statutory sources in 2006–07 totaled £12 billion, a year-on-year increase of 5 percent (NCVO, 2009a). This source now accounts for more than a third of all income received by the sector. More than 70 percent of all interactions between government and the voluntary sector take place at local level (Local Government Association, Improvement Development Agency and Local Government Information Unit [LGA, IDeA, and LGIU], 2006). Therefore it is not surprising that the £5.7 billion from local government is the largest single source of statutory income (47 percent). Central government's contribution is rising but in 2006–07 was £3.3 billion (NCVO, 2009a).

Much of this recent growth has come from the outsourcing of public services, which began under the Conservatives. This is particularly the case for certain public services such as personal social care and social housing. However, despite the increased involvement of the sector with the state, particularly in public service delivery, the NCVO (2009a) estimate that three quarters of voluntary organisations (around 117,000) receive no public money at all. The NCVO (2008a) categorise charities into three types: *onlookers* which do not seek for or rely on income from government; *associates* with important funding relationships, but perhaps not critically dependent; and *full partners* that rely heavily on government funding.

The state has a financial relationship with some 40,000 voluntary organisations, of which 27,000 rely on statutory funding for 75 percent of their income. Most of these are medium or large organisations (NCVO, 2009a). The largest organisations (those with an income of £1 million or more) receive more than three quarters of all the statutory funding provided to the sector. But it is the medium-sized organisations (with an income between £100,000 and £1 million) that are most dependent on the state. While they receive a smaller proportion of the overall government budget for the sector, this represents almost 40 percent of their total income (NCVO, 2009a).

Labour opened up the range of services likely to be delivered by the voluntary sector. In the past—at least since the creation of the welfare state— where public services were provided by the voluntary sector, it was usually in niche specialist areas or to fill in gaps in public provision. Previous

Conservative governments started to move away from this but with more of a focus on private provision and in fairly limited areas, such as in social care. The Commission for Social Care Inspection (CSCI) reported that in 1992 only 2 percent of home care hours in England were delivered by the independent sector (comprising the private and voluntary sectors), whereas this had risen to 73 percent by 2005 (CSCI, 2006). Conservative Government policy in the 1990s combined cutbacks in local government funding with an encouragement (an actual obligation in England) to increasingly outsource the provision of home care. A massive shift to the private and voluntary sector occurred, reflected in the ownership of registered domiciliary care agencies: by March 2006, 80 percent were in the private or voluntary sectors (CSCI, 2006). All political parties remain committed to further outsourcing, so that this process is set to continue (Carey, 2008).

More than 70 percent of social care is now provided by the private and voluntary sectors (Department of Health, 2006a). The Department of Health (2006b) provisionally estimates that, in England alone, there are more than 26,000 voluntary organisations delivering health and social care services, with a combined annual income of more than £13 billion.

The Charity Commission's survey report (Stand and Deliver, 2007) found that around a third (31 percent) of all public services delivered by charities are in health and social care, followed by education (15 percent) and children's services (14 percent). The NCVO (2009a) show that there are five subsectors in which voluntary organisations receive more than 50 percent of their income from statutory funding: employment and training (71 percent); law and advocacy (54 percent); education (52 percent); housing (51 percent); and social services (51 percent).

Within the overall growth in statutory funding, there is a 'strong comparative shift from grant funding to contract funding' (NCVO, 2008a, 32), and this shift has increased in pace in the last year for which data is available. The value to the voluntary sector of grants and contracts from statutory sources in 2006–07 was, respectively, £4.2 billion and £7.8 billion (NCVO, 2009a, 34). Grant-based statutory funding has been relatively flat for several years (NCVO, 2008a), suggesting that, whereas grants have not been cut much in value terms, statutory funders increasingly prefer to use contracts as the mechanism for additional funding for the sector. Therefore, grant levels have fallen as a proportion of income from the public sector and in 2006–07 were 31 percent of funding from central and local government (NCVO, 2009a).

THE EVOLUTION OF GOVERNMENT POLICY
TOWARD THE VOLUNTARY SECTOR

Labour has fundamentally altered the relationship between the voluntary sector and the state. This section outlines the development of government policy and the way that Labour has attempted to graft a neoliberal programme of public service reform onto a social democratic tradition while resolutely denying any ideological content to its approach. It also examines the government's view of the voluntary sector as an attractive lever for change in public service provision—for reasons that draw on both the neoliberal present and the social democratic past.

As outlined earlier, the provision of public services by the voluntary sector is not new—the sector provided many services before the creation of the welfare state. But in the present climate of what Suzi Leather, the Charity Commission chair, describes *as 'the all-party love-in with charities and the voluntary sector'* (Leather, 2007), it is well to remember the reasons for the creation of the welfare state in the first place. David Miliband (2006) put it very well. He said that the state did not 'squeeze out' 19th-century cooperative and charitable provision. On the contrary, the failure of the voluntary and market sectors demanded the development and then the expansion of state provision of public services, and it was:

> the growing problems of bankruptcy, inefficiency, and patchy provision within the third sector that necessitated the wider pooling of risk and the emergence of a welfare state.

Not only did charitable provision precede that of the state, but even after the creation of the welfare state, charitable provision continued in some areas—particularly in niche or specialist fields. This arrangement carried on for decades, but from the early 1990s and the subsequent election of successive Labour Governments from 1997, the state embraced the voluntary sector and assigned it a central role in public service provision that has not existed in modern times. There are a number of reasons for this, drawing on two contradictory political traditions: neoliberalism and social democracy.

NEOLIBERALISM AS IDEOLOGY-FREE PRAGMATISM

The new Labour Government came to office determined to confound its Conservative opponents and prove its economic competence. In an apparent effort to fend off potential critics, it pledged to abide by Conservative public expenditure plans for the first two years of the new administration. This disappointed traditional Labour supporters but was accepted as a tactical manoeuvre. Indeed, when first elected, New Labour was less hostile to the public sector and, after the first two years, committed to an expansion of public investment that rejected previous Conservative hostility to state provision.

The 1997 Labour party manifesto proclaimed that New Labour is 'a party of ideas and ideals but not outdated ideology. What counts is what works' (Labour Party, 1997). Blair repeatedly returned to this idea of a nonideological, technocratic pragmatism. Shortly after becoming prime minister, he made a speech in which he contrasted his objectives with those of his predecessors, declared that government should be *'pragmatic and rigorous about what does and does not work,'* and that the new government would *'find out what works, and we will support the successes and stop the failures'* (Blair, 1997). In 1999 the *Modernising Government* White Paper (Cabinet Office, 1999, 15) focused on the need for evidence-based policy:

> Government must be willing constantly to re-evaluate what it is doing so as to produce policies that really deal with problems; that are forward-looking and shaped by the evidence rather than a response to short-term pressures.

Once Labour was established in office, the reality of public-sector investment and reform under New Labour was very different. While emphasising its commitment to nonideological pragmatism, the government rapidly introduced a public sector reform programme with a strong neoliberal influence. The public sector was seen as locked in inefficiency and torpor with an underachieving and uncooperative workforce. After flirting with ideas of stake-holding (W. Hutton, 1995) and then partnership, the government repeatedly returned to the position that public sector problems require private sector or market solutions (Grimshaw, Vincent, and Willmott, 2002).

As a consequence, there was a wholesale acceptance of what Le Grand and Bartlett (1993) called public service 'quasi-markets' (albeit with some modifications to the Tory model, such as the replacement of Compulsory Competitive Tendering [CCT] with Best Value). Labour adopted the idea of an 'enabling state' using markets and contracts—the reinvention of government model associated with the influential American public administration theorists Osborne and Gaebler (1992). The state could then 'stick to the knitting' (Peters and Waterman, 1982) and focus on its 'core' activity as a commissioner, increasingly leaving 'peripheral' activities and service delivery to the private or voluntary sector.

THE VOLUNTARY SECTOR AS A LEVER FOR PUBLIC SERVICE REFORM

This approach had four levers (Cabinet Office, 2006b) to exert pressure: top-down from government itself (performance management); from citizens (choice and voice); from competition (markets); and capability and capacity building (for civil and public servants in central and local government). Key drivers in the model include the purchaser-provider split. competition and contestability, and market incentives to improve efficiency. One of the key principles is *'the promotion of alternative providers and greater choice'* (Blair, 2001), and the voluntary sector has an important role to play within that principle.

Labour's commitment to the notion that competition, markets, and choice are the mechanisms to improve public services intensified from 1997. Typical was the objective set out in the Local Government White Paper, *Strong and Prosperous Communities,* (Department for Communities and Local Government, 2006, 145):

> [T]o stimulate new markets in order to secure alternative provision and enable both commissioner and user choice in areas of local government which are currently uncontested or not fully contested . . . [and to] . . . increase the capacity and competitiveness in existing supply markets.

Public services are redefined as services funded by the public purse, rather than necessarily *delivered* by the public sector (Blair, 2006), and integrating the third and private sectors in the provision of public services is an important part of New Labour's concept of joined-up government (Clark, 2002). This reflects the continuing impact of the ideas of New Public Management and American public sector reformers like Osborne and Gambler (1992), with their emphasis on 'steering not rowing.' These ideas were previously highly influential on the Thatcher/Major governments, and the continuities can be seen by contrasting the views of ministers from the two periods. Nicholas Ridley (one of Mrs Thatcher's key ministers) predicted:

> a much more diverse pattern of provision in the future by a variety of different agencies working alongside local authorities. The role of the local authority will no longer be that of the universal provider. But it will continue to have a key role in ensuring that there is adequate provision. (Ridley, 1988, 16–17)

In the same vein, then Secretary of State for Business and Enterprise John Hutton (2006, 3) argued that:

> government must be ever sharper and more adept at creating and managing contestable forms of service delivery. Alternative providers, whether in the private, public, or third sectors, should be the norm, not the exception.

A change of prime minister did not lead to a change in policy. Writing in the *Financial Times*, Gordon Brown (2008, p. 9) noted:

> A greater diversity of providers, more choice, and in many areas more competition will continue to ensure that services that fail to deliver are legitimately challenged and standards are forced upwards.

In the context of the opening up of public services to market forces, ministers aim to place voluntary sector provision firmly in the mainstream, supplying services that were previously provided by the public sector. The government's Action Plan (Cabinet Office, 2006a) for third sector involvement in public services identified correctional services; employment services; children's services, education and training; health and social care services; and 'other' local services as the areas where there is the greatest potential for the sector to contribute (with the latter three being obvious areas for local authorities).

MORE THAN JUST GOOD FRIENDS: THE ATTRACTION OF THE VOLUNTARY SECTOR TO LABOUR

The NCVO describes the current relationship with government as 'the most favourable the sector has experienced' (NCVO, 2005). In fact all three major parties have fallen over one another to praise the sector and assure it of their good intentions. Stephen Bubb of the Association of Chief Executives of Voluntary Organizations (ACEVO), proclaimed:

> I suspect we're going to see a bidding war for the ear of the sector, which is a fantastic position to be in. We'll see which party can offer us the best deal. (Thomas, 2006)

While there is much continuity with the policy of previous Conservative administrations, there are also differences. The governments of Margaret Thatcher and John Major concentrated on economic restructuring, cutting public expenditure, and expanding the role of the private sector in public services delivery. The voluntary sector did not have much profile in this. The Conservatives had an instrumental approach to the sector, seeing it as a service agent, rather than a partner—and even then, often as a provider of last resort (Haugh and Kitson, 2007).

The attraction of the voluntary sector for New Labour links back to what Labour considers to be the weaknesses and failings of the public sector. As previously mentioned, senior figures in New Labour accepted the Conservatives' analysis of the public sector as having low productivity, providing inefficient and poor quality services, with public expenditure 'excessively burdensome to the economy' (Kelly, 2007, 1008), and while there are pockets of public service excellence, the absence of market mechanisms 'generates complacency, conservatism, and a failure to put the needs of citizens first' (Hindmoor, 2002, 290). Labour regarded public services as stuck in a one-size-fits-all 1945 model, desperately in need of reform (Blair, 2002). This came with a number of provisos, the main one being that Labour believed that there was a need for a major injection of funding into public services, but in the debate on New Labour's first Queen's speech, Tony Blair (Hansard, 1997) spelled out the price to be paid for this investment:

We have reached the limit of the public's willingness simply to fund an unreformed welfare system through ever higher tax and spending.

The involvement of the voluntary *and* private sectors as public service delivery agents was part of this reform process. New Labour's interest in the sector goes beyond simply using it as a delivery agent and is based on three elements. The sector is seen as: providing a solution to perceived problems of the public sector (Kelly, 2007), such as the professional rigidities and 'self-seeking behaviour' about which ministers complain; offering a series of positive attributes not present in the public sector; and fitting in with the policy priorities of the government.

The 2005 Labour Party manifesto praised the voluntary and community sector as 'innovative, efficient, and effective. Its potential for service delivery should be considered on equal terms' (Labour Party, 2005). Ministerial endorsement of the virtues of the third sector involves a cocktail of (sometimes contradictory) components. Not only is third sector provision supposedly more efficient and innovative than in-house provision, but it is also claimed to bring additional benefits related to its advocacy role, its influence on policy development, and its positive impact in deepening democratic engagement and strengthening civic society.

Labour believed that there were three ways in which public services could be improved by working with 'local communities and the local third sector': first, by involving those who use services in their design and delivery; second, public servants can mobilise people to help one another; third, civic society can help deliver public services itself (HM Government, 2009, 31).

There were tensions between the different roles urged on the third sector by government, which many organisations have recognised, but which ministers appeared to view as unproblematic. In addition the government also sometimes referred to 'independent' providers, thereby incorporating the involvement of private sector, for-profit providers into the discussion about voluntary sector provision of public services.

In one form or another, the various attributes (service provision, voice, contribution to civic society, and so on) assigned to the voluntary sector were repeatedly listed by ministers as reasons for a closer relationship between the sector and the state (Armstrong, 2006; Blair, 2006; Byrne, 2006; D. Miliband, 2006; E. Miliband, 2006). In his *Foreword* to the Treasury's Cross-cutting Review (HM Treasury, 2002, 3), then Chief Secretary to the Treasury Paul Boateng said:

[W]e look again to the voluntary and community sector to help us rekindle the spark of civic services that fires the building of strong civic communities; to reform the operation of public services and build a bridge between the needs of individuals living in those communities and the capacity of the state to improve their lives.

Another attraction that is rarely mentioned (except in reference to better value) is that services provided by the voluntary sector are seen as cheaper than in-house provision. This is a source of disquiet for some in the sector (NCVO, 2006), especially as it is regarded as mistaken in any event. The NCVO make the point that the sector's specialist services (which ministers admire so much) in areas of market failure or niche markets are likely to cost more rather than less as there are fewer economies of scale.

In addition, the Labour government saw the sector as an ally in its drive for 'localism' or decentralisation as part of its desire to create 'choice' and 'personalised services' (Armstrong, 2006). Ministers regarded the voluntary sector as better placed than the state to articulate the needs of local communities because it is locally embedded (Haugh and Kitson, 2007). Social exclusion and the environment are important priorities for the government, and the voluntary sector is seen as both active and experienced in these areas (Haugh and Kitson, 2007).

Many commentators have also noted that whereas the public often remains sceptical about the supposed benefits of transferring public service provision to the profit-making private sector, charities and not-for-profits retain a considerable amount of public trust (MacErlean, 2005; Mathiason, 2005; Caulkin, 2006). For example, referring to 'political and cultural barriers' to opening up children's services to the market, Pricewaterhouse-Coopers (2004, 10) observed:

> There are many reasons for this, including ethical concerns about extending models of service delivery to private organisations driven by a profit motive, concerns about the quality of alternative service providers who have been previously un-tested, and some unfavourable attitudes towards developing contestability.

In an acknowledgment to Labour's social democratic past, ministers highlight a link between current policy on the voluntary sector and the party's historic association with the co-operative movement (Brown, 2006). This plays well within the Labour Party and obviously presents political possibilities for public service reform that would not exist if the only option on the table was private sector provision funded by taxpayers' money.

Labour's relatively new enthusiasm for markets allowed it to develop what Burnham (2001) describes as a governing strategy of 'depoliticisation,' or the adoption of a rule-based system in contrast to a discretion-based or 'politicised' system of economic management. Such a strategy does not remove politics from the stage, but places *'at one remove the political character of decision-making'* (Burnham, 1999), leaving the state with arms length control but with the supposed benefit of being able to distance itself from the impact of the decision. Contracting out is a part of such an approach because it diminishes direct state control of the provision of public services via the use of markets and reliance on semi-independent or independent regulatory or audit bodies.

In the run-up to the 2010 general election, there has been something of a softening of the government's approach. Speaking at the King's Fund in September 2009, Health Secretary Andy Burnham declared the NHS to be the 'preferred provider' of health services (Department of Health, 2009). This provoked a furious response from the supporters of marketisation, including ACEVO and Julian Le Grand, who claimed that it would have *'a detrimental impact on the future stability of the voluntary sector'* (Asato et al., 2009). Ministers sought to calm troubled waters by emphasising that 'this does not represent a change in commissioning policy but signals an improvement in commissioning practice' (Hansard, 2009). In fact, Burnham's commitment was arguably just a robust development of the government's previous statement to the Public Administration Select Committee that it is *'not looking at a wholesale transfer of services to the third sector'* (PASC, 2008b, 3). This in turn recognised the Committee's observation that the debate 'should not be about transferring responsibility for delivering large areas of public service out of the State and into the third sector,' partly because *'third sector organisations are ill-equipped to provide universality and equity to service users'* (PASC, 2008a, 20). The Committee described this as

> a significant evolution of policy. The Government's position has moved from actively pursuing the transfer of services to allowing a more ready transfer 'where appropriate.' (PASC, 2008a, 21)

DEVOLUTION AND THE VOLUNTARY SECTOR

Labour's devolution programme has run in parallel with its turn toward the voluntary sector. In early 1999 the government created the Scottish Parliament (with a Scottish Executive—from 2007 known as the Scottish Government) and the National Assembly for Wales (and Welsh Assembly Government—WAG). With periods of suspension, Northern Ireland followed suit with its own Executive and Assembly (based on the 1998 power-sharing 'Good Friday Agreement').

Even before devolution, the voluntary sector had its own umbrella organisations within the UK countries complete with separate national identities and structures. The NCVO only operates in England, working closely with its equivalents in Scotland, Wales, and Northern Ireland—the Scottish Council for Voluntary Organisations (SCVO), the Wales Council for Voluntary Action (WCVA), and the Northern Ireland Council for Voluntary Action (NICVA).

Separate governmental structures have also developed. The Office of the Third Sector (OTS), set up in 2006, is responsible for policy development and delivery for England and has its own minister for the third sector (elevated from a parliamentary undersecretary to minister of state in June 2009). Other England-based programmes include the Compact, a national framework for government and sector relations; and various support programmes such as Futurebuilders England (now Social Investment Business), ChangeUp (Capacitybuilders since 2006), and Communitybuilders.

Within Scotland the relevant body is the Third Sector Division within the Directorate for Public Services Reform. Scotland has its own Future-builders Scotland programme and a Scottish Investment Fund, as well as a Scottish Compact, based on the one in England. The Welsh Assembly Government has a statutory duty to promote the interests of voluntary organisations in the exercise of all its functions (Welsh Assembly Government, 2008). The government is required to:

> *make a scheme setting out how it proposes in the exercise of its functions, to promote the interests of relevant voluntary organisations.* (Government of Wales Act 1998, Section 114).

It is claimed that this statutory Voluntary Sector Scheme is 'unique to the United Kingdom and probably to the world' (Welsh Assembly Government, 2008, 9). Wales has a Third Sector Unit located in the Communities Directorate within the Department for Social Justice and Local Government. The government also convenes a Third Sector Partnership Council of twenty-five third sector representatives, chaired by the minister, to advise on policy implementation, operation, and review.

In Northern Ireland, responsibility for the voluntary and community sector and social enterprise is split between, respectively, the Voluntary and Community Unit within the Department for Social Development and the Social Economy Unit within the Department of Enterprise Trade and Development. The re-imposition of direct rule between 2002 and 2007 meant that a number of English policy initiatives were introduced (such as a Northern Ireland Compact, Building Real Partnership). Consequently, there has been little development of an independent Northern Ireland approach.

Alcock (2009, 3) describes the devolution of policy toward the third sector as 'significant' and notes:

> the creation of four separate policy regimes for the third sector across the four countries of the UK. What is more these governance and policy differences have been developed for, and with, third sector practice communities which already had distinct histories, structure, and cultures within the four nations.

Despite the divergence in policy regimes, he sees the direction of third sector policy as 'remarkably similar' (Alcock, 2009, 3): all of the UK countries have moved toward a partnership approach with a common commitment to policy intervention and support for the sector to build its capacity.

POTENTIAL IMPACTS OF VOLUNTARY SECTOR PUBLIC SERVICES DELIVERY

The government's turn toward the voluntary sector to deliver public services on a large scale has provoked a lively debate within and beyond the sector. The introduction of competition and quasi-markets was supposed to offer choice to empowered customers and to drive up standards as public, private, and voluntary sector providers all competed to deliver the service (Le Grand and Bartlett, 1993). Against this backdrop, much of this debate has revolved around the likely impacts of the policy on service quality and on the voluntary sector itself, particularly its relationship with the state.

As the role of the sector has expanded, it has gained access to new sources of funding but has also become subject to greater regulatory control by the state. This has brought with it a certain bureaucratisation and 'professionalisation.' The government increasingly uses the voluntary sector as the vehicle for some of its policy goals—such as personalisation—in certain public services. Arguably there is a tension between some of these factors.

Social care was one of the first areas in which outsourcing was implemented, and, yet, it is alleged that *'many of the promises made about privatisation, including that it would create a more efficient and effective structure for the delivery of social care, have never materialised'* (Carey, 2008, 918). The specific claims about widening choice and meeting individual needs in a more flexible and innovative way are challenged by Scourfield (2006) and Drakeford (2000), who have drawn attention to the bureaucratised ineffectiveness of markets in social care.

Nevertheless, the government has repeatedly claimed that outsourcing to the third sector improves the quality of services; allows more local flexibility; gives individuals more control over the services they receive; and achieves better outcomes. Its cheerleaders within the sector have enthusiastically endorsed this. Stephen Bubb of the Association of Chief Executives of Voluntary Organisations (ACEVO) called for a 'step change' in outsourcing and asset transfer to the third sector (Brindle, 2006), and National Autistic Society Chief Executive Mark Lever has asserted that *'healthcare, employment services, and social care could all be delivered by independent organisations in the voluntary and private sectors'* (Lever, 2006).

However there is very little hard evidence that outsourcing to the voluntary sector has improved outcomes. The Commons Public Administration Select Committee (PASC, 2008a) examined the government's routine claims that the third sector has more specialist knowledge and expertise; is more innovative; provides higher quality service; and is inherently well suited to public service provision because of distinctive characteristics.

On all of these, the Committee was unconvinced. In relation to what it described as the government's 'central claim'—that third sector organisations can deliver services in distinctive ways which will improve outcomes for service users' (2008a, 3)—it *was 'unable to corroborate that claim'* and complained that *'too much of the discussion is still hypothetical or anecdotal'* (2008a, 3). Going further, the Committee questioned whether there are common characteristics across the entire sector that particularly equip it for public service provision—the *'evidence is simply not there to judge'* (PASC, 2008a, 83).

The Committee further commented that although the sector is cited as having a distinctive focus on service users, this user focus is not unique to the third sector and noted that it 'can be lost when organisations provide services to a large, general population' (PASC, 2008a, 28). Similarly, it also felt that it had 'not been provided with sufficient evidence' to prove the claim that the sector has more specialist knowledge than other sectors (2008a, 28), considered that flexibility of service and innovation—what it described as *'the very crux of third sector distinctiveness'*—had more to do with commissioning practice than with whether the service was provided by the third sector or not (PASC, 2008a, 29), and concluded that whereas innovation was not impossible under contractual conditions, 'contracts and innovation are uneasy bedfellows' (PASC, 2008a, 63). This observation therefore seems to add weight to the view that the retention of grant-based funding is needed in order to support innovation (Unwin, 2004; Curley, 2006).

The Public Administration Select Committee (2008a) additionally referred to 'general risks of contracting out public service delivery,' and the Communities and Local Government Committee noted:

> Constant cycles of competitive tendering are burdensome and expensive and this has a disproportionate impact on Third Sector and smaller providers. (Communities Local Government Committee 2009, 24)

In line with this, Cunningham and Nickson (2009, 1) report the views of Scottish social care organisations that re-tendering involves an enormous waste of time and resources and is becoming *'a major challenge to the financial stability of voluntary sector organisations.'* Indeed, the more general emphasis on tendering has been found to lead to organisations developing expertise in the process but not necessarily to improve service provision; as organizations may set out on 'market-friendly, not client-friendly, paths of development' (Evans, Richmond, and Shields, 2005, 93).

A great deal of discussion has focused on the dangers of voluntary organisations losing their independence by too close an embrace with the state (for instance, NCVO, 2008b). The Public Administration Select Committee (2008a) was unconvinced that the delivery of public services compromises a voluntary organisation's ability to independently campaign. Yet Fyfe (2005) points to the tension in the government's wish to use the third sector both to deliver professional and cost-effective public services and to assist in the reinvigoration of civic society. He argues that if third sector bodies play the role of 'neighbourhood-based, grassroots groups,' they are unlikely to be able to contribute to service delivery as the government hopes. Furthermore, he argues that those that do professionalise and restructure, risk disempowering citizens both inside and outside the organisation. Creating a hierarchical structure will inevitably divide volunteers and paid staff while reproducing the bureaucrat-client relationship typical of state organisations.

Additional potential problems identified include the concern that heavy reliance on state funding of any kind can make voluntary organisations vulnerable to changes to policy and funding priorities or to governmental change. The (roughly) one third of charities that have a significant reliance on government funding now face tighter government spending. So the NCVO (2008a, 33) recommends that *'it would be wise for these charities to look for other sources of income.'*

Government funding is also likely to accelerate a change in behaviour. Blake, Robinson, and Smerdon (2006) comment that third sector organisations are making compromises in order to win contracts. There are fears of 'mission drift' (Cunningham, 2008, 19). There is a risk in being resource-led rather then needs-led, serving the target regimes of the funding body rather than the identified mission of the third sector organisation. The NCVO (2005) similarly warn of the danger of voluntary and community organisations making a 'dash for cash,' bidding for and winning contracts that neither meet their constituency's needs nor help reach their organizational objectives.

Women's Aid Federation England (2009, 7) argue that one of the negative impacts of a tendering regime is

> distrust and conflict between previously cooperative organisations. This poses a threat to effective partnership working to meet the needs of survivors and their children.

Institutional pressures are also likely to change the way that voluntary organisations operate more generally. Kelly (2007, 1015), through utilizing DiMaggio and Powell's framework (1983), identifies three categories of isomorphic pressure that will change behaviour: coercive, mimetic, and normative. By agreeing to deliver public services, voluntary organisations will come under coercive pressure through public service accountability frameworks, above and beyond the terms of the contract. Mimetic pressure comes from the public sector commissioner's expectation of shared good practice, which will quickly become standardised. It is also there in the pressure to adopt private sector business methods and to 'professionalise' the sector. Normative pressures come from sources such as the qualification systems for middle and senior managers such as the MBA. Added to that are the likely impact of any future central initiatives from government with which the voluntary sector will be expected to comply.

The increased reliance on contracts can also change the relationship that the sector has with its client base. Voluntary sector organisations will gain a different set of users. The Charity Commission (2007, 21) notes that an expansion in charitable provision of public services will mean that:

> The users of these services will, in future, be clients of charities, rather than of statutory bodies, which will bring more complex issues of accountability.

Commissioning bodies are aggregating contracts under the pressure of the drive for efficiencies (Curley, 2009), effectively excluding the smaller organisations from bidding. The Charity Commission (2007, 21) has drawn attention to this, warning:

> there may be a risk of creating a restricted market where only those charities above a certain size and capacity can successfully compete for future delivery of public services.

The only alternatives for these smaller organisations are to enter into consortia or to act as subcontractors for larger organisations. In an attempt to remedy this problem, the government has issued guidance on working within consortia (Office of the Third Sector, 2008). In a separate but possibly related development, the Charity Commission (2009) is encouraging charities to consider collaborating if not full merger.

Given that contracting out public services to the voluntary sector is seen as the acceptable face of outsourcing (Brindle, 2005) and that a senior CBI official (Bentley, 2006) described the voluntary sector as 'the weapon of choice for those engaged in the ongoing battle over public service reform,' it is possible that the voluntary sector could unwittingly act as 'a Trojan horse' (Walker, 2006) for further private sector penetration into public services. The close collaboration of voluntary and private sector providers in the push for employment services contracts supports this view (Davies, 2008). ACEVO is a fervent advocate of contracting out public services, but its chief executive, Stephen Bubb, reported 'huge anger in the sector' (ACEVO, 2007) when the Department of Work and Pensions (DWP) expanded its 2007 tendering programme for the Pathways to Work project and awarded fifteen contracts to five private companies but just one to a third sector organisation. Others were not so taken by surprise. A year earlier, Neil Cleeveley of the National Association for Voluntary and Community Action (NAVCA) (2006) warned of the problem of *'the frequent lumping together by the government of the private and voluntary sectors'* and (correctly) predicted that although media coverage suggested that the DWP contracts would go to the third sector, the 'private sector is well placed to win most of the work.' He argued that the CBI *'wants the voluntary sector to act as its outrider for outsourcing'* (Cleeveley, 2006).

Others have urged caution for similar reasons. Writing on the prospects for health care contracting, Lewis, Hunt, and Carson (2006, 21) cautioned that 'there is a distinct danger that for-profit providers will sweep into primary and community care unchallenged' and staff- and patient-led organisations may find that by the time they are able to bid there will be little remaining. In evidence to the Health Select Committee (2006, Ev 91), the British Heart Foundation (BHF) expressed concern over the possibility that private companies might *'cherry pick the most profitable areas of cardiac care and as the nation's heart charity we could be expected to pick up the rest and potentially less profitable services.'*

Providing public services raises important issues of transparency and accountability and possible conflicts of interest for the voluntary sector. Concern has been expressed about the facts that, unlike the public sector, the voluntary sector providers of public services are not covered by either the Human Rights Act or the Freedom of Information Act; and 69 percent of charities overall and 40 percent of those delivering public services do not even have complaints procedures (PASC, 2008a). The Public Administration Select Committee called for the extension of coverage of both Acts to cover all organisations providing public services, including contractors (PASC, 2008a). In July 2009, following a consultation run by the Ministry of Justice, the UK government announced that it was making some modest extensions to the coverage of the Freedom of Information Act (to include the Association of Chief Police Officers, the Financial Services Ombudsman, the Universities and Colleges Admissions Service, and Academy schools). After lobbying from business interests, the government rejected a general expansion of coverage to contractors but

> intends to keep this matter under review, particularly in relation to prisons, detention centres, and foster care homes provided by private sector contractors on behalf of public authorities. (Ministry of Justice, 2009, 12)

Scotland began a separate consultation in Spring 2010 on extending coverage of its Freedom of Information Act (Scottish Government, 2009).

The House of Commons, House of Lords Joint Committee on Human Rights (2009, 43) examined the extension of the provisions of the Human Rights Act and concluded:

> We have heard nothing new in this inquiry to suggest that we should change our view that legislative change is necessary to restore the original intention of Parliament, that all private bodies performing public functions should be subject to the duty to act compatibly with human rights. We are concerned that the Government's approach panders

to the unjustified concerns of some in the private sector in order to maintain the market for contracted-out services and represents a significant shift from its earlier view that the scope of the HRA 1998 should be clarified.

The Joint Committee (2009, 44) referred to the evidence of the Equality and Human Rights Commission emphasising the 'uncertainty' felt by the voluntary sector over this question and urged the government to clarify the definition of a public authority within the meaning of section 6 of the Act to cover all providers of public services.

CONCLUSION

Outsourcing public services to the voluntary sector is now a key part of the UK government's public sector reform programme. It is a position shared by all the main political parties and is unlikely to change whatever the result of the next election. Enthusiasm for the project appears to be in inverse proportion to the hard evidence to support the claims behind the policy. As Will Werry of the Commissioning Joint Committee told the Public Administration Select Committee, '*It is surprising that a major national exercise is based on . . . supposition*' (PASC, 2008a, 34).

Nevertheless, more charities are now more dependent on statutory funding than ever before, and more are more involved in the delivery of public services than at any other time in the postwar period. Marketisation, the continuing shift from grants to contracts and, by extension, the public service reform agenda, has even been extended to services that were never provided by the public sector such as citizen's advice (AdviceUK, 2008).

Despite these major shifts, there is little evidence for the claimed benefits of outsourcing public service provision to the voluntary sector. Ministerial assertions of higher standards of service, greater choice and control for service users, and improved outcomes remain unproved. Even the sector's own declarations that they are more innovative and have greater specialist knowledge and a distinctive focus on service users have been questioned by the Public Administration Select Committee (2008a). The access to new levels and sources of funding means that the sector is increasingly subject to a range of new pressures and regulatory controls from the state. We do not yet know how far this process will go or whether it will push some parts of the sector into a form of parasitical role, with new questions about accountability, nor do we know how the sector's independence will be affected. The increasing reliance on contracts will undoubtedly change organisational behaviour, and there is some evidence that this is already taking place. Whether this will result in 'mission drift' or a decline in the capacity for innovation remains to be seen. We can also only speculate if and how the sector's relationship with its clients will be affected in the longer term, or how vulnerable the sector now is to major changes in government policy and competitive pressure from the private sector. What we can say is that a new series of tensions has been created as a result of the changes over the last decade or so.

Although expressed as a meeting of equals—the 'benign language of partnership' (Evans, Richmond, and Shields, 2005, 78)—outsourcing public services has involved a fundamental restructuring of the relationship between the state and the sector, in which increased power is wielded by the state through the commissioning of contracts. The end of the period of expanding public expenditure will inevitably bring with it forceful downward pressures on costs within those voluntary organisations delivering public services. This comes at the same time as increased demand from users, tighter regulatory controls, and policy changes, such as personalisation, with a potentially expensive price tag. Finally, although we are at a relatively early stage of the process, running through all of the above commentary are the fault lines around employment relations and pay and conditions, upon which outsourcing will have a profound impact.

BIBLIOGRAPHY

ACEVO (2000) *ACEVO Launches independent enquiry into Pathways to Work* contracts. Press release, 14 September 2007. London: ACEVO.

AdviceUK. (2008). *It's the system, stupid! Radically rethinking advice.* Report of AdviceUK's RADICAL Advice Project, 2007–2008. London: AdviceUK.

Alcock, P. (2009). *Devolution or divergence? Third sector policy across the UK since 2000.* TSRC Briefing Paper 2. Available at http://www.tsrc.ac.uk/LinkClick/aspx?fileticket=%2F71U8WqGcCI%3D&tabid-500. Accessed 12 December 2009.

Armstrong, H. (2006). *Breakfast briefing. The National Council for Voluntary Organisations* (NCVO). 8 November. Available at http://umbrl.cabinetoffice.gov.uk/media/cabinetoffice/corp/assets/publications/speeches/armstron/pdf/nevo001.pdf. Accessed 31 May 2010.

Asato, J., Kyle, P., Blake, S., Swain, J., Le Grand, J., Corrigan, P., Burke, S., and Ogden-Newton, A. (2009). *Letter to Andy Burnham.* 23 November. Available at http://www.progressonline.org.uk/Magazine/article.asp?a=4990. Accessed 11 December 2009.

Bentley, N. (2006). More room for the third sector. *Public Finance*, 4 August 2006. Available at http://www.publicfinance.co.uk/feature/2006/more-room-for-the-third-sector-by-neil-bentley. Accessed 31 May 2010.

Blair, T. (2006). *Voluntary sector speech at the Future Services Network Conference.* 22 June 2006. Available at http://webarchive.nationalarchives.gov.uk/+/http://www.number10.gov.uk/Page9714. Accessed 31 May 2010.

Blair, T. (2002). Speech at the 2002 Labour party conference, Blackpool, 1 October 2002. Available at http://politics.guardian.co.uk/labour2002/story/0,,802604,00.html. Accessed 31 May 2010.

Blair, T. (2001). Speech on public service reform. 6 October. Available at http://webarchive.nationalarchives.gov.uk/+/www.number10.gov.uk/output/Page1632.asp. Accessed 31 May 2010.

Blair, T. (1997). *The will to win.* Speech at Aylesbury Estate, 2 June 1997. Available at http://archive.cabinetoffice.gov.uk/seu/newsa52f.html?id=400. Accessed 1 December 2009.

Blake, G., Robinson, D., and Smerdon, M. (2006). *Living values.* London: Community Links.

Brindle, D. (2006). Marking out the territory. *The Guardian,* 20 Septembe 2006. Available at http://www.guardian.co.uk/society/2006/sep/20/guardiansociety-supplement.publicservices. Accessed 31 May 2010.

Brindle, D. (2005). Charity body jibs at transfer of services. *The Guardian,* 30 May 2005. Available at http://www.guardian.co.uk/society/2005/may/30/charities. charitymanagement. Accessed 31 May 2010.

Brown, G. (2008). Time for the third act in public sector reform. *Financial Times,* 9 March 2008. Available at http://ft.com/cms/s/0/c96a2baa-edfc-11dc-a5cl-0000779fd2ac.html. Accessed 31 May 2010.

Brown, G. (2006) *The Future of Britishness.* Speech at the Fabian New Year Conference. London: 14 January 2006. Available at http://www.fabians.org.uk/events/speeches/the-future-of-Britishness. Accessed 31 May 2010.

Bubb, S. (2006). Choice and voice—The unique role of the third sector. November 2006. London: ACEVO.

Burnham, P. (2001). New Labour and the politics of depoliticisation. *British Journal of Politics and International Relations,* 3 (2), 127–149.

Burnham, P. (1999). The politics of economic management in the 1990s. *New Political Economy,* 4 (1), 37–54.

Byrne, L. (2006). *Third sector public service delivery.* eGov Monitor, 13 March. Available at http://www.egovmonitor.com/node/5089. Accessed 31 May 2010.

Cabinet Office. (2006a). *Partnership in public services: An action plan for third sector involvement.* London: Cabinet Office, Office of the Third Sector.

Cabinet Office. (2006b). *The UK government's approach to public service reform—A discussion paper.* London: The Prime Minister's Strategy Unit, June 2006.

Cabinet Office. (1999). *Modernising government.* March. White Paper, Cm 4310.

Carey, M. (2008). Everything must go? The privatization of state social work. *British Journal of Social Work,* 38 (5), 918–935.

Caulkin, S. (2006). How the not-for-profit sector became big business. *The Observer,* 12 February. Available at http://www.guardian.co.uk/money/2006/feb/12/publicfinances.business. Accessed 31 May 2010.

Charity Commission. (2009). *Making mergers work: Helping you succeed.* Liverpool: Charity Commission.

Charity Commission, (2007), *Stand and deliver: The future for charities providing public services.* Liverpool: Charity Commission.

Clark, T. (2002). New Labour's big idea: Joined-up government. *Social Policy and Society,* 1, (2), 107–117.

Cleeveley, N. (2006). Taking care of business. *Public Finance,* 1 September 2006. Available at http://www.publicfinance.co.uk/features/2006/taking-care-of-business-by-neil-cleevely. Accessed 31 May 2010.

Commission for Social Care Inspection (CSCI). (2006). *Time to care? An overview of home care services for older people in England.* London: CSCI.

Communities and Local Government Committee. (2009). *The supporting people programme.* (Vol. 1, Report, together with formal minutes. HC 649-I, 3). November. London: The Stationery Office Limited.

Cunningham, I. (2008). *Employment relations in the voluntary sector.* Abingdon: Routledge.

Cunningham, I., and Nickson, D. (2009). *A gathering storm? Procurement, re-tendering, and the voluntary sector social care workforce.* Scottish Centre for Employment Research. Glasgow: University of Strathclyde.

34   *Steve Davies*

Curley, K. (2009). *Threats and opportunities facing the local third sector—Can we handle them?* One Voice, County Durham Conference, 25 March 2009. NAVCA. Available at http://www.navca.org.uk/NR/rdonlyres/4F3FA30A-A6D4-4755-89D9-6DF4CED6DC73/0/Durham.doc. Accessed 31 May 2010.

Curley, K. (2006). *Charities and public services delivery: A grassroots perspective.* Speech at Charity Commission conference, 21 March 2006.

Davies, S. (2008). Contracting out employment services to the third and private sectors: A critique. *Critical Social Policy*, 28, (2), 136–164.

Department for Communities and Local Government (DCLG). (2006). *Strong and prosperous communities.* White Paper. (Vol. 1, October, Cm 6939-I). Norwich: HMSO.

Department of Health. (2009). *The NHS as preferred provider.* Letter from David Nicholson, NHS Chief Executive, to SHA and PCT Chief Executives, 13 October 2009. Available at http://www.dh.gov.uk/prod_consum_dh/groups/dh_digitalassets/documents/digitalassets/dh_107127.pdf. Accessed 31 May 2010.

Department of Health. (2006a). *Our health, our care, our say: A new direction for community services.* Cmnd 6737. London: The Stationery Office Limited.

Department of Health. (2006b). *No excuses. Embrace partnership now. Step towards change!* Report of the Third Sector Commissioning Task Force. DH press release, 11 July 2006. Available at http://www.dh.gov.uk/prod_consum_dh/groups/dh_digitalasserts/@dh/@en/documents/digitalasset/dh_4137177.pdf. Accessed 31 May 2010.

DiMaggio, P. J., and Powell, W. W. (1983) .The iron cage revisited: Institutional isomorphism and collective rationality in organisational fields. *American Sociological Review*, 35, (1), 147–160.

Drakeford, M. (2000). *Privatization and social policy.* Harlow: Pearson Education Limited.

Evans, B., Richmond., T., and Shields, J. (2005). Structuring neoliberal governance: The nonprofit sector, emerging new modes of control, and the marketisation of service delivery. *Policy and Society*, 24 (1), 73–97.

Fyfe, N. R. (2005). Making space for 'neocommunitarianism? The third sector, state, and civil society in the UK. *Antipode*, 37 (3), 536–557.

Government of Wales Act 1998. (c. 38) London: HMSO.

Grimshaw, D., Vincent, S., and Willmott, H. (2002). Going privately: Partnership and outsourcing in UK public services. *Public Administration*, 80, (3), 475–502.

Hansard. (2009). *Written answers. NHS: Independent sector.* Answer from Baroness Thornton to question from Lord Warner. House of Lords, 22 October, Column WA92.

Hansard. (1997). *Debate on the Queen's speech*, House of Commons, 14 May 2007: Column 65. Available at http://www.publications.parliament.uk/pa/cm199798/cmhansrd/vo970514/debtext/70514-08.htm. Accessed 31 May 2010.

Haugh, H., and Kitson, M. (2007). The third way and the third sector: New Labour's economic policy and the social economy. *Cambridge Journal of Economics*, 31 (6), 973–994.

Health Committee. (2006). *Changes to primary care trusts: Second report of session, 2005–06.* HC 646. London: The Stationery Office. .

Hindmoor, A. (2002). Public policy—Developing a distinctive identity? *Parliamentary Affairs*, 55, 287–298.

HM Government. (2009). *Putting the frontline first: Smarter government.* December, Cm 7753. Norwich: The Stationery Office.

HM Treasury. (2002). *The role of the voluntary and community sector in service delivery: A cross cutting review.* September. London: HM Treasury.

House of Lords, House of Commons Joint Committee on Human Rights. (2009). *Any of our business? Human rights and the UK private sector.* First Report of Session 2009–10. (Vol. 1, HL Paper 5-I, HC 64-I). London: The Stationery Office Limited.

Hutton, J. (2006) *Speech at the 21st century public services—Putting People First Conference.* QE2 Conference Centre. London, 6 June 2006. Available at http://www.nationalschool.gov.uk/news_events/psrc2006/downloads/speech_john_hutton.pdf. Accessed 26 January 2010.

Hutton, W. (1995). *The state we're in* London: Jonathan Cape.

Kelly, J. (2007). Reforming public services in the UK: Bringing in the third sector. *Public Administration,* 85 (4), 1003–1022.

Labour Party (2005) Britain Forward Not Back. Labour Party manifesto. http://image.guardian.co.uk/sys-files/Politics/documents/2005/04/13/labourmanifesto.pdf. Accessed 31 May 2010.

Labour Party (1997) New Labour because Britain deserves better. Labour Party manifesto. http://www.labour-party.org.uk/manifestos/1997/1997-labour-manifesto.shtml Accessed 31 May 2010.

Leather, S (2007) Speech to the NCVO Annual Conference Wednesday 21 February 2007 http://www.ncvo-vol.org.uk/documents/2007-annual-conference-keynote-speech-dame-suzi-leather-february-2007 Accessed 5 November 2010.

Le Grand, J., and Bartlett, W., eds. (1993). *Quasi-markets and social policy.* London: Palgrave Macmillan.

Lever M (2006) 'Opportunity Knocks', Guardian, 28 June 2006. http://www.guardian.co.uk/society/2006/jun/28/comment.politics Accessed 26 January 2010.

Lewis, R., Hunt, P., and Carson, D. (2006). *Social enterprise and community based care.* King's Fund Working Paper. London: King's Fund.

LGA, IDeA & LGIU (2006) Comprehensive Spending Review (CSR) 2007: The Future Role of the Third Sector in Social and Economic Regeneration Joint submission from LGA, IDeA and LGIU. http://www.lga.gov.uk/lga/aio/105274 Accessed 5 November 2010.

MacErlean, N (2005) 'Social Enterprise: the Issues', Observer, 20 November 2006. http://www.guardian.co.uk/business/2005/nov/20/politics.publicservices Accessed 31 May 2010.

Mathiason, N (2005) Social Enterprise: Business Phenomenon of the Century Observer, 20 November 2005. http://www.guardian.co.uk/business/2005/nov/20/politics.publicservices Accessed 31 May 2010.

Miliband, D (2006) Putting People in Control Speech to NCVO Annual conference, 21 February 2006. http://www.guardian.co.uk/society/2006/feb/21/localgovernment.politics1 Accessed 26 January 2010.

Miliband, E (2006) Charities, Campaigns and Progressive Change Speech at Britain's Most Admired Charities Awards, 29 November 2006. http://www.cabinet-office.gov.uk/media/cabinetoffice/corp/assets/publications/speeches/milibande/doc/bmaca.doc Accessed 5 November 2010.

Ministry of Justice. (2009.) *Freedom of Information Act 2000: Designation of additional public authorities. Response to consultation.* CP(R) 27/07, 16 July. London: Ministry of Justice.

National Council for Voluntary Organizations (NCVO). (2009a). *The state and the voluntary sector.* London: NCVO.

National Council for Voluntary Organizations (NCVO). (2009b). *UK civil society almanac, 2009.* London: NCVO.

National Council for Voluntary Organizations (NCVO). (2008a). *UK civil society almanac, 2008.* London: NCVO.

National Council for Voluntary Organizations (NCVO). (2008b). *Standing apart, working together*. London: NCVO.

National Council for Voluntary Organizations (NCVO). (2006). *Response to the HM Treasury/Cabinet Office review of the future role of the third sector in social and economic regeneration*. September.

National Council for Voluntary Organizations (NCVO). (2005). *The reform of public services: The role of the voluntary sector*. London: NCVO.

Office of the Third Sector (OTS). (2008). *Working in a consortium: A guide for third sector organisations involved in public service delivery*. London: Cabinet Office.

Osborne, D., and Gaebler, T. (1992). *Reinventing government: How the entrepreneurial spirit is transforming the public sector*. Reading, MA: Addison-Wesley.

Peters, T., and Waterman, R. (1982). *In search of excellence: Lessons from America's best run companies*. Profile.

PricewaterhouseCoopers. (2004). *Scoping the market for children's services*. Report for the Department for Education and Skills, October. London: PricewaterhouseCoopers LLP.

Public Administration Select Committee. (2008a). *Public services and the third sector: Rhetoric and reality*. (Vol. 1, HC 112-II, 9 July). London: The Stationery Office Limited.

Public Administration Select Committee. (2008b). *Public services and the third sector: Rhetoric and reality: Government response to the Committee's eleventh report of session 2007–08*. HC 1209, 4 December. London: The Stationery Office Limited.

Ridley, N. (1988). *The local right: Enabling not providing*. London: Centre for Policy Studies.

Scottish Government (2009) Extending coverage of FOI Act. Press release, 8 December 2009. http://spoxy4.insipio.com/generator/en/www.scotland.gov.uk/News/Releases/2009/12/08113806 Accessed 26 January 2010.

Scourfield, P. (2006). "What matters is what works?" How discourses of modernisation have both silenced and limited debate on domiciliary care for older people. *Critical Social Policy*, 26 (1), 5–30.

Thomas, N (2006) 'Reform in public services "will lead to bidding war"', Third Sector, 27 September 2006. http://www.thirdsector.co.uk/news/archive/613281/Politics-Reform-public-services-will-lead-bidding-war/?DCMP=ILC-SEARCH Accessed 26 January 2010.

Unwin, J. (2004). *The grantmaking tango: Issues for funders*. London: Baring Foundation.

Walker, D. (2006) 'Are We Backing a Trojan Horse?' Guardian, 12 July, 2006. http://www.guardian.co.uk/society/2006/jul/12/futureforpublicservices.comment Accessed 31 May 2010.

Welsh Assembly Government. (2008). *The Third Dimension—A strategic action plan for the voluntary sector scheme*. January. Cardiff: WAG.

Women's Aid Federation England (2009) Evidence from Women's Aid Federation England. Submission to the Communities and Local Government Committee Inquiry into Supporting People, June 2009. http://www.publications.parliament.uk/pa/cm200809/cmselect/cmcomloc/memo/support/ucm11302.htm Accessed 31 May 2010.

3 Trends in Voluntary Sector Employment

Jenny Clark and Karl Wilding

INTRODUCTION

For those with only a passing knowledge of voluntary organisations, the idea of paid employment in the voluntary sector—what might be called working for a charity—often continues to arouse a mix of confusion, suspicion, and, on occasion, disdain. Much is based upon misconception, chief among which is that paid employment in the 'voluntary' sector is an oxymoron. Yet, against this background of misconception, the UK voluntary sector workforce has experienced substantial growth over the last ten years, throwing such issues into sharper relief.

Debates around the transfer of public services to the voluntary sector, and in particular concerns regarding the pay and conditions of staff and senior managers, have also framed discussions of employers and paid employment in the sector. Moreover, as the number of paid employees and employers within the voluntary sector has increased, so has interest in the role of the sector as an employer. Governments in the UK and overseas have long-identified the sector as a source of new employment (Davidman, Betcherman, Hall, and White, 1998), and more recently the recession has furthered interest in the extent to which voluntary organisations can provide a route into formal work, whether via volunteering or intermediate labour markets. In some cases, though, there remains suspicion that in the public services unpaid voluntary work is in effect substituting for paid work.

Perhaps unsurprisingly, much of the public debate has been hindered by a limited awareness of evidence regarding levels of employment, workforce characteristics, employment practice, and remuneration in the voluntary sector. This chapter therefore explores and examines trends in the size, scope, sectoral and organisational location, and characteristics of the voluntary sector workforce, and areas of skills shortages and skills gaps. A central focus of the chapter is on how the trends and findings identified are linked to the developments that have occurred with regard to the voluntary sector's increased involvement in the delivery of public services.

CONTEXT: THE RISE OF THE UK VOLUNTARY SECTOR

Any exploration of the voluntary sector workforce first needs to contextualise change by summarising the broader expansion in the voluntary sector over the 2000s. Using a narrow definition of the sector based upon registered charities, but excluding those organisations that are controlled by government, independent schools, and faith groups, evidence suggests that between 2000–01 and 2007–08 the UK voluntary sector's income increased on average by 5.3 percent to £35.5 billion (Clark, Kane, Wilding, and Wilton, 2010). Concurrent increases in the number of organisations have also occurred, driven first by new establishments and second by a shift or blurring in the boundaries between the public, private, and voluntary sectors. The emergence of social enterprises (at the boundary with the private sector) and the 'charitisation' of functions, such as leisure services previously administered by statutory bodies (much as other services were privatised in the 1980s), have, as a result, additionally been notable throughout the decade (Cater, 2002).

A closer relationship with the state has driven much of the expansion in the voluntary sector, particularly a bigger role in the delivery of public services. Income to the voluntary sector from statutory sources[1] totaled £12.8 billion in 2007–08, a sum that has increased every year since 2000 (Clark et al., 2010). Approximately one fifth (22 percent) of voluntary organisations now have a direct financial relationship with the state.

The antecedents of this expansion were sown in the 1980s when a desire to shift the burden of responsibility for welfare provision to individuals and communities, plus a dissatisfaction with the big state, and local authorities in particular, initially led to the greater involvement of voluntary organisations in social services via compulsory competitive tendering. More recently, the establishment of The Compact framework (Craig et al., 2005) for voluntary sector–government relations and subsequent policy initiatives (particularly reports associated with comprehensive spending reviews) have created what in future might be viewed as a 'golden age' for the voluntary sector. Thus not only have these developments been associated with, as noted above, increased levels of statutory funding, but also with significant efforts to build the capacity of voluntary organisations to deliver publicly funded services and steps to encourage a broader, deeper role for them. However, the recent debate over the role of voluntary organisations in the running of prisons points to the fact that this expansion has not been uncontentious (Neilson, 2009).

In recent years there have been two changes both in the nature and purpose of statutory funding that have had a bearing on the sector's workforce. First, voluntary organisations now play a greater role in delivering services on behalf of government, services which were previously provided by the public sector. Second, statutory funding for a range of activities is now more likely to be in the form of contracts rather than grants. Contract income from statutory sources was worth £9.1 billion in 2007–08, an increase of £5.1 billion in seven years: a substantial change in the context of our evidence that only 38,000 voluntary organisations have a direct financial relationship with government (Clark et al., 2010). Indeed, a continuous upward trend in the total value of contract income is evident, and the pace of growth has quickened since 2004–05. Over the same time period, statutory grants to the sector declined by £400 million to £3.7 billion, although the decline may appear deeper to the sector because of an increase in grants earlier in the decade (Clark et al., 2010).

In turn, trends such as the rise in contracting and involvement in service delivery have raised the question of the extent to which the voluntary sector remains distinctive: is it becoming too much like the public or private sectors? Are services being 'transformed' (based on the presumption that the sector and its staff are different from other sectors) or simply transferred (Paxton, Pearce, Unwin, and Molyneux, 2005)? Has the pursuit of income from the delivery of services under contract inherently changed the dimensions, characteristics, and values of the sector and its workforce? A key dimension of this argument has been the professionalisation of the sector, a somewhat contested term with both positive (a more professional approach) and negative (loss of altruism; impact on volunteers [Russell and Scott, 1997]) connotations. This has been visibly manifested by an increase in employees moving between sectors, and therefore a rise in the number who view employment in the voluntary sector as simply a stage in their career (Lewis, 2008). Arguments for professionalisation have also been driven by a substantial expansion in the number of paid staff working in the voluntary sector, the subject of the next section.

THE UK VOLUNTARY SECTOR WORKFORCE: OVERVIEW[2]

To explain the pattern of employment in the voluntary sector it is first useful to understand the different types of voluntary organisations and the implications for employment. Table 3.1 shows the voluntary sector workforce continuum. Voluntary organisations are situated across this continuum, though many will move toward the right during their life cycle as they formalise and attract resources. Typically an organisation may start life with the involvement of trustees only. As the organisation gathers momentum, it attracts volunteers and growth and becomes more formalised. Paid staff are employed to supplement and coordinate volunteers and then to do some of the work once carried out by volunteers. These categories are of course blurred in reality, and the overlap between trustees, volunteers, and beneficiaries is sometimes considerable. The creation of organisations with charitable or mutual status (see above) is challenging this life-cycle model; moreover, the shift to delivering more services and the associated risks and complexity of contracting have led to arguments that trustees should be paid. Like other dimensions of the debate around public services delivery, the issue of trustee remuneration continues to divide the sector (Charity Commission, 2008).

Table 3.1 also shows one of the defining characteristics of the sector, that is, the large numbers of volunteers who give their time freely. The majority of voluntary sector organisations continue to rely solely on volunteers. The Citizenship Survey estimates that 28 percent of adults living in England volunteer formally[3] at least once a month—a substantial human resource (Department for Communities and Local Government [DCLG], 2009). Many deliver public services. Moreover, it is also worth noting that many volunteers give their time directly to public bodies—the 1997 National Survey of Volunteering estimated that more than five million people have volunteered for a public sector body (Davis-Smith, 1998). A more recent survey estimated that 23 percent of volunteers helped public sector bodies (Office of the Third Sector [OTS], 2007).

However, it is with the paid workforce that this section is largely concerned. Estimates of the dimensions and characteristics of the voluntary sector workforce are drawn from the UK Labour Force Survey (LFS), a quarterly survey of individuals undertaken by the Office for National Statistics (ONS, 2009). Using methods originally developed by Kendall and Almond (2000) to combine different survey waves, and therefore to produce a dataset sufficiently large to enable statistically significant analysis, the LFS provides the basis for an exploration of many dimensions of paid work.[4]

Our analysis of the LFS suggests that there were 668,000 paid employees within the UK voluntary sector in 2008[5] (see Table 3.2). The number of paid employees within the voluntary sector has increased by nearly one-quarter (23 percent), or 124,000 employees, in ten years. As already noted, this employment growth reflects almost 20 years of public service delivery being contracted out by central and local government agencies to the sector (Kendall, 2003). Moreover, it also reflects the gradual shift to a service-based economy seen in all advanced industrialised nations (Leete, 2006): most voluntary sector employees work for service-delivering organisations. International comparative work by Anheier and Salamon (2006) suggests that, as a proportion of the economically active population, the UK voluntary sector paid and unpaid workforce is proportionately large, although

Table 3.1   The Voluntary Sector Workforce Continuum

No staff (trustees only)	Volunteers only	Mainly volunteers and some paid workers	Predominantly paid workers and some volunteers	Paid workers only
		Trustees		

less so than in some other countries, including the Netherlands, Belgium, and Ireland.

At the time of writing (April 2010), there are significant questions over whether such growth will continue. A significantly tighter public spending envelope is widely forecast to constrain, and possibly contract, expenditure on publicly funded services. This may imply a scenario where the role of voluntary organisations delivering services reduces in line with other providers; alternative scenarios based upon a 'smarter government' delivering more services through the sector imply a larger role, though it is far from clear whether such a role entails a larger paid workforce in the voluntary sector (HM Government [HMG], 2009). Either scenario clearly creates a quandary for unions that represent both voluntary sector and public sector employees (Unite, 2009a).

EMPLOYMENT STATUS: PART TIME STAFF AND TEMPORARY/FIXED-TERM CONTRACTS

Part-time work is a significant part of voluntary sector employment, with nearly four out of ten workers in the UK voluntary sector (37 percent) working part-time, equating to 247,000 employees. This proportion is much higher than in the public (29 percent) and private sectors (23 percent). Part-time working has implications for the management of human resources in terms of both organisational and individual development. For example, effective information and knowledge management systems need to be implemented and sufficient working arrangements, resources and guidance in place to facilitate it. While the prevalence of part-time employees suggests that many voluntary organisations have put such policies and practices in place, there continues to be evidence that all but the largest organisations continue to find such arrangements both difficult and costly,

Table 3.2   Total UK Workforce by Sector, 1996–2008 (Head Count, Thousands)

	1996	*1999*	*2002*	*2005*	*2008*
Voluntary sector	483	544	567	611	668
Public sector	6,135	6,112	6,441	6,978	7,016
Private sector	18,517	19,680	20,218	20,536	20,805
Total workforce	25,141	26,339	27,231	28,130	28,489

Source: Labour Force Survey
Base: All people aged 16 and over

with the affordability of dedicated human resources support cited as a particular barrier (Wainwright, 2004).

Fewer than one in ten (8 percent) voluntary sector part-time employees are working part-time because they could not find a full-time job, equating to 20,000 employees. More than eight out of ten (81 percent) of them (200,000 employees) do not want a full-time job. The fact that so many part-time employees do not want to work full-time suggests that they are attracted to the part-time opportunities that the voluntary sector offers. To maintain this attraction, it is important that the voluntary sector encourages and develops work-life balance policies.

A higher proportion of voluntary sector employees are on temporary contracts. Just over nine in ten employees (91 percent) in the sector are on permanent contracts. Both the private and public sectors have a higher proportion of employees on permanent contracts (96 percent and 93 percent, respectively). Between 1998 and 2008, the number of private sector employees on temporary contracts decreased by 27 percent, 273,000 employees, while the number of public sector ones on such contracts decreased by 16 percent, 97,000 employees. Conversely, the number of voluntary sector employees on temporary contracts increased by 15 percent, 8,000 employees, a situation the unions continue to highlight as a major cause of concern for their members (Unite, 2009b). Voluntary sector employers recognise such concerns, plus additional mission-related risks. Employees with poor job security or short-term contracts are relatively difficult to recruit and retain, with resignation before the completion of a fixed-term contract perceived to be a common problem (Cunningham and James, 2007).

Most voluntary sector employees on temporary contracts are on fixed-term ones. More than two out of three temporary voluntary sector employees (67 percent) are on contracts of this type; this equates to 40,000 employees. In the public sector a smaller proportion are on fixed-term contracts (60 percent), and in the private sector only 29 percent of temporary employees are. Between 1996 and 2008 the proportion of temporary voluntary sector employees on fixed-term contracts fluctuated between 56 percent and 72 percent. The higher usage of such contracts in the voluntary sector is likely to be related to the fact that many voluntary sector organisations depend to a considerable extent on short-term funding, evidence suggesting that a high level of funding volatility is relatively common (Clark et al., 2010).

Voluntary sector employees are mainly concentrated in small workplaces with one-third of voluntary sector workers (32 percent) employed in workplaces with fewer than 10 employees[6]. This is markedly different from both the private sector (25 percent) and the public sector (7 percent). These findings, particularly when combined with the prevalence of part-time employment and short-term contracts, have real implications for voluntary sector employment policy and practice. With most voluntary sector employees located in small workplaces, the task of providing support, such as training and development, becomes incredibly difficult (Wainwright, 2004). Small workplaces are less likely to provide internal training courses and have less capacity for peer support. Small workplaces are also less likely to have central services departments, such as human resources (HR), on site or an HR department at all. Research, for example, shows that more than two-thirds of small and medium-sized voluntary sector organisations do not have a dedicated HR specialist (Cunningham and Newsome, 2003), a feature which means that it is unlikely that the training and HR needs of their employees are being met.

FROM SECTOR TO INDUSTRY: WHAT AREAS ARE VOLUNTARY SECTOR EMPLOYEES WORKING IN?

Analysis of the voluntary sector workforce using the 1992 Standard Industrial Classification (SIC[92]) (ONS, 1997) helps to identify the areas of activity that employees work in. The SIC was designed to disaggregate industrial activities and so is not ideal when exploring the workforce of the voluntary sector. It does however provide an indication of the changing boundaries between the sectors.

More than half (56 percent) of all voluntary sector employees—374,000 employees—are employed in social work activities. Of this, 86 percent are employed in social work activities without accommodation. Overall, voluntary sector organisations providing social services receive a much larger amount of statutory income than any other subsector: £4.2 billion in 2006–07. The period 1996–2008 saw a huge increase in the number of voluntary sector workers employed in social work activities—from 202,000 employees in 1996 to 374,000 in 2008—an increase of 85 percent. The transfer of social care activities from the public sector may in part explain this substantial increase. Over the same period the number of employees working in social work activities in the public sector decreased from 480,000 to 424,000, a decrease of 13 percent.

There are 39,000 voluntary sector employees (6 percent) working in 'real estate activities' (for example, housing). Between 1996 and 2008 employment in this area has increased in both the private and voluntary sectors (by 52 percent and 46 percent, respectively), whereas in the public sector such employment has decreased (by 25 percent). This is likely to reflect the continuing transfer of housing provision from local authorities to the private and voluntary sectors.

The number of voluntary sector employees in the combined category of primary, secondary, special, and technical education has decreased between 1996 and 2008 from 65,000 to 50,000 (a decline of 22 percent). Both the public and private sectors have seen a substantial increase in employees in this area (an increase of 34 percent and 112 percent, respectively). Much of this expansion can be attributed to the primary education category, presumably a result of government policy in relation to class sizes.

WORKFORCE CHARACTERISTICS

More than two-thirds of the voluntary sector workforce are women (68 percent). This compares with the public sector (65 percent) but contrasts with the private sector (39 percent). The high proportion of women in the voluntary sector has implications for the sector's employment policies and practices, such as maternity leave, part-time working, and flexible working practices.

Just over two in five female employees in the voluntary sector are employed part-time (43 percent) compared to just over one in five (23 percent) of males. The number of women in the sector has seen a continual steady increase between 1996 and 2008. However the proportion of the voluntary sector workforce that is female has also remained relatively static. The proportion of women who work part-time has fluctuated but has remained basically unchanged. The proportion of men working part-time in the sector has, in contrast, increased from 14 percent in 1996 to 23 percent in 2005. The growth in the proportion of men who work part-time in the voluntary sector could reflect the growing number who view the voluntary sector as providing an alternative career path and wish to take up the sector's flexible working practices.

The voluntary sector workforce contains a higher proportion of disabled people than the public and private sectors. Nearly one in five people (19 percent) working in the voluntary sector has a disability compared to 14 percent of the public sector workforce and 12 percent of the private sector one. The proportion of disabled people working in the voluntary sector has increased from 14 percent in 1999 to 19 percent in 2008. The voluntary sector's policies on employment such as part-time hours, flexible working, and encouragement of diversity among its workforce may make it a good prospective employer for disabled people, but these statistics also reflect the traditional role of voluntary organisations in finding or even creating work (for example, through work integration schemes) for 'disadvantaged' groups in society (Aiken, 2007).

The ethnicity of more than nine in ten of the voluntary sector workforce is white (93 percent). This is slightly higher than in the public and private sectors (each equating to 91 percent). Between 2002 and 2008, the proportion of white employees has decreased slightly across all sectors by just over 1 percent.

Voluntary sector employees are relatively highly qualified. Two out of three voluntary sector employees (71 percent) have a qualification at 'A' level or beyond, and nearly four-in-ten (38 percent) have a degree-level qualification. The voluntary sector employee profile of qualifications is very similar to that of the public sector (68 percent and 37 percent, respectively). In the private sector just over half the employees (52 percent) have an 'A' level qualification or higher, and nearly one in five (19 percent) has a degree or equivalent qualification. Between 1998 and 2008 the number of voluntary sector employees with a degree increased from 147,000 to 252,000, an increase of 71 percent. This again gives weight to the suggestions that there has been a professionalisation of the voluntary sector and that both current and potential employees increasingly see a career path within the voluntary sector.

LEVELS OF PAY WITHIN THE VOLUNTARY SECTOR

Levels of pay and remuneration are increasingly argued to be a key factor in the recruitment and retention of paid employees. Unfortunately for both policy and practice, reliable evidence on levels of pay in the voluntary sector remains sparse. However, with increasing levels of public service delivery being contracted to the voluntary sector, it is increasingly important to understand the role of employment costs in what are labour-intensive service delivery activities.

Using Labour Force Survey data, Rutherford (2008) explored labour and nonprofit wage differentials in the health and social work industries. He identified that public sector wages were the highest, followed by the voluntary sector, with wages in the private sector significantly lower. There appeared to be a significant gap between the private sector and the other two sectors, whereas the wages within the public and voluntary sectors were broadly similar. Further analysis also found strong evidence of higher levels of unpaid overtime among employees in the voluntary sector, particularly female employees. However, basic hours wage equations identified a premium for both male and female workers (Rutherford, 2009).

Pay has been a particularly contested area in the field of social care, where many voluntary sector employees work. The Social Care Employers' Consortium identified particular issues between the public and the voluntary sectors with regard to pay (Social Care Employers' Consortium, 2008). Whereas the pay of voluntary sector care providers had increased by between 2 percent and 3 percent each year for the last three years, combined with a 15 percent increase in the national minimum wage, the increase was much less than the 35 percent increase in pay levels that local authority staff had experienced. With competition for care staff at a high level, the lower level of pay in the voluntary sector makes a voluntary organisation's task of recruiting high calibre staff more difficult. The report concluded that 'the government's commitment to working in partnership with the voluntary sector can only be achieved by its open acknowledgement that more effort and resources has to be put into creating a level playing field between local authorities and the voluntary sector.' These may well, however, be the concerns of a specific subsector, albeit one that is the majority employer within the sector. Indeed, while accurate intersector comparison remains difficult, the 'blurring of the boundaries' between sectors has led, we believe, to a more general narrowing—though not an eradication—of pay differentials.

FIT FOR PURPOSE? SKILLS WITHIN THE VOLUNTARY SECTOR WORKFORCE

As has already been noted, the enabling public policy environment that has been responsible for driving increased service delivery by voluntary organisations has been accompanied by a generic capacity building programme that has aimed to address the perceived weaknesses of voluntary organisations. Capacity building (or what McLaughlin [2004] refers to as 'modernisation') has addressed a range of issues, including funding, strategy development, performance management, ICT, and, relevant for this discussion, workforce and skills.

The skills agenda is of central importance to any discussion of the voluntary sector and public service delivery. In other words, does the voluntary sector workforce have the capacity to take on the public services role increasingly envisioned for it (Davidman et al., 1998)? The drive for 'world class' public services and expansion in activity in the main service delivery areas—health, social care, housing, education—have in turn created problems of recruiting and retaining appropriately skilled staff for employers in the voluntary, private, and public sectors (Public Services Forum, 2009). The voluntary sector's skills needs—whether skills shortages (an inability to recruit employees or volunteers with appropriate skills) or skills gaps (where existing staff or volunteers do not have the requisite skills to deliver the organisation's mission)—are therefore worthy of investigation. Our analysis draws upon evidence from a large-scale (N = 2,564) representative survey of skills shortages and skills gaps in the UK voluntary sector paid workforce (Clark, 2007) and a subsequent qualitative study (Clark and Jochum, 2008).

As the sector has taken on activities undertaken by public and private organisations and adopted management approaches undertaken in other sectors, it is perhaps unsurprising that many of the skills required to work within voluntary organisations are similar to those required in other sectors. These can be broadly defined as generic and specialist skills. Generic skills include literacy, numeracy, team-working, and communication skills. Specialist skills include legal knowledge and contract management. There are also skills that are specific to job roles found predominantly (though not exclusively) within the voluntary sector. These include fundraising, campaigning, and volunteer management.

RECRUITMENT PROBLEMS AND SKILLS SHORTAGES IN THE VOLUNTARY SECTOR

Our evidence suggests that skills shortages continue to inhibit the voluntary's sector's ability to deliver public services. Recruitment problems were evident across the voluntary sector with one-quarter of employers reporting hard-to-fill vacancies within their organisation (24 percent). For most functions[7], vacancies were more likely to be identified as hard to fill.[8] Whereas micro and small organisations[9] were less likely than large organisations to have vacancies within their organisation, they were more likely to report those they did have as hard to fill.

Employers most frequently identified hard-to-fill vacancies within youth work, social care, and health care (8 percent, 8 percent, and 7 percent, respectively). In social care, however, there is some evidence that recruitment difficulties have eased, though substantial proportions of employers continue to report difficulties in what is perceived to be an increasingly competitive market for staff (Social Care Employers' Consortium, 2008). Skills shortages were at the heart of hard-to-fill vacancies, with more than one-third of employers with hard-to-fill vacancies reporting skills shortage vacancies[10] (37 percent). In particular, nearly a quarter of employers cited a lack of specialist skills and/or experience in applicants (24 percent each). Only 13 percent of employers, however, reported a lack of qualifications as a problem.

There are a number of other contributory factors to hard-to-fill vacancies. Just under one quarter of employers cited few or no applicants as the reason behind their hard-to-fill vacancies (24 percent). While this inevitably reflected a relatively tight labour market, other reasons for hard-to-fill vacancies included an organisation's location, a perceived lack of career progression, and the type of job offered. Importantly, terms and conditions were mentioned by almost one fifth of employers (18 percent).

SKILLS GAPS IN THE VOLUNTARY SECTOR

Over the last two decades, the level of skills required for jobs has risen significantly. The proportion of jobs requiring at least level 4 qualifications (a certificate in higher education or above) has risen from 20 percent in 1986 to 30 percent in 2006.

On average, jobs in 2006 required a longer period of training. Thus, a training period of two years or more accounted for 30 percent of jobs in Britain compared to 22 percent in 1986 (Felstead, Gallie, Green, and Zhou, 2007). For voluntary organisations delivering public services, the increasingly widespread introduction or up-rating of quality standards has therefore been a double-edged sword: while improvements in quality are likely to result in better outcomes for beneficiaries (Forder, Netten, Caiels, Smith, and Malley, 2007), the associated costs of employment and training are argued by many to have not been incorporated into contracts (Parry and Kelliher, 2009).

Skills gaps[11] are apparent across the sector with around three in ten employers (29 percent) reporting underskilled staff within their organisation. Small organisations are more likely to report skills gaps. This is likely to be due to the staff having to be multiskilled to perform a variety of functions. Specialist skills gaps were a particular problem: more than one-quarter of employers reported skills gaps within strategic use of IT, legal knowledge, and fundraising (27 percent, 26 percent, and 25 percent, respectively). Some of the specialist skills were 'niche' skills (particularly in the field of health care), which made the gaps experienced by organisations harder to address. Soft skills such as communication and team working were also mentioned by one fifth of employers (21 percent and 19 percent, respectively). Skills gaps in management were perceived by organisations to have the greatest impact, with strategic management and people management cited most frequently.

SKILLS NEEDS: EMPLOYERS' RESPONSES

Our evidence indicates a clear link between skills gaps and lack of available resources for training and development, a problem most acute in small voluntary organisations. Both lack of funding and lack of time for training and development were identified as the main causes of skills gaps (57 percent and 47 percent, respectively). In a similar vein, approximately one-third of employers reporting skills gaps identified that there was a lack of suitable internal or external training available to them (33 percent and 29 percent, respectively).

Overall, just under three-quarters of employers formally assessed whether individuals have gaps in their skills and/or hold a training and development policy. Two-thirds of employers (66 percent) had an annual training and development budget. The average annual training budget per organisation was approximately £3,877, rising to £7,491 if employers who do not have a training budget are discounted.[12] This equates to an average of £121 per employee, rising to £234 per employee if employers who do not have a training budget are discounted.

Other than training, organisations had addressed skills shortages and gaps using a number of tactics, but a common impact appears to have been an increased burden upon other employees. Reorganisation of workloads (44 percent of employers) and substitution of paid staff with volunteers (25 percent) are the most common responses, though both responses in-turn can generate different management difficulties, particularly given widespread evidence of difficulties in recruiting volunteers (for instance, Skills for Justice, 2009).

CONCLUSION

It has been argued in this chapter that a substantial expansion in the size, scope, and activities of the formal voluntary sector has been shaped by large-scale investment in public services and an enabling public policy environment that has sought to build the role and capacity of the voluntary sector with regard to their delivery. In turn, this has driven-up employment levels in the 'core' voluntary sector and increased the number of employers, making the sector a more visible and tangible career option for employees who might traditionally have thought in terms of just the public or private sectors. At the same time, it has also been argued that policy and practice might benefit from a more nuanced understanding of perceptions of the voluntary sector as an employment option, particularly among older workers who will in future constitute a majority of the UK workforce.

There is also an increasing prevalence of 'boundary-changers'—employees moving between the public, private, and voluntary sectors, often at a senior management level—that in part reflects the closer relationship between a mainstreamed voluntary sector and other public sector bodies; in some cases, employees have found themselves working in the voluntary sector as a result of service transfers. This closer proximity between the two sectors has, we believe, contributed to changing organisational cultures and approaches to management within the voluntary sector, with evidence of both professionalisation and bureaucratisation. The isomorphic tendencies of statutory bodies and commissioners have therefore been a force for good and bad for the voluntary sector and its workforce. In particular, concerns remain that the contract market relating to the delivery of public services has impacted negatively on the terms and conditions of those transferring from the public sector. These concerns point, on the basis of the evidence reviewed, to a need for a more robust empirical understanding of how far this has been the case.

We have also argued that the expanded service delivery role for voluntary organisations has brought additional capacity, but also new challenges in relation to workforce and employment issues. If current labour market surveys are correct, by 2012 the number of working adults available for employment will decline. As such, it is hard to see some of these challenges going away.

An ongoing shortage of suitably skilled employees in areas such as social care has been compounded by funding mechanisms that have emphasised short-term arrangements and failed to address the core costs associated with being a good employer or the costs of managing volunteers. Volunteers are still too often perceived as free labour, when much of the evidence suggests otherwise. In addition, the relationship between paid staff and volunteers has received insufficient attention and is a subject that deserves further research, particularly in relation to the delivery of public services. For example, do paid staff crowd out volunteers, and if so, why? Anecdotal evidence suggests too many voluntary organisations are not good employers and, in some cases, volunteer managers. Again, policy and practice would benefit from further investigation by the research community to quantify such concerns.

How might these trends and challenges unfold in the future? Much has currently been written about the forthcoming 'era of austerity,' when public services may well be scaled back significantly. As we have already noted, some commentators are arguing that this situation represents a huge opportunity for the voluntary sector to demonstrate it can run services more cheaply and effectively. However, a clear danger is that this approach may pander to existing misconceptions about the use of volunteer labour. Moreover, the pursuit of this agenda implies a 'race to the bottom' in terms of the cost and quality of public services. This scenario, where services delivered by voluntary organisations are no different from those delivered by the statutory bodies they seek to replace (and improve on), has been referred to as 'public service transfer' (Paxton et al., 2005). An alternative scenario, 'public service transformation,' implies a role for voluntary organisations based upon the value and values, such as proximity to users, which are characteristic, if not unique, to the voluntary sector. It is perhaps encouraging therefore that a continuing interest in values (Blake and Smerdon, 2006; Jochum and Pratten, 2009), and the need to remain distinctive, is evident among many voluntary organisations, including those that deliver public services under contract.

Finally, it is worth noting that although our knowledge of the dimensions and characteristics of the voluntary sector workforce has improved measurably over the last decade, there remain substantive areas where empirical evidence and detailed understanding are weak. Whether the voluntary sector paid workforce continues to expand or begins to recede, there is nevertheless certainty that employment in the sector will continue to be an issue deserving of more attention from the research community.

NOTES

1. This includes resources from UK central, local, and devolved administrations, international bodies, and overseas governments.
2. Thanks must go to Stephen McKay at the Third Sector Research Centre, University of Birmingham, who provided the Labour Force Survey data tables on which these findings are based.
3. Formal volunteering is defined by giving unpaid help through groups, clubs, or organisations to benefit other people or the environment.
4. Kendall and Almond (2000) highlight a key characteristic of the survey: that of self-definition by participants in terms of sector of employer. Evidence produced by the Scottish Council for Voluntary Organisations in relation to the Scottish voluntary sector workforce suggests that self-definition, combined with the structure of the LFS question on sector, leads to underenumeration of voluntary sector employees. Contact the authors for a more detailed discussion of this problem.
5. For more information on the voluntary sector workforce and a discussion of these estimates, please see the *UK Civil Society Almanac, 2010* (Clark, Kane, Wilding, and Wilton, 2010).

6. The size of the workplace refers to the total number of employees at the respondent's workplace.
7. During the survey, it did not matter whether a staff member had a different job title, but whether they conducted that function within their work. It is therefore possible for one member of staff to work in multiple functions.
8. *Hard to fill vacancies* are those vacancies described by employers as being hard to fill.
9. A four-category size classification was implemented: microenterprises (2–9 employees), small employers (10–49 employees), medium employers (50–99 employees), and large employers (100+ employers).
10. Skills shortage vacancies are those hard-to-fill vacancies which are the result of either lack of required basic or specialist skills, qualifications, or experience in the applicants.
11. Skills gaps are defined in terms of staff being underskilled in their function. In the survey, respondents were asked to indicate for each of a number of functions if they considered any member of staff to be underskilled. All those which identified at least one function where staff were underskilled were identified as having a skills gap.
12. These figures cannot be compared to the figures presented within the *National Employers Skills Survey* (NESS) because of the large variation between the questions. The *National Employers Skills Survey* uses a 24-question additional survey to explore training expenditure in more detail (Learning and Skills Council ([LSC], 2008).

BIBLIOGRAPHY

Aiken, M. (2007). *What is the role of social enterprise in finding, creating, and maintaining employment for disadvantaged groups?* London: .Office of the Third Sector.

Anheier, H., and Salamon, L. (2006). The nonprofit sector in comparative perspective. In W. Powell, and R. Steinberg (eds.), *The nonprofit sector: A research handbook* (2nd ed., pp.). New Haven: Yale University Press, pp. 86–116.

Blake, G., and Smerdon, M. (2006). *Living values.* London: Community Links.

Cater, N. (2002). Creeping 'charitisation' threatens public services. *The Guardian.* Available at www.guardian.co.uk/society/2002/sep/30/charities.comment. Accessed December 2002.

Charity Commission. (2008). *Trustee remuneration: Views from the sector.* Available at www.charity-commission.gov.uk/enhancingcharities/trindex.asp. Accessed March 2008.

Clark, J. (2007). *UK voluntary sector skills survey, 2007.* London: UK Workforce Hub.

Clark, J., Kane, D., Wilding, K., and Wilton, J. (2010). *The UK civil society almanac, 2010.* London: NCVO.

Clark, J., Kane, D., and Wilding, K. (2009). *The state and the voluntary sector: Recent trends in government funding and public service delivery.* London: NCVO.

Clark, J., and Jochum, V. (2008). *Third sector skills research, 2008: Further evidence and recommendations on skills gaps.* London: NCVO.

Craig, G., Taylor, M., Carlton, N., Garbutt, R., Kimberlee, K., Lepine, E., and Syed, A. (2005). *The paradox of compacts: Monitoring the implementation of compacts.* London: Home Office.

Cunningham, I., and James, P. (2007). *False economy? The costs of contracting and workforce insecurity in the voluntary sector.* London: UNISON. Available at www.unison.org.uk/acrobat/B3258.pdf. Accessed December 2009.

Cunningham, I., and Newsome, K. (2003). *More than just a wing and a prayer: Identifying human resource capacity among small and medium sized organisations in the voluntary sector.* London: NCVO.

Davidman, K., Betcherman, G., Hall, M., and White, D. (1998). Work in the nonprofit sector: The knowledge gap. *The Philanthropist,* 14 (3), 34–48.

Davis-Smith, J. (1998). *The 1997 national survey of volunteering* London: Institute for Volunteering Research.

Department for Communities and Local Government (DCLG). (2009). *Citizenship survey: 2009–10 (April–June 2009), England.* London: DCLG.

Felstead, A., Gallie, D., Green, F., and Zhou, Y. (2007). *Skills at work, 1986–2006.* Oxford: ESRC.

Forder, J.,Netten, A., Caiels, J., Smith, J., and Malley, J. (2007). *Measuring outcomes in social care: Conceptual development and empirical design.* Kent: University of Kent PSSRU.

HM Government (HMG). (2009). *Smarter government: Putting the frontline first.* London: The Stationery Office.

Jochum, V., and Pratten, B. (2009). *Values into action: How organisations translate their values into practice.* London: NCVO.

Kendall, J. (2003). *The voluntary sector: Comparative perspectives in the UK.* London: Routledge.

Kendall, J., and Almond, S. (2000). *Paid employment in the self-defined voluntary sector in the late 1990s: An initial description of patterns and trends.* Civil Society Working Paper 7. London: LSE.

Learning and Skills Council (LSC). (2008). *National employers skills survey, 2007.* Coventry: LSC.

Leete, L. (2006). Work in the nonprofit sector. In W. Powell and R. Steinberg (eds.), *The nonprofit sector: A research handbook* (2nd ed., pp.). New Haven: Yale University Press, 159–179.

Lewis, D. (2008). Using life histories in social policy research: The case of third sector/public sector boundary crossing. *Journal of Social Policy,* 37 (4), 559–578.

McLaughlin, K. (2004). Towards a 'modernized' voluntary, and community sector? *Public Management Review* 6 (4), 555–562.

National Institute of Adult Continuing Education. (2009). *Narrowing participation for adults,* Leicester: NCVO.

Neilson, A. (2009). A crisis of identity: Nacro's bid to run a prison and what it means for the voluntary sector. *The Howard Journal of Criminal Justice,* 48 (4), 401–410.

Office for National Statistics. (ONS) (1997) UK Standard Industrial Classification of Economic Activities UK SIC(92) Methodological Guide. Online. Available at http://www.statistics.gov.uk/methods_quality/sic/contents.asp. Accessed October 2008.

ONS. (2009). *Labour force survey user guide, volume 1: Background and methodology.* Newport: ONS.

Office of the Third Sector (OTS). (2007). *Helping put: A national survey of volunteering and charitable giving.* London: Cabinet Office.

Parry, E., and Kelliher, C. (2009). Voluntary sector responses to increased resourcing challenges. *Employee Relations,* 31 (1), 9–24.

Paxton, W., Pearce, N., Unwin, J., and Molyneux, P. (2005). *The voluntary sector delivering public services: Transfer or transformation?* York: JRF. ,.

Public Services Forum. (2009). *Quality skills ,quality services: Final report of the public services forum learning and skills task group.* London: Cabinet

Office. Available at www.cabinetoffice.gov.uk/media/211487/quality skills.pdf. Accessed December 2009.

Russell, L., and Scott, D. (1997). *Very active citizens? The impact of contracts on volunteers.* Manchester: University of Manchester.

Rutherford, A. (2009). *Where is the warm glow? Donated labour and nonprofit wage differentials in the health and social work industries.* Stirling Economics Discussion paper, University of Stirling. Available at www.econ.stir.ac.uk/DPs/ SEDP-2009–20-Rutherford.pdf. Accessed December 2009.

Rutherford, A. (2008). *Exploring voluntary sector pay at the industry level: Evidence from the UK labour force survey.* Paper presented at the NCVO/VSSN Researching the Voluntary Sector Conference, September 9–10, Warwick University, England.

Skills for Justice. (2009). *Skills in the justice sector: A survey of third sector employers, 2009.* Sheffield: Skills for Justice.

Social Care Employers' Consortium. (2008). *Social care: Has anything changed? A report into the recruitment and retention of the voluntary sector social care workforce.* Social Care Employers' Consortium. Available at www.lcdisability. org/?lid=8122. Accessed December 2009.

Unite. (2009a). *Charities are being used as 'the privatisation Trojan horse' in the NHS.* Available at www.unitetheunion.com/news__events/latest_news/charities_are_being_used_as_%e2%80%98t.aspx. Accessed November 2009.

Unite. (2009b). *Unite recommendations for funding in the sector.* Available at www.unitetheunion.com/sectors/community_youth_workers/campaigns-1/ funding_campaign/unite_recommendations_for_fund.aspx. Accessed November 2009.

Wainwright, S. (2004). *A stitch in time: The provision of HR support by voluntary sector infrastructure organisations to their clients and ,members.* London: NCVO.

4 Trade Union Organising in the Voluntary Sector

Mike Short

INTRODUCTION

This chapter explores the issue of trade union organising in the voluntary sector from the perspective of a trade union official engaged in it on behalf of one of Britain's largest unions, UNISON. More specifically, it does so by reference to the experiences of the author and his union in seeking to expand membership, workplace organisation, and employer recognition in the sector.

The chapter starts by providing an overview of UNISON's presence in the voluntary sector and moves on to describe the key issues and concerns union members in it face and how UNISON is seeking to address them. The nature, theoretically, of trade union organising and how UNISON has been pursuing it are then considered, along with some evolving strands of the union's organising strategy.

WHERE ARE WE NOW? UNISON'S PRESENCE IN THE SECTOR

Of UNISON's 1.3 million members, more than 60,000 work in the community and voluntary sector. These members are spread across various types of organisations. More than a third work for housing associations. A large proportion work for large charities (for example, the union has more than 1,000 members in Barnardo's, approaching the same number in Mencap, and several hundred in various other 'big-name' charities). Others, meanwhile, are spread more thinly across a wide range of smaller organisations.

Members located in the community and voluntary sector are an important and integral part of the union and are committed, dedicated, and highly motivated workers who do vital jobs, working in the hearts of communities, and responding to their needs. Trade union organisation can, and does, provide members with a powerful collective voice at work, effective workplace representation, and highly developed communications and information-sharing networks across the voluntary sector.

UNISON has seen very rapid growth in its voluntary sector membership over the last few years. Between 2004 and 2008, it rose from 40,000 to 60,000 members—an increase of 50 percent. Some of this increase has been what might be termed 'organic' in that it is the product of the recruitment of brand-new members. But a lot of the increase (although it is difficult to say precisely how much) is due to transfers of staff arising from outsourcing that have led to members moving across from the public sector—a traditional UNISON stronghold. Either way, the union's membership in the sector is rising rapidly, and the challenges presented in terms of member participation, representation, and bargaining are growing accordingly.

A key determinant of a union's strength and influence in the workplace is its density of membership—the *proportion* of the workforce that is in membership. Union density across the voluntary sector is difficult to calculate, not least because there are so many different definitions of what the sector is and where its boundaries lie. But the union estimates that density for all unions combined is somewhere around 25 percent.

UNISON's main activists are known as stewards—workplace trade union representatives who have been trained and carry out a wide variety of tasks, such as representing individuals and negotiating with their employers. UNISON has 1,500 stewards in the voluntary sector. Set against our membership level, that is one steward for every 40 members—a very healthy activist-to-member ratio that is comparable to that in other sectors. But the average amount of steward activ*ism* (or activity) per member is much less. The reasons for this discrepancy, and the implications of it, will be explored further below.

WHAT'S GOING ON? THE ISSUES FOR UNISON MEMBERS IN THE VOLUNTARY SECTOR

Although the subject under discussion is trade union organising in the voluntary sector, this activity does not take place in a vacuum. It is influenced by the underlying aim of helping members achieve fairness at work and defending and improving their terms and conditions of employment. So it is important to describe some of the problems faced by members and potential members working for voluntary sector organisations which give rise to the need for organising.

The underlying cause of many of the problems faced by UNISON's voluntary sector members is the funding regime in which many of their employers operate.

As a result of the government's increasing use of the voluntary sector to provide public services, and the consequent shift in statutory funding for the sector away from grants and more toward contracts for service provision, many employers are now competing for contracts (Davies, 2007). In order to win these contracts, employers are cutting costs in a variety of ways—such as awarding a very low cost-of-living pay increase (or, in some cases, freezing pay completely); making staff redundant and leaving those that remain to cope with the workload; downgrading workers; and restructuring entire reward systems to remove pay increments and other commitments arising from the Transfer of Undertakings (Protection of Employment) (TUPE) Regulations (Cunningham and James, 2007). At the time of writing, for example, some organisations had recently brought forward radical proposals to alter fundamentally the terms and conditions of entire workforces—in effect dismissing and re-engaging all staff on inferior terms and conditions, with less chance for progression and less generous conditions of service.

The short-term nature of many of these contracts for the delivery of public services means that many voluntary sector workers are permanently insecure in their jobs, in some cases being served with a redundancy notice every year.

Other common problems relating to terms and conditions in the voluntary sector are the presence of two-tier workforces (workers alongside each other, doing the same job, getting paid different amounts), poor training provision, health and safety concerns (particularly violence at work), and deteriorating occupational pensions provision. A survey of housing association workers carried out by UNISON and Income Data Services in 2007 revealed that 20 percent of housing association workers have either no occupational pension or just a money purchase one (Storry and Melis, 2007).

It is consequently clear that the government's desired level playing field between public and voluntary sector providers does not exist. Driven down by cost-based competition, terms and conditions for voluntary sector workers providing public services are inferior to those of workers providing equivalent ones in the public sector. Competing with more reliable funding, comprehensive training strategies like the National Health Service's (NHS's) Knowledge and Skills Framework and the major public sector pension schemes, it is therefore no surprise that voluntary organisations can find themselves struggling to recruit and retain the staff that they need (Nickson, Warhurst, Dutton, and Hurrell, 2008).

These outcomes can be seen as the inevitable consequences of the current legislative and policy context within which public sector outsourcing is occurring. The TUPE regulations, for example, are not as strong as they could or should be: employers can engage in restructuring so as to avoid their requirements, and the protection of pensions granted by TUPE is weak (Cavalier and Arthur, 2007). Full cost recovery, a much-debated issue in the voluntary sector and a principle supported by the government (Home Office, 2005), is still not achieved by most voluntary sector organisations providing services on behalf of the public sector (Charity Commission, 2007). In addition, the definition of 'full cost' can vary—organisations may consider that they achieve full cost recovery, even if they do not budget for contractually guaranteed incremental pay increases, for example. At a broader level, the absence of social or fair wage clauses that serve to take terms and conditions out of the competitive offer means that voluntary sector organisations will continue to compete by cutting staffing costs, rather than on the basis of the different qualities and innovations they can bring to the service for which they are bidding.

If contracting out is to continue to happen in such a context, then UNISON is against it, because it leads far too often to a local authority's deciding to contract out a service, setting a fairly minimal threshold for service quality, and then creating a contest to find who can do it cheapest. This approach, as well as causing a constant downward pressure on labour costs, prompts more and more organisations to shift resources into the contracting field, at the expense of their longer-term innovative, community-based, and campaigning work. Nevertheless, it is this latter work which the Labour Government has given as a reason for wanting the sector to be more involved in public service delivery (Davies, 2007).

Clearly, a better approach would be for public bodies, like local authorities, to think first about the type of service they want and then consider who might help them best achieve it, with in-house bids from the appropriate public sector provider being actively encouraged. For, if contracts *are* to be used, they must be used in the interests of the service users; an issue that cannot, of course, be divorced from the need to treat staff fairly.

These matters of policy and politics are crucial for UNISON as it decides what its organising tactics for the voluntary sector should be. Whereas underlying universal principles of trade union organising do exist, their application must differ depending on the industrial realities of a sector.

WHAT IS ORGANISING? A BRIEF DISCUSSION

Organising is one of these words that gets talked about a lot in trade union circles and defined in different ways. There is consequently no indisputable and succinct definition.

Having spent several years as a union organiser, and also spending a lot of time working with community organising groups with which UNISON has close working relationships, I would define organising like this: *building your membership, in terms of size and activity, so as to increase bargaining power, building skills, and developing leadership, identifying collective issues and objectives, and facilitating member-led campaigns to achieve those objectives.*

For a trade union, organising therefore involves recruitment, identifying activists and training them, working with members and activists, communicating, bargaining, and negotiating around pay and conditions at work, and campaigning in different arenas, such as equalities and public service reform.

The nearest I can get to a pithy definition, then, would be: *using collective campaigning and bargaining to increase your size and strength, and using your increased size and strength to make your campaigning and bargaining more successful.*

But there are tensions within these definitions. One implication of the organising model suggested by these definitions is that unions should recruit people by appealing to whatever their 'issues' are, and then collectivise them. In the context of trade union organising, 'issues' tend to refer to concerns or situations affecting workers in their workplaces. Collectivising them should be easy enough for some of the 'big' issues, like pay and job security. But as we have seen, those issues are not the only ones faced by workers in the voluntary sector—in fact they may not even be the main concerns.

The results of the UNISON / Income Data Services housing association worker survey in 2007 made it clear that pensions are at least as big a concern as pay for workers in that part of the voluntary sector (Storry and Melis, 2007). The survey also found that equalities and workplace-based training are major concerns. Meanwhile, some members are more concerned about child care issues, as they are away from home a lot. Others prioritise health and safety—they work alone in challenging environments and are regularly at risk of being attacked at work. All of these issues are important; so if you recruit 100 new members, and each one has a different issue, how do you prioritise among them? The answer is that organising actually involves elements of education and leadership. A free vote on the number one issue, without any sense of direction, will often just end in confusion.

A slightly different insight into what organising is may be gleaned from the author's experience of organising alongside community groups. One variant version of the theory of organising rejects the principle of issue-based organising, in favour of *interest*-based organising. In this model, organisers are trained to speak to individuals and identify their concerns, beliefs, and priorities on a much broader basis, asking people probing questions to find out about their families, their religious beliefs, their personal circumstances—a wide range of interests which may not seem relevant to the domain you are operating in (for example, trade unionism). The advantages of this model are that organising can be based very accurately on individuals' own concerns, giving it a high degree of relevance to the targets of the organising, people are encouraged to build alliances and determine their own collective goals, and organisers can use knowledge of people's interests to develop appropriate collective goals, often with great success. A drawback, however, is that issues identified in this manner can be more difficult to collectivise at the workplace level.

KEY AREAS FOR TRADE UNION ORGANISING IN THE SECTOR

In this section, the application of these ideas and principles of organising to UNISON's current position in the voluntary sector is examined by reference to five crucial aspects of its work in it.

Recognition

In many of the voluntary organisations where UNISON has members, the union does not have recognition and therefore bargaining rights. As a result, the union is often precluded from negotiating with employers to improve workers' terms and conditions.

Under UK employment law, recognition, unless granted voluntarily by the employer, can only be obtained if half of the workforce is in membership or if majority support is obtained in a recognition ballot, with this support constituting 40 percent of those eligible to vote (Ewing, Moore, and Wood, 2003). Obtaining such levels of membership or support is probably the biggest headache facing the union.

People will tend to join a union very happily if they can see how their membership relates to the process for changing terms and conditions, how they can get involved in it, and what the results will be. For example, often, when the union convinces employers to grant voluntary recognition before 50 percent of the workforce is in membership, it does so by convincing them that workers want to join, but also seeking some sign that there will be a bargaining relationship. A good example of this is the mental health charity Together Working for Well-being, where UNISON's membership grew by 130 percent in the two and a half years after recognition was granted.

Without a negotiating relationship, members are left with weaker consultative arrangements, with representatives basically accountable to employers and elections organised by the employers. This lack of independence means that non-recognition-based consultation arrangements rely on the employer's goodwill and are usually toothless. They serve more as forums to discuss general organisational business than as a chance for employees to have a tangible stake in their own workplace issues. Thus, whereas the Information and Consultation of Employees Regulations 2004 (Welch, 2006) establish an extremely helpful minimum standard for employee engagement, the structures that these regulations require are no substitute for collective bargaining.

In organisations where trade union recognition is in place, the benefits to staff are clear. There is a proper mechanism for negotiating around pay and conditions, backed by the training and support of a trade union, and the outcomes for terms and conditions are demonstrably better than would be achieved without collective bargaining.

But there are benefits for employers too: access to a free source of human resource expertise (which is becoming an increasing asset as small voluntary organisations struggle to fulfil their infrastructure obligations to public sector funders in the face of ever-tighter funding); effective, trained, and confident representatives; and a cost-effective way to fulfil legal obligations through talking to staff. Of course, unions need to continue to make this case, rather than assuming that it will be immediately obvious to employers who perhaps have little or no experience of working with unions. But without more actual negotiating, the ratio of talking to action will continue to be unfavourable, and voluntary organisations will continue to waste a lot of time and money.

Aside from membership density, one of the other biggest barriers to unions organising for recognition is a cultural one which is specific to the voluntary sector.

A common perception is that voluntary sector employers are generally more pro-union than private sector ones and maybe more so than those in the public sector as well. But working with unions is much more common in these other sectors than in the voluntary one. In the public sector, negotiation with unions tends to take place because it always has—membership density is comparatively high, and engaging in negotiations is 'what you do.' In the private sector, employers are less likely to be happy with having a negotiating relationship, but may prefer to take the path of least resistance. They think *'Here's a union, they represent a lot of the staff, it would be better to get them into a constructive relationship than to set them up as an adversary from the outset.'*

In the voluntary sector, especially when union density is low, the employers' approach can often be summed up by the phrase 'what about the non-members?' They will talk to the union, but want arrangements which enable non-members to be represented, too. In addition, some parts of the sector seem wary of trade unions—with many charities seeming to favour a libertarian individualistic approach to helping people, as opposed to the unions' collectivist one—the organising model.

When they do take the plunge, most employers accept the clear benefits of negotiating with trade unions. Even organisations in which industrial action has been taken accept that an ongoing relationship with UNISON is the most effective way to resolve pay and conditions issues.

Some employers have developed models in which formal recognition is granted to the union, but which also enable nonunionised staff to be consulted. But employers need to accept that *bargaining* can only happen with workers who have formed an independent collective group, a union, and that only workers who join that group will be represented by a body that is both sufficiently independent, and sufficiently representative, to enable valid negotiations to take place.

Member Recruitment

So it is clear that in order to gain recognition in more voluntary sector workplaces, unions need to recruit more members. The basic principles guiding recruitment activities in the voluntary sector are no different from those for any other sector:

- Listening is more important than talking;
- Appeal to individuals' actual concerns;

- Discuss the benefits of building alliances and taking a collective approach to problems;
- 'Face to face' contact works better than remote communication;
- 'Like recruits like' can be a successful approach;
- Describe, demonstrate, and discuss the benefits of joining;
- Access new starters at induction so that you can approach potential members on or near day one;
- Employer support is useful, providing it doesn't come across as too close.

However, the way the voluntary sector tends to work, and the way the public sector is increasingly using the voluntary sector, can cause particular difficulties for trade unions in applying these principles to their recruitment efforts.

As has already been indicated, a large number of UNISON's members in the voluntary sector work in small organisations, or in small workplaces within large organisations. Twenty-three thousand, or nearly 40 percent, of UNISON's voluntary sector members are found in groups of fewer than five members, spread across 14 thousand workplaces. Two-thirds of those members are the only UNISON member in their workplace.

Although public service delivery is still only a small proportion of what the voluntary sector does, a large majority of UNISON's members in the sector are engaged in delivering public services through contracts between public sector bodies (usually local authorities) and voluntary sector employers. The kinds of services that tend to be transferred to the voluntary sector are those that deal with particularly challenging or vulnerable service users or situations, and which often require intensive service provision. This means that members in the sector might typically be employed in small community care teams, visiting widely spread service users; or in small residential care homes for people with profound mental ill-health requiring 24-hour care; or in floating support services, delivering housing-related support to older people across an entire local authority area.

This model of working is a specific result of the transfer of public sector work to the voluntary sector, in particular the decisions made about what sorts of services are transferred. If, for example, acute wards in hospitals are transferred, then the challenges posed for trade unions seeking to increase their membership are very different. As it is, the nature of the transfers to the sector has meant that it is very hard to get to potential members and try to recruit them. For example, often the workplace will be a service user's home because many UNISON members work in residential homes for people with severe mental health problems or learning disabilities. Sensitivity is therefore required. A workplace might even be a private house, which the worker visits to provide care or support. The increasing personalisation of public services will make this even more of an issue for trade union recruitment strategies.

Activism and Participation

Union organising is as much about encouraging activism as it is about increasing membership. It is an uncomfortable truth of trade union organising that people get active in their union when times are troubled. In other words, when things are bad, unions get more stewards.

If the link between 'bad times' for workers and unions' ability to recruit stewards were to hold, it would be expected that activist numbers in the sector would be good, and this, as already noted, is indeed the case. Thus, despite the fact that the union's organisation in the voluntary sector is less developed than in the public sector, the activist-to-member ratio is very similar. The difference is that, as noted earlier, *activism* in the sector is lower.

The key to encouraging activism with any type of employer is facility time; that is, paid time off given by the employer to enable representatives to carry out trade union duties. The provision of such time is a major problem in the voluntary sector.

Employers who recognise the union will usually grant facility time for union duties, like representation, if not broader union activities, like attending a conference. But employers who have not granted recognition give representatives little or no such time. With tight budgets, it is no surprise that employers are reluctant to grant facility time. However, as long as facility time is limited, the benefits unions can bring to organisations will also be limited.

It is consequently clear that trade unions in the sector need to be more robust in talking up the benefits for employers of facility time, such as:

- Quick and effective resolution of grievances and disciplinaries (in fact, often resolution of issues at a very localised and sometimes informal level);
- Better learning practices and a positive impact on the organisation's training strategy, through union learning representatives and learning partnerships;
- Healthier and safer workplaces due to health and safety representatives.

Lack of facility time is, though, not the only barrier to membership participation in voluntary sector unions. Even in places where there is a good facility time agreement, the type of work that the sector does means that often it just isn't possible to take it. A lot of members in the sector are, for example, engaged in residential social care work in isolated settings and find themselves unable to leave their workplaces at all.

Individual Representation

Individual representation is another of the significant challenges unions face while organising in the voluntary sector, for a number of reasons.

The first problem is the number and distribution of activists. A lot of paid organisers' time is taken up with individual representation; time which organisers should ideally be spending on other things (like campaigning on workplace issues, identifying and training activists, and helping build workplace structures which will enable a local organisation to become sustainable), but which they have to do. This is partly because there are not sufficient workplace representatives, or, more accurately, because these representatives are not distributed equally in relation to where members are. Indeed, most of UNISON's voluntary sector members do not have a representative in their own workplace.

Another reason for organisers' time being taken up with individual representation is the difficulty of training activists in the voluntary sector. In order to represent members effectively, representatives need training. Employers, however, often make the provision of training difficult. One major charity, for example, has acknowledged the value UNISON representatives can bring, but complains that there are not enough competent representatives, while refusing them time off to undertake basic representative training.

Facility time is also an important issue here. Representatives in the public sector have superior facility time arrangements, and so representation of individuals is much easier. In the voluntary sector, where human resource practices are less developed as it is, paid organisers often carry out individual representation. This means that members are not represented by a local workplace representative with knowledge of the employer and a feel for its culture, organisers are diverted from more strategic collective work, and members feel cut off from their union branches, which are sometimes dominated by their public sector counterparts already.

Pay

The first major issue in terms of pay is that, in a large number of voluntary sector organisations, there is no process for negotiating it. Instead, annual pay uplifts (or decisions to not provide them) are decided by the organisation and then reported to staff forums as part of what is inaccurately termed a 'consultative process.'

Another major issue for unions in engaging in pay bargaining with voluntary organisations is the financial arena in which they are operating. Undeniable shifts have taken place in the way that the sector is funded, and these are having a real effect on the manner in which unions do, and can, engage in pay bargaining.

Voluntary organisations, especially the large ones which employ many of UNISON's members, are becoming increasingly reliant on statutory funds (National Audit Office, 2007).Within that source of money, the balance of funding is, as already noted, shifting away from grant funding and increasingly toward contract funding—fees paid by a statutory body to a voluntary organisation in return for the provision of a service for a set period of time. The result, as again has already been observed, is that organisations are being forced to compete for contracts and in many cases can only win them by cutting costs. This puts a consistent strain on negotiations between employers and unions on the subject of staff terms and conditions.

At this point, a major qualification should be made. *Every* employer involved in pay negotiations with a trade union has financial constraints— sometimes self-imposed, sometimes coming from outside, sometimes both. A private company must bear in mind the expectations of shareholders. Government departments have to operate within Treasury restrictions. Some public bodies have funding dependent on results or ratings. So the voluntary sector's reliance on government policies is not unique.

Nonetheless, that reliance is a reality: voluntary sector employers *are* constrained in negotiations as a result of the low-cost competitive environment. UNISON is finding a diverse range of reactions to this situation from employers.

At one end of the scale, one major charity in which UNISON has many members is doing more than simply limiting pay increases in the face of funding pressures. They are actively scrutinising legal cases, seeking legal loopholes, to find any way out of paying a cost-of-living increase to different groups of staff. As a result, this charity has a lot of staff on 'frozen pay.'

Often, UNISON negotiators find themselves pleading with employers not to bid for work they cannot afford—and to factor in long-term staffing costs (including pensions provision, funding for training and career paths, and adhering to government codes of practice intended to prevent the emergence of a two-tier workforce). Too many employers agree but then bid anyway and stay afloat by freezing pay. Employers who have taken such steps have moved beyond the place where negotiation is possible. The result, in the case of the charity mentioned above, was industrial action. This action ended in success for the workers in question: following the transfer of the contract concerned to a different provider, and a TUPE transfer for the staff, the new employer agreed to give the pay increase which the previous employer had refused to honour.

At the other end of this spectrum of approaches to dealing with financial pressures, a large learning disabilities service provider has been much more open in recent years, telling the union exactly what uplift every local authority funder is paying them, and then negotiating on the basis of that information. This seems to be a much fairer tactic. It enables the union to make claims which are ambitious and yet realistic—and to use its experience to suggest ways to make the most of limited funding. So in this case, for example, negotiations have explored deleting the lowest pay scale points and raising payments for sleeping-in shifts, as well as a cost-of-living increase.

So UNISON's approach to negotiating with employers relies on developing an open and honest relationship. The employer needs to provide a good picture of what is going on and not bid for contracts irresponsibly. The union needs to use its experience to suggest ways to improve conditions, without threatening the organisation's sustainability, and must avoid making unrealistic promises to members that can hinder the negotiating process. Of course, alongside this, the union still campaigns to make the overall 'negotiating pot' bigger via political work, notably lobbying the government for changes in its treatment of public services and the voluntary sector.

TRADE UNION ORGANISING IN THE SECTOR—NEW WAYS OF WORKING

Over the last few years, UNISON has developed a number of organising initiatives which it believes are beginning to improve its response to the problems described above.

New Organising Projects

UNISON's ongoing identification of organising projects in the voluntary sector focuses very much on issues which are of specific concern to the sector in general and which have local relevance. The idea of this strategy is to increase membership from the 'bottom up,' attracting activists who are impressed by the union's ability to relate to concerns which to them are immediate and real, while also raising the union's national profile as one which is in tune with trends and developments in the voluntary sector as a whole.

For example, the most common health and safety complaint in the sector is violence at work—partly as a result of the fact that the voluntary sector is taking on many of the public services for the most challenging, vulnerable service users. So UNISON is raising awareness of how it can help deal with that, promoting the ways in which activists can negotiate constructively for effective workplace policies designed to deal with workplace violence.

The union is also beginning to organise around the problems caused by procurement and funding—the loss of campaigning and fund-raising functions and the trend toward mergers between organisations and the building of 'Chinese walls' within organisations. Mergers in particular are becoming more common in the voluntary sector, as organisations seek to benefit from economies of scale, reducing unit costs and increasing their chances of winning contracts. But at the same time, many such organisations are seeking to avoid the larger scale collective bargaining which is implied by the creation of new larger organisations, by setting up more complicated subsidiaries and divisions between different parts of the organisation. So, for example, a trade union recognition agreement in one part of an organisation might not necessarily apply to other groups of workers within it. Trade union organising campaigns may therefore need to be nuanced, to respond to the different approaches to industrial relations that may be encountered in different parts of the same organisation.

Occupational, Professional, and Sector-Wide Campaigns

Issue-based organising in the voluntary sector has tended to focus on 'bread and butter' workplace issues within a single employer, like health and safety, working hours, and pay. More sophisticated union organising campaigns, linking membership and participation to occupational issues and professional concerns, have in contrast tended to take place in the public sector—in local government and the NHS.

Such methods, it is now recognised, need to be extended to the union's voluntary sector organising work, and the union is consequently piloting occupation-based organising in the Northwest, looking at organising around the issues faced by domiciliary care workers for the elderly. This is a model that it is felt should be used a lot more, especially as it becomes increasingly clearer what the personalisation agenda will mean for the way public services are delivered by bodies other than those in the public sector.

There may also be the prospect of unionising entire areas within the broader voluntary sector. UNISON is currently attempting exactly this in the private sector, organising the cleaning and catering workers employed in public services, regardless of the organisation they work for.

As has been seen, many voluntary sector organisations compete for the same work in particular sectors and are becoming bigger than ever. UNISON is therefore considering the scope which exists for organising major groups in the voluntary sector across employer boundaries—groups like mental health workers or those providing learning disability services.

Members and potential members involved in work relating to equalities and diversity are of particular interest to UNISON in this context. In part, this is because a large proportion of them work for organisations which campaign in these areas, for example, Women's Aid and the Refugee Council. But it is also because one of the effects of the increasing focus on short-term, competitively awarded contracts in the sector has been that smaller, campaigning organisations have struggled to survive, compared with the larger, more corporate service-provision charities. With its strong record of organising and campaigning on equalities issues, UNISON is furthermore ideally placed to engage with such voluntary sector organisations and to organise the staff employed by them.

Organising Staff

The basis of the organising approach is that recruiting new members and representatives is a pre-condition of solving all of the other problems. Pay bargaining is easier when backed by more members; individual representation is easier with more representatives; and recognition is achieved when membership density is high.

UNISON is therefore employing an increasing number of organisers—staff who get down to the workplace level and do basic organising and training, leaving groups of members in a sustainable position, before moving on to a new target. In doing so, it is, however, taking care to use such staff in a strategic and flexible manner and avoid their becoming institutionalised in particular local workplaces or employer organisations.

New Structures

UNISON's branch structures were not always suitable for voluntary sector workers as they were based on large local authority branches to which groups of voluntary sector members were tagged. UNISON has therefore recently introduced the flexibility to change branch structures according to local needs, in response to members' wishes, and there are various experiments taking place designed to examine which options work best.

As opposed to the usual model of branches based in a locality, national branches for national charities are now being tried. A thriving national branch for Barnardo's has, for example, been developed that has enabled the union to increase membership by around 50 percent, develop a positive relationship with the employer, and work constructively with it on all aspects of terms and conditions via a single UNISON focal point (rather than a series of branch and regional offices). Such national branches stand or fall, however, on the employer's willingness to do business with them and on having activists who are able and willing to run the branch. Without those ingredients, another solution is needed.

At the national level, in 2009, UNISON's members voted for an exciting and radical structural change, which created a body for voluntary sector members which stands apart from equivalent ones in health and local government, and gives UNISON's work in the sector genuine parity and a new sense of direction. This change reflects the realisation by UNISON's lay leaders that the union's voluntary sector membership is developing its own sense of solidarity and shared concerns, despite the diverse range of organisations which make up the sector.

This change should ensure that members have a real voice within the union's structures, with key decisions being made by members at the level of their 'bargaining interest.' In other words, members with shared workplace interests can now come together nationally to make decisions about bargaining strategies and campaigns. So the union's bargaining policies with respect to the voluntary sector should become more focused on the problems caused for members' terms and conditions by the relationship with public sector funders, short-term contracts, competitive tendering, and TUPE. Moreover, UNISON's executive committee for the voluntary sector has made it clear that further devolution down toward coherent groups of members is desirable. For example, workers in large, national charities may feel that they have a coherent set of concerns and issues which is distinct from that of workers in other parts of the 'third' sector, like small community groups or housing associations. If so, they are now able to decide to organise as a 'large, national charities' sector.

The last time such a structural change took place for a group of UNISON members—for our Police Staff group—both recruitment and steward identification rose dramatically, as more organisational resources were devoted to them and they became more aware of the priority UNISON was giving them. There is a confidence that the same will happen in the voluntary sector.

The Internet

Another important strand to the union's work in the voluntary sector is electronic communication. UNISON has led the way in developing groundbreaking 'virtual branches'—interactive websites that encourage greater membership participation in the union, improve workplace organisation, enhance democracy, and provide fora for activists in disparate workplaces to discuss issues, raise concerns, and share best practice. As an increasing number of charities and housing associations merge, creating new organisations which cover much larger parts of the country than their predecessor constituent organisations, this form of communication will, it is believed, become increasingly vital. Already, UNISON's national virtual branch project includes two voluntary sector branches, Greater Belfast Voluntary Organisations branch (http://www.unisoncommunity.org/) and Quarriers national branch (http://www.quarriersunison.org.uk/).

Lifelong Learning

The development of a learning partnership is a positive offer that UNISON can make to employers which benefits both the corporate organisation and its staff. The union is therefore developing learning partnerships which provide learning opportunities for individuals, help the employer up-skill their workforces, and enable staff to improve their skills and develop career paths.

Work on such partnerships is being carried out in a number of organisations. For example, as part of its comprehensive training strategy, the learning disabilities service provider Dimensions will, it is hoped, be using courses provided by UNISON to fulfil the basic skills training requirements of its staff—such as information technology and English as a second language.

In the East Midlands area, UNISON has had a lot of success organising around learning issues. In Nottingham Community Housing Association, a 'Communication at Work' course has taken place as a result of UNISON working closely with the employer, and, more generally in the area, a large number of UNISON members based in the voluntary sector have signed up for 'Openings' courses provided by the Open University that are facilitated by UNISON, with support from their employers. These are short accredited courses, on subjects like Understanding Society, Understanding

Health, Understanding Children, and Understanding Management, which
serve as tasters for higher education level study.

Cross-Sector Bargaining Solutions

Although organising relies on a workplace-based approach, UNISON is
campaigning hard for a level playing field between providers. For voluntary organisations to recruit and retain staff, they have to be able to offer
pensions comparable to public sector schemes and training and career programmes that match the National Health Service's Knowledge and Skills
Framework (the career and pay progression strand of the NHS pay system,
which provides a single consistent, comprehensive and explicit framework
for staff reviews and development in the NHS).

Small organisations in particular are at a disadvantage in this respect.
As a result, the union has had talks with the Cabinet Office and the Pensions Trust about the promotion of charity final salary schemes—along the
lines of the already existing Social Housing Pension Scheme. In a similar
vein, it has been a long-time advocate of a skills body for the voluntary sector, an objective that has now been achieved via the setting up of Skills—
Third Sector.

These are just examples; the more general point is that, as the government
increasingly uses the voluntary sector as a core service provider, there may
be *political* solutions to those workplace issues which are most difficult to
resolve. All of Britain's mainstream political parties seem to want to see the
voluntary sector provide public services, and so it is crucial that pressure on
policy issues which have knock-on effects on the workforce is kept up.

CONCLUSION

It seems clear that the future of the voluntary sector as a provider of a
steadily increasing proportion of public services is secure.

Whatever UNISON's views are on whether this shift should take place,
and whatever national and local campaigns it engages in to keep services
in-house, the union has to make sure that it is in a position to represent and
organise the workers in the voluntary sector, whether they have transferred
into it or worked in the sector for a long time. The employment position of
workers in the voluntary sector is more precarious and less well rewarded
than in the public sector, and UNISON's role must be to work with them to
improve this situation, while also supporting their commitment to improving service quality and delivery.

Doing all of this presents real challenges, as much of what the union
encounters in the sector is a more pronounced version of what it encounters
in other sectors: particularly, small and dispersed workplaces, less capacity
for activism, and employer resistance. But the sector also gives UNISON a

massive opportunity to use new organising techniques, whose effects are already beginning to be seen. By combining core organising principles, focusing on members' direct workplace concerns, and developing member-led campaigns, with appropriate structural, staffing, and technological change, the union has put itself in a strong position to build real union organisation in the voluntary sector and make genuine gains for and with its members. It is important that UNISON now makes the most of this position.

BIBLIOGRAPHY

Cavalier, S., and Arthur, R. (2007). *Providing a service? The new TUPE regulations.* Liverpool: Institute of Employment Rights.

Charity Commission. (2007). *Stand and deliver: The future of charities providing public services.* London: Charity Commission.

Cunningham, I., and James, P. (2007). *False economy? The costs of contracting and workforce insecurity in the voluntary sector.* London: UNISON.

Davies, S. (2007).*Third sector provision of local government and health services.* London: UNISON.

Ewing, K., Moore, S., and Wood, S. (2003). *Unfair Labour practices: Trade union recognition and employer resistance.* London: Institute of Employment Rights.

Home Office. (2005). *Funding and procurement: Compact codes of good practice.* London: Home Office.

National Audit Office. (2007). *Public funding of large national charities.* London: NAO.

Nickson, D., Warhurst, C., Dutton, E., and Hurrell, S. (2008). A job to believe in: Recruitment in the Scottish voluntary sector. *Human Resource Management Journal*, 18 (1), 8–33.

Storry, R., and Melis, S. (2007). *Terms and conditions in housing associations: A research report for UNISON.* London: Income Data Services and UNISON.

Welch, R. (2006) .*The information and consultation regulations: Wither works councils?* Liverpool: Institute of Employment Rights.

Part III

Employment Policies and Practices

5 Shaping HRM in the Voluntary Sector
The Influence of Government
Emma Parry and Clare Kelliher

INTRODUCTION

This chapter is concerned with examining the role that government has played in recent years in shaping the approaches adopted to managing human resources (HR) in voluntary sector organisations. Historically, the voluntary sector has developed an approach to operating, which has distinguished it from the public and private sectors (Armstrong, 1992; Billis, 1993; Lloyd, 1993; Tassie, Zohar, and Murray, 1996; Palmer, 2003). This distinctive approach has developed, at least in part, as a result of the context in which it operates (Armstrong, 1992). There is some evidence to suggest, however, that this approach has been subject to change in recent times by becoming increasingly professional and more similar to approaches that are characteristic of the public and private sectors (Kellock Hay, Beattie, Livingstone, and Munro, 2001; Palmer, 2003; Parry, Kelliher, Mills, and Tyson, 2005; Rodwell and Teo, 2004; Parry and Kelliher, 2009).

Recent years have seen significant growth across much of the voluntary sector in many countries (Kendall, 2003). Estimates suggest that in the UK more than 600, 000 people are in paid employment in the voluntary sector (National Council for Voluntary Organisations [NCVO], 2009). The sector has seen a growth in employment of more than 26 percent over the ten-year period since 1996 (NCVO, 2007). Much of this growth can be attributed to the development of the so-called mixed economy of care policy initiated by successive governments from the 1980s (Kendall, 2003). This policy enabled voluntary and private sector organisations to compete with the public sector for the provision of publicly funded services, principally in the areas of health and social care. As a consequence of this, the voluntary sector has become an important provider of publically funded services in health, social care, and housing (Cunningham, 2001).

The fact that much of the growth in the sector has been as a result of changes to government policy, and that in many cases government has become a major source of income for voluntary sector organisations, raises the question over the degree to which government has influenced the way in which such organisations conduct themselves and has also been responsible for the changes in approaches to management observed by some commentators (Leat, 1993; Harris, 2001; Alatristra and Arrowsmith, 2004; Cunningham, 2008). In this chapter we will examine this question principally in the context of how employment matters are managed in the voluntary sector.

We start by examining first how the state may influence employment matters and, by reference to institutional theory, consider how this may occur within voluntary sector organisations that are providers of publically funded services. Second, we present a brief overview of developments in substance misuse treatment services—the sector in which our own research has been based. Third, we examine the findings of three studies that the authors have undertaken to explore the changing nature of HRM in this sector and the factors that have influenced it, and locate these in the context of other extant factors. Finally, drawing on this material, we will present a number of observations about the nature of the influence which has been exercised by the state and some assessment of the impact of this influence.

THE INFLUENCE OF GOVERNMENT

Governments may affect employment and related matters in a number of ways. First, they may influence the debate concerning, and practice in employment through the development of policy, which may in some cases be backed up by legislative provisions. Second, where the state is a large employer itself and public sector employment constitutes a significant proportion of total employment in an economy, practice in the public sector is likely to have a major effect on the labour market. Third, as a purchaser of goods and services, the government may influence employment practice by requiring potential providers to meet defined employment standards and to provide evidence of employment policies as part of the tendering process. In the current context of the voluntary sector, it is possible that the voluntary sector will play a particularly significant role, given how governments have increasingly contracted with organisations in it for the provision of services.

Institutional theory may be instructive in understanding how governments can influence practice in the voluntary sector through their purchasing power. Institutional theory posits that coercive, mimetic, and normative isomorphic pressures influence how an organisation operates (DiMaggio and Powell, 1991). Coercive isomorphism occurs where formal and informal pressures are exerted on an organisation by another on which it is in some way dependent. For example, management approaches adopted by the voluntary sector may be the result of government-enacted legislation or, in a contracting situation, procedural requirements under which tenders are only invited from supplier organisations who comply with certain specified minimum criteria or standards. Mimetic influences are where organisations conform to the behaviours adopted by others in order to minimise risk and uncertainty. For example, voluntary sector organisations might offer employees 'market-rate' terms and conditions or ones similar to the public sector in order to minimise risk in recruitment. Normative pressures are related to what should be done in a particular context. While normative influence may come into play as a result of the value-led nature of many voluntary sector organisations (Armstrong, 1992), approaches to management advocated by government may also be internalised by them. Thus, to summarise, there appears to be considerable scope for government to exert coercive influence through the contracting process (Chew & Osborne, 2009), and, drawing on existing work, there is evidence to suggest that, as the involvement of the voluntary sector in the provision of publicly funded services has grown, there has also been a tendency for it to exhibit mimetic behaviours in relation to employment in order to assist in the recruitment of staff (Cunningham, 2008; Parry and Kelliher, 2009).

These three sources of institutional pressure may, however, create different pressures for organisations, which may be in conflict. Voluntary sector organisations competing to provide publicly funded services may face pressures from commissioners to adopt certain approaches to employment, while trying to contain costs in order to be competitive, either of which factors may or may not sit comfortably with the values of the organisation.

THE SUBSTANCE MISUSE SECTOR

Before examining existing evidence on the practice of, and sources of, change, in HRM in the substance misuse sector, it is important to provide some background to recent developments in this sector. In 1998 the UK Government launched a ten-year strategy, 'Tackling Drugs to Build a Better Britain' (HM Government, 1998), which included the key target of doubling the availability of drugs treatment services by 2008. This strategy involved a number of initiatives including the formation of a National Treatment Agency (NTA) in 2001. The NTA is effectively a special health authority within the NHS, set up to improve the availability, capacity, and effectiveness of treatment for drug misusers in England. The NTA's role is enacted through nine regional teams that support local drug action teams (DATs) that aim to ensure that available funding is spent effectively. Public funding for drug treatment services has increased since 2001, with the NTA being allocated £406 million in central government funding in 2009–10 (www.nta.nhs.uk).

The NTA has attempted to influence practice in the substance misuse sector through the launch of a number of occupational standards. First, Quality in Alcohol and Drugs Services (QuADS) standards (Drugscope, 1999) were launched as a result of a 1996 Task Force to Review Standards for Drug Misusers which highlighted the variable quality of drug treatment services and especially the variations in the areas of management systems, monitoring systems, and forward planning. QuADS are a set of quality standards against which drug treatment providers are expected to audit their organisational practices and to identify necessary changes if they do not meet them. The standards cover both aspects of service provision and the management of service provider organisations, including the management of human resources. Organisations bidding to provide publicly funded services are required to demonstrate that they can meet these standards.

In addition to QuADS, a set of Drugs and Alcohol National Occupational Standards (DANOS) was developed by the NTA in partnership with Skills for Health,[1] which details the skills levels to which substance misuse workers should be qualified. DANOS details standards in the three areas of service delivery, management of services, and commissioning of services. The NTA requested that all job descriptions in these three areas be written in terms of DANOS standards by December 2004. The DANOS standards have since been included in a number of qualifications, including the NVQ levels 3 and 4 in Health and Social Care and NVQ level 3 on Working with Offending Behaviour.

The Department of Health's targets set out in the ten-year plan to double the number of people in treatment between 1998 and 2008 was achieved, as was an increase in the percentage of those successfully completing or continuing treatment year on year (www.nta.nhs.uk).

In the light of these developments, it can be argued that government has not only increased funding and service provision in the substance misuse sector, but that it has also attempted to exert an influence over the way in which the sector manages itself. Specifically, funding, contracting arrangements, and standards such as QuADS and DANOS might be expected to act as pressures on organisations to adopt particular HRM or general management practices.

HRM CHANGE IN THE SUBSTANCE MISUSE SECTOR

To explore changes in the management of HRM in the sector and the factors that have influenced it, we examine three studies that we have undertaken to investigate the response of voluntary sector organisations to the government's ten-year plan "Tackling Drugs to Build a Better Britain." First, we discuss the findings of two previously published studies (Parry, Kelliher, Mills, and Tyson, 2005; Parry and Kelliher, 2009), conducted in 2002 and 2003, approximately five years into the ten-year plan. Second, we present evidence from more recent research conducted to coincide with the conclusion of the time period of the ten-year plan. We will present findings from a series of interviews which focused on the sources and causes of changes in the approaches adopted to managing human resources.

The 2002 and 2003 Studies

The first of these studies focused solely on Greater London and surveyed 96 organisations by means of a postal questionnaire. Sixty percent of responses were from the voluntary sector, with the remaining 40 percent being mainly public sector (NHS Trusts). In addition to data on workforce demographics, the survey gathered data on approaches to recruitment, training, and workforce planning and the problems associated with recruitment and retention. These findings were supplemented by a small number of interviews with HR managers to provide richer data on the areas covered in the questionnaire. The second study was similar in design, but included service providers throughout England, excluding those in Greater London. On this occasion 181 responses were received from voluntary sector organisations. In addition to the questionnaire, forty-one semistructured interviews were conducted with managers in voluntary sector organisations who had responsibility for managing human resources and twenty-three with members of drug action teams (DATs) (the commissioning bodies). A comparison of HR practice in the voluntary and public sectors has been made using the London data (Parry et al., 2005). The nationwide data has been used to examine how the voluntary sector responded to the dual challenges of the significant increase in public funding to provide services and the need for nonprofit organisations to adjust their management practices in order to demonstrate their compliance with the quality standards required to compete for the provision of services (Parry and Kelliher, 2009).

Broadly speaking and in line with other research, both of our studies found evidence of an increasingly professional approach to the management of people in the voluntary sector (Batsleer, 1995). This was in contrast to much of the earlier literature in the field which suggested that HRM in the voluntary sector was lacking in sophistication (Butler and Wilson, 1990; Lloyd, 1993; Cunningham, 2000; Akingbola, 2004), and that the management of people had taken a backseat in comparison to activities such as fund raising and service delivery (Zacharias, 2003). Rather, we found that for many HR activities the voluntary sector adopted an approach similar to that of the public sector. However, we did observe that factors such as the irregular nature of funding experienced by many voluntary sector organisations impeded their ability to offer competitive (in comparison with the public and private sectors) terms and conditions of employment (Parry et al., 2005).

In spite of evidence of voluntary sector workers being prepared to work for lower extrinsic rewards, because of the opportunity for intrinsic rewards, the so-called ethos discount (Lloyd, 1993), we found that this factor had implications for their ability to be competitive in a labour market in which competition for appropriately qualified and experienced staff had been intensified by the rapid increase in service provision. Nevertheless we also found that a number of voluntary sector organisations had sought other ways of attracting candidates, such as offering flexible working arrangements. We also found evidence of organisations using the offer of training and career development to attract recruits and retain existing staff (Parry and Kelliher, 2009).

Approximately halfway through the implementation of the ten-year plan our evidence therefore suggested that quite considerable change was taking place in the approach to HRM in voluntary sector organisations. We found that these employers had made changes to their practices in order to respond to the quality standards laid down by government, which had resulted in greater similarity with public sector providers. However, the pressures of the contracting environment and the uncertain nature of funding had also required them to develop different approaches from the public sector, in order to improve their labour market position.

The findings obtained from these earlier studies echo those of others that have also found varying degrees of government influence over employment in the voluntary sector, as a result of its increased involvement in the provision of publicly funded services (Cunningham, 2001; Akingbola, 2004; Barnard, Broach, and Wakefield, 2004). However, Cunningham (2008) has questioned the degree to which the accompanying cost pressures result in an inevitable 'race to the bottom.' Drawing on a study of the relationships between twenty-four voluntary sector organisations and seven local authorities, he found that although all organisations reported considerable pressures on pay and conditions and the labour process, differences emerged in their responses and the outcomes for employment. He argued that these were dependent upon the degree of competition, their existing customer base, and their access to other sources of finance. This suggests that while voluntary sector organisations have closer relationships with government and are subject to their influence (Chew & Osborne, 2009), there still remains scope, under certain circumstances, for a degree of autonomy to be exercised. Furthermore, in relation to the establishment of standards, it should be recognised that organisations may respond to them in different ways, which may not always have significant implications for practice, but equally they may be used by managers as a lever for change (Paton and Foot, 2000).

More Recent HRM Developments

At the conclusion of the ten-year plan, we conducted a further set of interviews with managers in voluntary sector substance misuse provider organisations. This allowed us to update our previous work once policies had been bedded-in and to examine the influence of government on the conduct of HRM in the sector over a longer period of time. Twenty interviews with managers or HR managers of voluntary sector substance misuse treatment providers were conducted. Interviewees were identified via contact with DAT coordinators who were asked to provide a list of the substance misuse treatment providers in their areas. Representatives from a variety of organisations, in different geographical locations and of different sizes, were interviewed in order to obtain a wide range of information. Whereas a number of the organisations included in this later study were the same as those in the earlier ones (particularly in the case of the larger substance misuse treatment providers), none of the interviewees were the same, probably because of relatively high turnover and other changes (such as organisational mergers) within the sector.

An interview protocol was constructed based upon the literature and the results of the two earlier studies. The interviews contained a number of questions about HRM policies and practices, recent changes in these areas, and the impact of government and other influences on HRM. Each interview was recorded and transcribed in full. A content analysis of the transcripts of these interviews allowed us to identify a number of themes related to the influence of government on HRM.

First, we found continued evidence of changes to the conduct of HRM within voluntary sector substance misuse treatment providers. A number of interviewees described how steps had been taken to improve practices within their organisations, resulting in greater sophistication and coherence in HR policies and practices. One interviewee, for example, explained:

> We've moved to a much more robust HR administrative system. . . . it's a much more electronic HR system now and, in terms of tying up loose ends, we've an Investors in People programme, which is quite helpful in pulling together all the different threads into something more consistent.

Some organisations had specifically recruited experienced HR professionals from outside the sector in the belief that this would facilitate this process. For example, one interviewee explained that they personally were recruited to:

> Introduce a bit more structure and some professional knowledge and some legal knowledge into the HR practices.

There was also evidence of organisations recruiting other managers from the private sector in the belief that they could achieve a new (more professional) focus for the organisation. A small number of interviewees also discussed the changing role of the HRM function more generally, reporting that there had been a move to a more strategic role and in some cases toward to a business partner approach (Ulrich, 1997), as the following quote illustrates:

> I think the big thing is probably the same as . . . in the HR world. . . . that whole thing about [being] much closer to what the business needs; closer to the business ambitions. Having me as part of the executive team helps

obviously, because a lot of HR departments struggle with not having a voice at the very senior table . . . our influence in the organisation grows as we get more involved with the strategic level of operations.

More specifically, the interviews provided some background to the reasons behind these changes in HRM. The influence of government can be broadly speaking divided into those which were direct and those which were indirect. The direct influences were largely brought about through coercive and normative pressures and the indirect influences by mimetic ones.

Direct Government Influences

Legislation—Several interviewees described the impact that the introduction of an increasing quantity of employment legislation over the past five years had had on their HRM practice. One commented:

> There is a need [and] awareness [that] actually we can't do things in the way we've always done them because there are new laws such as disability discrimination. . . . every five minutes it seems like there's a new regime for maternity pay.

Another interviewee described the challenge of keeping up with the increasing volume of employment legislation:

> One thing that is sometimes very difficult is . . . trying to keep up with the raft of legislation that seems to be constantly changing.

In particular there was some concern over the increased requirement for reference checks such as Criminal Records Bureau (CRB) ones.

A number of interviewees reported that they dealt with these regulatory demands by relying on support from their professional association, for example, the Chartered Institute of Personnel and Development (CIPD) or government organisations, such as ACAS, to keep up-to-date with developments in employment legislation. A small number of respondents indicated that they had also used law firms to support them in this process. Thus legislation appears to have acted as a strong coercive influence on particular aspects of HRM practice. This influence is of course not unique to either the substance misuse or voluntary sectors and may therefore have the effect of creating greater similarity in practice between employers in those areas subject to legislative developments.

National Occupational Standards and the skills agenda—All interviewees referred to general pressure from government, via the NTA, to improve the skill levels of substance misuse workers. In particular, this had been driven by the introduction of DANOS and a requirement for employees to be qualified up to NVQ level 3 in substance misuse work. One interviewee, for example, observed that: '*In the drugs world, DANOS has changed the landscape.*'

Another explained how the introduction of DANOS and the QuADS management standards, as well as the wider workforce development plan that focused on improving skills levels and qualifications in the substance misuse workforce, had put pressure on them to encourage their staff to seek qualifications:

> We had QuADS, then DANOS, and then the training needs analysis and then the workforce development plan. And that workforce development plan was to get all the unqualified drug and alcohol workers to be qualified.

Specifically in relation to QuADS, one interviewee described how the introduction of these standards had improved the quality of HRM policies and practices:

> Before QuADS . . . I'll say this profession was slapdash . . . some of the organisations I've worked for didn't record information. They didn't even record who was coming through the door . . . I think what it has done is upped the ante of our professionalism.

The DANOS standards in particular appear to have been widely adopted, with most interviewees describing how they had developed job descriptions and person specifications based upon them. Other organisations reported that they had developed training programmes based on the DANOS standards and the requirement for employees to have NVQ level 3:

> We offer a huge in-house training programme, all mapped on DANOS and professional standards . . . it's accredited by the Open College Network, so we fund people to go through that, to build their portfolios to get to level 3.

There was some feeling however that, despite the early emphasis on the DANOS standards, this had not been followed up with appropriate levels of support or information for provider organisation:

> There was a great press and a lot of push towards doing this [DANOS] about three years ago. We had all of our job descriptions include DANOS standards and a lot of our training courses will actually have DANOS standards against them. However . . . I was expecting there to be an NVQ . . . very specific for the sector with the DANOS standards, the core standards, plus extras.

A number of interviewees also expressed concern that whereas on the one hand providers were expected to enhance the skills levels of employees, they had not been provided with the necessary resources and additional funding in order to do this.

In addition to those initiatives specific to the substance misuse sector, there have been a number of external programmes, such as the Agenda for Change in the NHS, which were also found to have had an influence on the organisational priorities for developing their employees. One organisation, for example, had developed its own set of standards based on DANOS and a number of others.

> We've got our own internal quality assessment tool. . . . Thirty-nine standards and every agency is assessed. We have to evidence our practice around every single one of those standards and those standards range from everything from service provision to HR to personal development. . . . they include everything that we do.

This emphasis on skills has resulted in a number of provider organisations setting up their own training units. Meanwhile, one organisation described how it had set up a partnership arrangement with other organisations to work on workforce development.

> Workforce development is one area where we could actually work together and put aside the whole competitive tendering process . . . it's been mainly information sharing but in terms of the new apprenticeship scheme that we have, it will be joint. So we'll look at how we share resources.

Other direct influences from the NTA—Perhaps surprisingly, the opinion offered by a number of interviewees was that the NTA, as the government body responsible for substance misuse treatment, did not have a sufficiently direct influence over HRM or workforce development in the sector. Several interviewees discussed the fact that the NTA had originally pushed for the workforce skills levels but then appeared to have dropped the workforce agenda.

> I think the NTA not having a direct role in HR practice is a real issue. There was a real thing about 'this is the target, you've got to get X percent through NVQ level 3 or 4 or whatever' and then they just dropped it. . . . I think that's a real gap and that's why DANOS isn't as useful as it could be for us . . . nobody's really developing it.

However, one interviewee suggested that the 'reviewed drug strategy' had, in fact, had a direct impact on their training and development.

> The reviewed drug strategy, that's put a good focus on [the] safeguarding agenda [and] has required us to send staff on CAF training and assessment training.

Indirect Government influence

Organisational growth—A number of the interviewees described how their organisations had grown considerably over the past five years, leading to a need to develop HRM practices:

> The volume of HR work has increased tremendously, certainly in this organisation . . . because of our growth it has been enormous.

This growth was attributed to increased activity arising from the winning of additional contracts for services. When a contract, which had previously been operated by another provider, was won, the existing staff were taken on by the new contractor (in accordance with TUPE legislation[2]), and when a contract which had not previously existed was won, additional staff were recruited to service it. More generally, however, the level of new business activity clearly reflected the growth in the sector that had been prompted by the goal of the ten-year plan to increase service provision:

> You've got some more money going out, you've got people asking for different things, you've got more provision to provide.

Funding and competition—HRM within the sector had also been influenced by the need to compete for funding through the tendering process. There was some suggestion by interviewees that the nature of HRM was affected by the resultant pressure to contain costs:

> This last year [Area] DAT had to find £100,000 through efficiencies. We managed to work together as a team and got that down to £70,000 or £80,000, and it all came out of overheads, training budgets, buildings, you know, economies of scale in overheads this year. But next year we're looking at £178,000 office costs unless we can get more people into treatment.

There was also some feeling that voluntary providers were under particular pressure to keep budgets down, in order to compete with provider organisations in the statutory sector:

> I've got a bit of a feeling that they get us almost cheap. If I'm putting other people to do work, what I add on is nothing like what the NHS would add on to the cost of individual posts.

The competitive tendering process also had a more direct influence on HRM, through normative pressures. Providers felt the need to have a more professional approach to HRM in order to work in partnership with the statutory sector, as can be seen from the following quote:

Working in partnership with your statutory providers, they're not going to drop their level, we've got to raise our bar so to speak to interface
with them in some way that is acceptable. We won't get the funding if
we can't work with these providers. . . . they do not recognise you if
you don't have certain qualifications . . . so to be competitive in that
market we, as a charity, we come in at a lot lower price but we can now
throw in the governance as well, 75 percent of our staff are trained in
health and social care.

CONCLUSIONS

Our research among voluntary sector substance misuse organisations
has suggested that the way in which human resources are managed has
been subject to change in recent years. This has been stimulated by three
main developments. First, voluntary sector organisations have increasingly
become involved in the provision of publicly funded services, thereby developing a closer, contracting relationship with government. Second, because
this has been an area of significant growth in the past ten years, organisations have responded to the opportunities presented, often resulting in
growth in the organisations themselves. Third, and linked to the increased
public funding in the area, a number of occupational standards have been
developed, and service providers have been required to demonstrate how
they meet these standards.

The findings from our recent research have supported our earlier work
and have provided more detail on the nature and source of human resource
management changes. Overall, we found that voluntary sector substance
misuse treatment providers have been adopting a more professional
approach to human resource management and have been developing more
coherent HRM policies and practices as a result of both coercive and normative pressures. This process of reform can be seen to cast doubt on the
continued validity of the view that the voluntary sector lacks a sophisticated approach to HRM (Lloyd, 1993; Cunningham, 2000).

Many of these changes in HRM can be attributed to the influence
of government in some form or another. The government has exerted a
direct and coercive influence on management practice, both through the
introduction of standards such as QuADS and DANOS within the sector and through employment legislation affecting employers more widely.
In addition, voluntary sector providers reported that they were directly
influenced by the nature of the contracting and funding environment
(Osbourne, 1997) and monitoring from the National Treatment Agency.
There was also some evidence of mimetic effects through the espoused
need for voluntary sector organisations to adopt practices in line with the
public sector providers that they work in partnership with. Thus, it was
found that organisations often attempted to mimic public sector practice

as this was seen as the most low-risk strategy when working with public-sector organisations.

Interestingly, there was also some evidence of HRM in the voluntary sector being influenced by trends in the wider HRM arena. For instance, interviewees described the need for the HR function to operate in a more strategic fashion and to become a business partner. This is in line with the trend in the private sector for HR to operate in a way that is closer to business needs (Ulrich, 1997; Paauwe, 2004) and may be seen as evidence of normative pressures prompting voluntary sector HRM to become more sophisticated and more similar to that in the private and public sectors (Parry et al., 2005). This, of course, serves to raise questions about the extent to which this model of HRM is appropriate for a sector which has a number of distinct characteristics (Armstrong, 1992).

Our earlier work found significant evidence of mimetic pressures on HRM through the perceived need to modify HRM practices in the belief that this would enable them to attract suitable recruits to the organisation. This however was not apparent in our later study, perhaps because the focus had moved away from recruitment since the completion of the ten-year plan. Furthermore, there was some evidence that organisations had moved away from competing to attract and retain staff and instead had started to work together in order to address the need for increased skills levels through collaboration in workforce development.

Our research is obviously limited by the use of a small sample of interviewees in a single sector. However, it does provide some insight into the effect of government influence on HRM and on wider management in the voluntary sector. Further investigation is, however, needed to establish whether our findings are generalisable to voluntary sector organisations outside the substance misuse sector.

NOTES

1. Skills for Health is the Sector Skills Council (SSC) for the UK health sector. There are twenty-five SSCs in the UK who each hold responsibility for skills and workforce development in a particular industry.
2. The Transfer of Undertakings (Protection of Employment) (TUPE) regulations are designed to protect UK employees' terms and conditions when a business (or part of one) is transferred to a new employer.

BIBLIOGRAPHY

Akingbola, K. (2004). Staffing, retention and government funding: A case study. *Nonprofit Management and Leadership*, 14 (4), 4534–4565.

Alatrista, J., and Arrowsmith, J. (2004). Managing employee commitment in the not-for-profit sector. *Personnel Review*, 33 (5), 536–548.

Armstrong, M. (1992). A charitable approach to personnel. *Personnel Management* (December), 28–32.

Barnard, J., Broach, S., and Wakefield, V. (2004). *Social care: The growing crisis.* London: Report on Recruitment and Retention Issues in the Voluntary Sector by the Social Care Employers Consortium.

Batsleer, J. (1995). Management and organisation. In , J. Davies-Smith, C. Rochester, and R. Hedley (eds.), *An introduction to the voluntary sector* (224–248). London: Routledge.

Billis, D. (1993). *Organising public and voluntary agencies.* London: Routledge.

Butler, R. J., and Wilson, D. C. (1990). *Managing voluntary and non-profit organisations: Strategy and structure.* London: Routledge.

Chew, C. and Osborne, S. P. (2009). Exploring strategic positioning in the UK charitable sector: Emerging evidence from charitable organizations that provide public services. *British Journal of Management,* (20) 1, 90–105.

Cunningham, I. (2008). A race to the bottom? Exploring variations in employment conditions in the voluntary sector. *Public Administration,* 86 (4), 1033–1053.

Cunningham, I. (2001). Sweet charity! Managing employee commitment in the UK voluntary sector. *Employee Relations,* 23 (3), 226–239.

Cunningham, I. (2000) 'Prospects for union growth in the UK voluntary sector—The impact of the Employment Relations Act 1999. *Industrial Relations Journal,* 31 (3), 192–205.

DiMaggio, P. J., and Powell, W. W. (1991). Introduction. In P. J. DiMaggio, P. J. and W. W. Powell (eds.), *The new institutionalism in organisational analysis* (1–38). Chicago: University of Chicago Press.

DrugScope. (1999). *Quality in Alcohol and Drugs Services (QuADS): Organisational standards for alcohol and drug treatment services.* Available at www.drugscope.org.uk. Accessed 17 February 2010.

Feiock, R. C., and Jang, H. S. (2009). Nonprofits as local government service contractors. *Public Administration Review,* 69 (4), 668–680.

Harris, M. (2001). Voluntary organisations in a changing social policy environment. In M. Harris and C. Rochester (eds.), *Voluntary organisations and social policy in Britain* (213–229). Basingstoke: Palgrave.

HM Government. (1998). *Tackling drugs to build a better Britain.* London: HMSO. Available at http://www.archive.official-documents.co.uk/document/cm39/3945/3945.htm. Accessed 17 February 2010.

Kellock Hay, G., Beattie, R., Livingstone, R., and Munro, P. (2001). Change, HRM and the voluntary sector. *Employee Relations,* 23 (3), 240–255.

Kendall, J. (2003) *The voluntary sector.* London: Routledge.

Leat, D. (1993). *Managing across sectors.* London: VOLPROF.

Lloyd, T. (1993). *The charity business.* London: John Murray.

National Council for Voluntary Organisations (NCVO). (2009). *The Civil Society Almanac, 2009.* Available at http://www.ncvool.org.uk/publications. Accessed 27 March 2009.

National Council for Voluntary Organisations (NCVO). (2007). *The Voluntary Sector Almanac, 2007* Available at http://www.ncvovol.org.uk/publications. Accessed 27 March 2009.

Osborne, S. (1997). The voluntary and non-profit sector & the provision of social welfare services in Britain. *Aston Business School Research Paper RP9711.*

Paauwe, J. (2004). *HRM and performance.* Oxford: Oxford University Press.

Palmer, G. (2003). *Employee relations in the voluntary sector.* Paper presented at the British Universities Industrial Relations Association Annual Conference, Leeds, 3–5 July.

Parry, E., and Kelliher, C. (2009). Voluntary sector responses to increased resourcing challenges. *Employee Relations,* 31 (1), 9–24.

Parry, E., Kelliher, C., Mills, T., and Tyson, S. (2005). Comparing HRM in the voluntary and public sectors. *Personnel Review*, 34 (5), 588–602.

Paton, R., and Foot, J. (2000). Non-profit's use of awards to improve and demonstrate performance: Valuable discipline or burdensome formalities? *Voluntas*, 11 (4), 329–353.

Rodwell, J. J., and Teo, S. T. T. (2004). Strategic HRM in for-profit and non-profit organizations in a knowledge-intensive industry. *Public Management Review*, 6 (3), 311–331.

Tassie, B., Zohar, A., and Murray, V. (1996). The management of change. In S. Osborne (ed.), *Managing in the voluntary sector: A handbook for managers of charitable and non-profit organisations*. London: International Thomson Press, pp. 137–153.

Ulrich, D. (1997). *Human resource champions*. Cambridge: Harvard Business School Press.

Zacharias, L. (2003). Small change. *People Management* (May), 24–27.

6 'We Could Take on the World if We Had the Space'

Understanding Graduate Recruitment Problems in the Voluntary Sector

Scott A. Hurrell, Chris Warhurst, and Dennis Nickson

INTRODUCTION

In Scotland, as in the rest of the UK, the state is being hollowed out as some public services are contracted out to the voluntary sector. As part of this process, voluntary sector organisations (VSOs) are being required to become more 'business-like.' This, in turn, is serving to increase these organisations' demand for graduates, as part of a more general desire to upgrade workforce skills. However, despite an expanding supply of graduates in the labour market, the sector confronts difficulties in meeting its demand for this source of highly skilled labour.

This chapter draws on existing evidence and exploratory empirical research conducted in the social care subsector of the Scottish voluntary sector. The chapter focuses on graduates possessing university degrees in subjects such as business and social sciences who may be suitable for employment in VSOs' business support functions. In seeking to explain the sources of graduate recruitment difficulties, two main sources are highlighted. First is a *systems failure* caused by poor information exchange between the voluntary sector and potential labour supply, leading to a mismatch between the demand for and supply of graduates in the sector. Second is a compounding *administrative failure* in which the demand for graduates in VSOs providing subcontracted services for the government is constrained because funds are not provided to meet their business support costs.

In what follows, existing literature is initially used to establish the likely relevance of these two types of failure. The authors' new primary data is then used to reinforce and further support the contribution that these failures made to the voluntary sector's graduate recruitment problems.

VOLUNTARY SECTOR JOBS AND GRADUATE LABOUR

Over the past twenty years in the UK, social services have been contracted out by central and local government. The transfer of these social services from the public to the voluntary sector is seen as 'a more palatable alternative to outright privatisation' (Labour Research, 2007a, 14; see also Labour Research, 2007b).

According to Davies (in this volume) voluntary sector income from the public sector rose from £8 billion in 2000–01 to £11 billion in 2004–05. Consequently, funding of the voluntary sector by both central and local government has increased significantly over recent years with a particular increase in the use of subcontracting of services rather than grant-based income (Brown, 2007). Thus, in 2002, 47 percent of government-derived income came from such contracts; in 2006, 62 percent (Little, 2008). Indeed, 2005–06 was a watershed; thereafter most VSOs' income became earned rather than resulting from donations (Brindle, 2008).

As the state's role in the provision of social services has been hollowed out, there is related pressure from government on VSOs to improve their service delivery through improved cost effectiveness and having appropriately qualified staff (Meyer, 2009). The increase in subcontracting has also necessitated that VSOs improve their accountability and operate in a more 'businesslike' and 'professional' manner (Scottish Council for Voluntary Organisations [SCVO] 2007a; Dart, 2004; Wilson and Larson, 2002). As a result the management and organisation of functions and staff are now paramount, and VSOs' business functions are becoming increasingly important (Parry, Kelliher, Mills, and Tyson, 2005).

Despite the 'voluntary' label, the sector is not just about *volunteering* but has many job opportunities for paid staff. In Scotland, the voluntary sector employed 137,000 staff in 2009 (SCVO, 2010a) and accounted for approximately five percent of the workforce, a figure that has remained relatively stable since the early 2000s (Wilding, Collis, Lacey, and McCullough, 2003; SCVO, 2010a). Furthermore, recent job growth has been strong, with the Scottish voluntary sector experiencing a 55 percent increase in employment between 1996 and 2005 (Clark, 2007a). The rate of employment growth in the voluntary sector in Scotland between 1996 and 2005 was more than twice that in the UK as a whole (26 percent) and was substantially higher than in the private and public sectors (11 percent and 14 percent, respectively) (Clark, 2007a).

Although a growing source of employment, VSOs report recruitment difficulties. The 2007 UK wide skills survey conducted by the National Council for Voluntary Organisations (NCVO) revealed that 8 percent of Scottish voluntary sector employers reported skills shortages (as defined by the existence of a vacancy which is 'hard to fill' because applicants lack the correct skills) (Clark, 2007b). This figure was supported by the earlier 2004 Scottish Employers Skills Survey in which skills shortages were reported by 9 percent of voluntary sector establishments, compared to 5 percent of establishments in the public and private sectors (Futureskills Scotland, 2005). Furthermore, a key problem is the recruitment of *graduates* (Shah, 2004a).

An HM Treasury report (2004, 55) highlighted that VSOs had 'significant skills gaps' in business support functions such as leadership, management, administrative and technical support, and ICT. Similarly Clark and Wilding (in this volume) report survey data showing key skill gaps in IT strategy, legal knowledge, strategic planning, and fundraising. Wilding, Collis, Lacey, and McCullough (2003, 1) have also stated that: '*Voluntary organisations' priority skills needs for the future include management skills such as planning and organising, project management and strategic planning . . . team working and partnership working . . . leadership, and fundraising.*' Such skills are developed at university (Mason, 2001), and so, not surprisingly, the demand for graduates is rising. Unfortunately, whereas VSOs need more graduates, they are failing to attract them.

This failure is occurring despite graduate labour being plentiful. The UK government has intentionally expanded higher education, with around 50 percent of young people in Scotland (that is, those aged under 21) now participating in higher education in recent years (Scottish Government, 2008). However, there are now difficulties for graduates to find 'graduate' jobs, suggesting that supply is outstripping demand. Recent UK-wide figures suggest that the supply of workers with degrees outstrips employer demand for them by approximately 1.1 million (Felstead, Gallie, Green, and Zhou, 2007). There is clearly both a supply and demand for graduate labour within the sector that needs to be married in order to address VSO's priority skills deficits. The plentiful supply of graduate labour highlights that there is no *market failure* (Keep and Mayhew, 1999) in terms of an inadequate supply of skills on which VSOs can draw; instead as the next section argues, a *systems failure* is apparent.

'SYSTEMS FAILURE' AND ATTRACTING THE PURISTS

With poor pay rates, a question arises as to whether the sector can realistically expect to attract graduates. Managers (jobs for which graduates might be suited) in the UK public sector, for example, earn considerably more than those in the voluntary sector. In Parry et al.'s (2005) study of London-based drug and alcohol services, the average wage for managers in the voluntary sector was £27,531 compared to £35,706 in the public sector. In Scotland the relative overall pay disparity within the voluntary sector translates to an average weekly pay differential of 13 percent with the private sector and 20 percent with the public sector (Barnard, Broach, and Wakefield, 2004; Shah, 2004b).

However, research suggests that despite poor pay the attraction of staff is still possible because of an 'altruism payoff' in which VSOs' employees are willing to 'trade off' lower salaries against task significance and the values of the organisation as work in the sector has a high perceived social importance (Wilson and Larson, 2002; Parsons and

Broadbridge, 2006; Nickson, Warhurst, Dutton, and Hurrell, 2008). This focus on task significance has been labeled by Cunningham (2008) as a 'voluntary sector ethos' through which workers in the sector display a high 'affective commitment' (Meyer and Allen, 1991) to their organisations.

The possibility of levering value congruence to attract graduates through this affective commitment is revealed in Brown and Hesketh's (2004) study of the values that are important in graduates' job choices. This research identified two extreme types of behaviour in graduates applying for jobs: *players* and *purists*. Players, as the name suggests, 'play the game' and use information gathered from companies beforehand to 'market [themselves] in ways that conformed to the broader requirements of employers' (p. 127). By contrast, purists carefully research organisations in order to match their values with those of potential employers, applying for those organisations that fit their 'authentic selves' (p. 142).

Because of the existence of both graduate vacancies and purist graduates *market failure* is not an adequate explanation for graduate level skills shortages in VSOs. Instead there seems to have been a failure in the way that the sector attempts to attract graduates. Such a failure represents a *systems failure* relating to the inadequacy of employer strategies to maintain equilibrium between graduate supply and demand (Keep and Mayhew, 1999). In other words, an appropriate supply of skills exists in the labour market, but is not being matched to employer demand, as the systems used to attract graduate recruits are not taking advantage of the available supply. Most obviously, the recruitment polices and practices of VSOs are not efficacious.

The voluntary sector, in fact, has become aware of this systems failure. A report of UK-wide research commissioned specifically to address the problem of attracting graduates into the voluntary sector states that *'Although there is a need to attract high-calibre new talent, there appears to be a lack of awareness among graduates and school leavers about the range and scope of career opportunities within the sector'* (ATA Management, 2006, 5). Other research reveals that knowledge of the sector among potential employees is poor. A survey of 500 thirteen to nineteen year olds by market research company Zebra Square, commissioned by the NCVO, found that 31 percent knew nothing of the sector while a further 54 percent knew only 'a little.' Further qualitative research highlighted that most of the young people interviewed associated the sector with volunteering, believing that only managers were paid (Zebra Square, 2006). When asked to name voluntary sector jobs, most respondents could only cite charity shop work and believed that no qualifications were required to work in the sector. The image of the sector was also poor—regarded as out of touch and populated by old, retired, 'kind-hearted' women. These findings suggest that the voluntary sector is not good at communicating information about itself to potential applicants—graduates or otherwise.

FUNDING, UNCERTAINTY, AND IMPLICATIONS
FOR GRADUATE STAFFING

Systems failure may not, however, fully explain an unfulfilled demand for graduate level staff, as many VSOs are constrained by funding in that they do not receive 'full cost recovery' (FCR) for subcontracted services from the government. FCR is defined as:

> the principle by which third sector (voluntary) organisations are paid not only for the direct costs they incur by providing a service . . . but also for the indirect or overhead costs associated with delivering the service such as office space, information technology support, and other support costs. (National Audit Office [NAO], 2007, 2).

FCR has been a key tenet of UK governments' policy interventions in the voluntary sector. The Treasury's 2002 'Cross-Cutting Review' and a 'Strategic Funding Review' conducted by the Scottish Executive[1] both made commitments to use FCR when contracting public services to the voluntary sector (HM Treasury, 2004; Wainwright, Clark, Griffith, Jochum, and Wilding, 2006; NAO, 2007). FCR is thus essential to ensure that costs not directly associated with service provision, such as business support, are met in full. Indeed, the Association for Chief Executives of Voluntary Organizations states:

> 'Struggling to secure funding for overhead costs leads to underinvestment in: management and leadership, internal and external infrastructure and strategic development and governance. This difficulty is historically exacerbated by a trend on the part of the third sector's funders towards funding the direct costs of projects rather than overheads or "core funding". Failure to secure funding for overhead costs makes important services, including public services, and the organisations that deliver them, unsustainable . . . Government and the sector's representatives have agreed on a solution: *Full Cost Recovery*' (ACEVO, 2010: *Emphasis in Original*)

However, in practice, the Scottish Council of Voluntary Organisations (SCVO) notes that FCR remains the exception (SCVO, 2010b). A 2004 Treasury review of voluntary sector involvement in public service provision also concluded that FCR had largely not been implemented (HM Treasury, 2004). A further report by the National Audit Office (NAO, 2007) reported that many government departments had not implemented FCR since the 2002 review, leading the NAO to suggest that *'[t]he Office of the Third Sector and HM Treasury should expand their commitment to the implementation of full-cost recovery'* (p. 3). Labour Research (2007a) also estimated that FCR was still not widely practiced and that by 2007 only one in eight UK VSOs received FCR from government for the provision of transferred services. A further survey of 100 Scottish VSOs commissioned by the Scottish Executive revealed that 71 percent of contracts with central or local government were not based on FCR. Further qualitative investigation of VSO managers revealed that where FCR was not evident, staff costs tended to be cut (Hayton, Percy, and Crawford, 2007, 3).

Business support areas in which graduate skills are most required have thus been those worst affected by the absence of FCR, with related pressures on staff costs. Furthermore, the lack of FCR in the sector also has implications for pay, with the SCVO (2007a) believing that VSOs' service contracts are often awarded on the basis of being a 'cut price option,' with wages below the 'going rate' for public service workers. Moreover, contracting arrangements between VSOs and either central or local government are often highly uncertain. Short-term funding arrangements make it difficult for VSOs to plan for the future and deflect already scarce resources onto the need to constantly reapply for funding (HM Treasury, 2004). As HM Treasury admits, many VSOs are on renewable one-year contracts, and, in Scotland, even where contracts are longer, they often fall short of the 'officially recommended three years' as had been championed by the Scottish Executive (see end note 1 above) (SCVO, 2010; see also SCVO, 2007a). The resultant job insecurity in addition to lower pay rates potentially affects the attractiveness of the sector for graduate recruits even where VSOs can afford to employ them. In this respect the lack of FCR creates what Keep and Mayhew (1999) refer to as an *administrative failure*—or, more bluntly in this case, the inefficient allocation of resources to the sector.

This chapter empirically explores the possibilities of both systems failure and administrative failure, drawing on research undertaken in the social care subsector. To analyse these possibilities, four particular issues are examined: first, whether a demand for graduates actually exists in the social care subsector; second, whether voluntary sector organisations are an attractive employment option for graduates; third, whether graduates have misperceptions about the voluntary sector and work within it; and finally, whether graduate demand in the sector is constrained financially.

AN OUTLINE OF THE RESEARCH

The social care subsector is the largest single employer in the voluntary sector in both the UK and Scotland (Barnard, Broach, and Wakefield, 2004; Shah, 2004 a) and is also the subsector that relies most heavily on subcontracting (SCVO, 2007a). Initial research concerned an exploration of recruitment difficulties in the voluntary sector (see Nickson et al., 2008) and encompassed seven leading and anonymised Scottish-based social care VSOs (Supportco, Stratos, Houseco, Liveco, Nimbus, Diversico, and Kidco). The organisations provided a range of services for disadvantaged groups including the physically and mentally impaired, single parent families, and vulnerable children. The organisations were medium to large size, having between 180 and 1,400 employees. The research methods included telephone interviews conducted with 100 front-line, nonmanagerial staff and 30 managers across all organisations. Face-to-face interviews with the human resource (HR) director from each organisation and an HR assistant from Kidco were also conducted. This chapter is mainly drawn from the HR director interviews.

In order to specifically explore the graduate recruitment process, the fieldwork was extended to consider other stakeholders. The director of a pilot graduate placement scheme run by a Scottish organising body for voluntary organisations (Umbrellaorg) was twice interviewed; once during and once after the scheme had finished. This pilot scheme was funded by the EU and placed new graduates on projects within VSOs where a demand for graduate abilities was unfulfilled. Interviews with representatives from three employers attending a conference designed to attract graduates to the sector were also conducted. One of these respondents was from Stratos, while the other two representatives were first from Schoolco, an educational service provider employing about 300 people; and, second from Eastnet, a regional organising network. Eastnet had also been part of the graduate placement scheme. To ascertain supply-side issues five careers advisers from three Scottish universities (Westuni, Eastuni, and Northuni) were interviewed; three from Westuni and one each from the other institutions. A focus group was also conducted with final year arts, business, and social science students from Westuni.

RESEARCH FINDINGS

The findings from the above study are presented as follows. First, the way in which the growing professionalisation of VSOs has served to prompt an increased demand for graduates is examined. Second, consideration is given to the extent to which VSOs have to date been successful in attracting graduates. Third, the manner in which the attraction of graduates has been hampered by misconceptions concerning the nature of the voluntary sector is addressed. Finally, the discussion turns to the way in which funding issues have acted to limit the ability of VSOs to recruit the graduates that they need.

Professionalisation and the Demand for Graduates in the Voluntary Sector

All the human resource (HR) directors and the director of the pilot graduate placement scheme emphasised that the sector was undergoing significant change, particularly in terms of business support functions. All HR directors had faced pressures to align human resource practices with those in the public and private sectors, with each stating how their HR departments were growing and becoming more 'business like.' This trend was epitomised by the HR director of Stratos who stated that work in the sector was *not just tea and sympathy . . . you're running a project . . . [people think the sector is] cardigans—soft and woolly, but that's not what it's like, it's actually a lot more business focused.*' As each organisation's HR department was expanding, so, as a consequence, was the demand for graduates. Kidco now had two and half professional posts requiring graduates, with Supportco and Nimbus also developing further professional posts in HR, while the HR director in Stratos had managed to 'source' a graduate to help her develop a staff appraisal system.

In all of the organisations the growth of other business support functions was evident alongside a related demand for graduates. Houseco had experienced ICT problems and believed that the organisation's ICT infrastructure needed further development, offering a job opportunity for a graduate in this field. Within Nimbus, the public relations/marketing function had been developed with the recent appointment of a director of communications, and the intention was to expand the department further. Similarly Liveco had a well-developed business service division including marketing, finance, administration, and training. Kidco also had an IT specialist and a media/marketing department as well as a growing administrative function. The HR directors of Stratos and Schoolco stated that the demand for graduates was primarily in business support functions, ICT, and public relations. The graduate placement offered by Eastnet was explicitly because the organisation needed someone with marketing expertise. The growth of these support functions was attributed to the fact that the organisations' service provision was expanding rapidly.

It was partly because of the ubiquitous expansion in VSOs' business functions that Umbrellaorg's pilot graduate placement scheme had been developed. The director of the scheme stated that the placements overwhelmingly demanded '*either graduates . . . to develop a marketing strategy or IT and . . . showed us there was a skills shortage there.*' This skills shortage was attributed to the fact that organisations were becoming less of an 'Aunt Sally'[2] and more professional in operation.

Attracting Graduates to the Voluntary Sector

Given the demand for graduates in the voluntary sector, a key issue is whether the sector is an attractive option for graduates. Perhaps the biggest potential problem in this respect, as noted earlier, is poor pay. This problem was affirmed by the HR directors in the initial research, although predominantly in relation to front-line care jobs rather than graduate positions (see Nickson et al., 2008). The funding problems caused by a lack of FCR were seen as a major reason why pay rates were not competitive. The HR director of Liveco typified the role of funding in low pay rates, saying: '*We put our salaries up a thousand [pounds] but we still can't enter into the high wage bracket because we're restricted to the money that the social work department [of the local council] will give us to meet this package.'*

A further concern was the perception that career development and job security in the sector were 'poor.' Indeed none of the graduates placed in the voluntary sector pilot placement scheme has subsequently secured permanent employment within those organisations because of a lack of funds.

Notwithstanding these problems with pay and permanency, the voluntary sector could still be potentially attractive for graduate recruits. The HR directors attending the careers conference believed that the relatively informal and flat structures of many voluntary organisations actually offered graduates *more* opportunity to use their skills than might be the case in private or public sector organisations, sometimes because of funding issues:

> The voluntary sector offers a range of opportunities that aren't necessarily available in the public or private sector because the same things that are challenges for us, particularly the fact that we are tightly resourced and money is scarce, means that often when somebody comes in to do a particular job, they often have the opportunity to get involved in other areas of the business. (HR director, Stratos)

The HR director from Schoolco believed that graduates with particular expertise would be 'listened to' in voluntary sector organisations to a greater extent than in the private sector, and because of tight resourcing graduates could gain considerable responsibility at an early stage in their career. The Schoolco HR director also revealed that many people applying for administration posts were graduates with Schoolco tending to *'grow a lot of functions out of people [graduates] who joined us as admin staff.'* Indeed, Parry and Kelliher (this volume) note that many of the VSOs in their survey attempted to 'grow their own' staff and had a higher spend on training than comparable organisations in the public sector.

Significantly, even where permanent graduate positions were not available because of funding, short-term job opportunities within VSOs still enable graduates to utilise their skills. Furthermore, such opportunities can then lever other jobs either within or outside the voluntary sector. This point was emphasised by the director of the graduate placement scheme. Such placements, he said, were preferable to graduates over 'shelf-stacking' because of opportunities for graduates to use their skills and develop their employability. The Eastnet representative revealed that one graduate placed with the organisation had attributed her success in securing a subsequent job in the private sector to experience gained while on the work placement. Another graduate trainee employed directly by Eastnet had reportedly used her experience to secure a position in one of Scotland's largest and best-known VSOs. The placement director also stated that at least two of the six graduates had completed additional short-term project work for either the placement provider or other VSOs. Although it is not possible to generalise from these findings, the opportunity for some graduates to undertake short-term project work within the voluntary sector can clearly offer a 'springboard' to other jobs.

In addition, the sector may be seen as attractive to graduates who display value congruence with VSOs. Indeed, the overwhelming finding from the original research encompassing the views of front-line employees and managers was that workers joined the voluntary sector because it was 'something to believe in.' Pay and working conditions were seen as relatively unimportant compared to the nature of caring work and the values of VSOs (Nickson et al., 2008). This affective commitment was confirmed by the HR directors in relation to both their staff and themselves. The human resource assistant in Kidco believed that her job was the 'ideal opportunity' for her in terms of her values, as she had 'always wanted to work in the voluntary sector.' The HR directors of Supportco, Nimbus, and Houseco also expressed contentment with working in the sector after becoming disillusioned with work in the public and private sectors. As Supportco's HR director stated: '[Supportco is] something I can actually be passionate about. It's quite hard to get worked up about bits of software or whatever.' Significantly, the HR directors also noted that value congruence could help attract graduates to the sector, with Nimbus, for example, recently taking on a couple of 'purist' graduates who had 'liked the idea of the sector.'

Misperceptions of the Voluntary Sector

Given that graduate opportunities clearly exist in Scottish VSOs and the sector is a potentially attractive place to work, the question arises as to why graduates are not being attracted to the sector. One possible explanation is the misconceptions of the sector held by graduates and students.

Umbrellaorg's graduate placement scheme had been developed partly because of the realisation that many graduates had little or no idea about jobs in the voluntary sector. The director of the scheme reported that:

> We very often are surprised ourselves at the surprise on graduates' faces [when they] learn that there are actually jobs in the voluntary sector . . . the assumptions seem to be that the voluntary sector is about volunteering and about do[ing] good works.

This lack of awareness of job opportunities in the sector was apparent in the focus group of final-year Westuni students. Two participants, for example, typified the view that the sector was 'working in charity shops, befriending in the community, community kind of work, that kind of stuff,' and 'working out of the goodness of your heart as opposed [to working] for cash.' Meanwhile, the majority of the students had little idea that paid jobs existed in the voluntary sector, let alone those that might be suitable for graduates. Indeed, when presented with information about job possibilities within the sector, respondents were genuinely interested, especially in marketing/media positions and project management.

The careers advisers also acknowledged the misperception problem for the sector. Westuni did inform students of the voluntary sector as a career option, although '*you have to make them [students] aware that you are talking paid jobs because the tendency is for them to think, "Well that would be nice but I can't afford to work for nothing."*' However, as another careers adviser stated: '*[O]nce they [students] start to look, they're quite amazed by the breadth of the types of organisations and types of jobs.*' The various respondents believed that misperceptions were caused by poor communication and information exchange between the voluntary sector and graduates. As a consequence, there was a perceived lack of awareness among graduates (and the public as a whole) about the extent and types of paid jobs within VSOs.

The director of the placement scheme believed that the misperceptions held by graduates arose partly because of the lack of direction from careers advisers but acknowledged that '*We stand condemned as well. . . . We have never really approached the academic world and careers advisers in any meaningful way. . . . We have failed miserably to promote the voluntary sector as a [graduate] career opportunity in the past.*'

The graduate placement scheme had highlighted to Umbrellaorg that the sector needed to act differently if it was to promote itself as a graduate career opportunity. Both the careers advisers and students shared this view. The careers adviser from Northuni stated:

> I think they [the voluntary sector] need to market themselves as graduate employers if they want to target students. I'm not aware that they do or that voluntary sector organisations have graduate training schemes. Other employers come and do presentations at the university to talk about the work they do.

Furthermore, the same respondent stated that when voluntary organisations did market themselves at careers fairs, they were often promoting *volunteering*. In a similar vein, the careers advisers at Westuni had no formal links with any voluntary sector organisations and believed that the sector was not proactive in promoting itself as a graduate employer. The advisers' view was supported by the students at Westuni, who believed that if VSOs were more visible on campus this presence would help to change the perceptions of students about the sector and associated graduate job opportunities within organisations. '*It would diminish the myth if they actually came out to the universities and said this is what we have to offer.*'

When reinterviewed after the cessation of the pilot graduate placement scheme, the director reaffirmed that communication with careers advisers and universities was one of the most important priorities for Umbrellaorg. To this end a training course for careers advisers had been arranged in

2007 to inform them of opportunities in the voluntary sector. This course
had been well received by all of its participants.

Demand Constraint

As well as problems noted previously with pay, respondents reported cases
where funding issues had *directly* impeded the creation of graduate level
positions, especially in business support functions. The directors of Stratos
and Nimbus, for example, wanted to employ more graduates in their HR
departments but simply did not have the resources to do so. The Diversico representative echoed the feeling of many that their HR departments
were 'reasonably sized (but) not big enough for the organisation' and so
needed more staff. Similarly, the opportunity identified in Houseco for an
IT graduate had not been implemented at the time of the research because
of funding issues. Kidco's human resource director highlighted the frustration caused by resource constraints:

> The most frustrating thing for me is that I am absolutely blessed to have
> such a great staff team and I cannot use them to the best advantage for
> the organisation, just simply because there are not those resources. We
> could take on the world if we had the space.

The graduate placement scheme was motivated, in part, to plug skills gaps in
organisations, typically in business support functions. Indeed demand out-
stripped supply, and requests from organisations for graduates were greater
than the number of graduates for which the scheme had funding to place.
The director claimed that constraints in the demand for graduates in VSOs
was mainly because of a lack of FCR: '[I]t's hard to convince them [funders]
that an organisation also needs HR, IT, etc. . . . our experience is that, in the
main, it is support functions which suffer.' He revealed that FCR was one of
Umbrellaorg's 'biggest bones of contention' and that much of the organisation's lobbying of government and funders was directed at this issue.

Furthermore, the pilot scheme itself had not run after its allocated year,
with no subsequent funding available from the Scottish Executive or other
sources, despite a real need from VSOs for graduate support. The director also revealed that following the training course for careers advisers an
approach was made to the Scottish Funding Council[3] to fund a sustained
programme to promote the sector as a career opportunity to higher and
further education students, to train careers advisers, and to offer more student placements. Despite many 'positive noises,' six months later no funding decision had been received, leading the director to conclude that there
was an 'appetite' for promotion of the sector but 'nae money.'

The director also revealed that a highly successful VSO student placement scheme funded by a private sector bank, which had been run by
a Scottish university for three to four years, had also folded because

funding had ceased. It is, thus, not only individual VSOs that suffer from poor funding but also umbrella bodies attempting to alleviate the problems associated with FCR, mirroring the situation in the sector as a whole.

DISCUSSION AND CONCLUSIONS

Despite an increased demand for graduates stimulated in a large part by the professionalisation of VSOs' business support functions and an expanding number of graduates in the labour market, the voluntary sector has difficulties attracting graduates. There is no market failure in terms of the supply of and demand for graduates. Instead the reasons, we have demonstrated, are a mixture of *systems failure* (the attraction of graduates) and *administrative failure* (the funding for graduates). *Systems failure* occurs in organisations that can fund graduate positions but cannot attract recruits because of misperceptions among graduates and students. These misperceptions are compounded by VSOs' failure to adequately communicate the job and career opportunities available in VSOs to graduates, students, and labour market 'gatekeepers' such as careers advisers. In the case of *administrative failure* funding constraints lead to unfulfilled demand for permanent graduate positions in many VSOs, especially in business support functions. That a funding deficit exists because of inadequate funding from government is ironic as it is because of the demands of subcontracting triggered by government that business support functions are growing and the demand for graduates expanding.

An important priority has to be the attraction of Brown and Hesketh's (2004) 'purist' graduates (those who seek employment commensurate with their own beliefs and values) to those organisations that *can* provide graduate level jobs. To do so requires the systems failure to be rectified through the provision of information about the opportunities and advantages of working in the sector. Primarily, the voluntary sector needs to better present itself to graduates. The key is to raise the profile of paid jobs in the sector and dispel the 'only volunteering' myth, most obviously through university careers services. The pilot graduate placement scheme and graduate careers conference reported here provide examples of initiatives to rectify this problem, but more needs to be done. Even where graduates do not have a purist orientation, opportunities to use skills and develop employability in VSOs can be mutually beneficial, even if only on a short-term basis; and should be promoted by VSOs as part of the better supply of information to prospective graduate recruits.

Currently FCR is sparse, and VSOs typically only receive funding for the direct costs of service provision rather than any 'extras' such as, for example, graduate-level expertise in marketing or IT. The instability of project funding that this situation inevitably creates in the sector is exacerbated by the fact that voluntary sector organisations in Scotland, as in the rest of the UK, are often required to regularly reapply for short-term funding. While many voluntary organisations would like to create permanent jobs suitable for graduates, financial barriers thus often exist.

Relatedly, pay is a long-standing problem that requires a long-term solution, with government needing to rethink funding formulas if the continued transfer of services is to be efficacious. The issue of pay in attracting recruits at all levels is pertinent, even though many employees work in VSOs for reasons of value congruence. Government should work with social care voluntary organisations to deal with the pay issue through 'real' full cost recovery so that voluntary organisations can meet the actual costs of their service provision and attract the staff that they require.

Administrative failure not only affects individual VSOs but also intermediary organisations, further impeding the attraction of graduates. The difficulty faced by intermediary bodies was demonstrated by the unsustainability of Umbrellaorg's graduate placement scheme, the lack of funding thus far for the proposed awareness raising exercise, and the collapse of another graduate placement scheme.

This chapter has identified that VSOs delivering public services certainly require graduate labour and that such organisations may be a highly attractive option for such employees. However, VSOs need to do more to attract graduates—although their actions alone can only partially rectify the problems in attracting graduates to the sector. Many VSOs find that they cannot fulfil their demand for graduate employees because of administrative failure in funding arrangements. If the hollowing out of the public sector is to continue, then resources should be allocated to ensure that VSOs can attract the staff they require to fulfil the demands placed upon them by the state.

ACKNOWLEDGMENTS

The authors would like to thank Eli Dutton for project managing the initial research reported in this chapter and Shiona Chillas for her research assistance in the second stage of the research.

NOTES

1. Now the Scottish Government.
2. A British phrase applied to objects of ridicule or abuse.
3. The Scottish Funding Council (SFC) is the body that distributes funding for teaching, research, and other activities in Scotland's colleges and universities.

BIBLIOGRAPHY

Association of Chief Executives of Voluntary Organisations (ACEVO). (2010). *Full Cost Recovery*. Available at http://www.acevo.org.uk/Page.aspx?pid=1024. Accessed 10 November 2010.

ATA Management. (2006). *Third sector, first choice: Exploring the viability of a new scheme to attract graduates to the voluntary and community sector as the first stage in building their career*. London: NVCO.

Barnard, J. Broach, S., and Wakefield, V. (2004). *Social care: The growing crisis*. London: Social Care Employers Consortium.

Brindle, D. (2008). All together now for community cohesion. *The Guardian*, 20 February, p. 2.

Brown, M. (2007). There may be trouble ahead. *Voluntary Sector Magazine* (June), pp. 22–23.

Brown, P., and Hesketh, A. (2004). *The mismanagement of talent: Employability and jobs in the knowledge economy*. , Oxford: Oxford University Press.

Clark, J. (2007a). *The UK voluntary sector workforce almanac, 2007*. London: Workforce Hub/NCVO.

Clark, J. (2007b). *Voluntary sector skills survey, 2007, England*. London: UK Workforce Hub/NCVO.

Cunningham, I. (2008). *Employment relations in the voluntary sector*. London: Routledge.

Dart, R. (2004). Being 'business like' in nonprofit prganisation: A grounded and inductive typology. *Non-profit and Voluntary Sector Quarterly*, 33 (2), 290–310.

Felstead, A. Gallie, D., Green, F., and Zhou, Y. (2007). *Skills at work, 1986–2006*. Oxford: Economic and Social Research Council.

Futureskills Scotland. (2005). *Voluntary sector: Scottish sector profile, 2005*. Glasgow: Futureskills Scotland/Scottish Council for Voluntary Organisations.

Hayton, K. Percy, V., and Crawford, K. (2007). *Full cost recovery in the voluntary sector—Impact assessment*. Edinburgh: Scottish Executive Social Research, Scottish Executive.

HM Treasury. (2004). *Voluntary and community sector review*. London: HM Treasury.

Keep, E., and Mayhew, K. (1999). The assessment: Knowledge skills, and competitiveness. *Oxford Review of Economic Policy*, 15 (1), 1–15.

Labour Research. (2007a). Voluntary sector faces bidding war. *Labour Research* (August), 12–14.

Labour Research. (2007b). Voluntary sector expansion is 'due to social care transfers. *Labour Research* (December), 4.

Little, M. (2008). Unions find more losers than winners. *The Guardian*, 20 February, p. 5.

Mason, G. (2001). *Mixed fortunes: Graduate utilisation in service industries*. London: National Institute for Economic and Social Research.

Meyer, J. P., and Allen, N. J. (1991). A three-component conceptualization of organisational commitment. *Human Resource Management Review*, 1 (1), 61–89.

Meyer, M. (2009). 'Wie viel Wirtschaft verträgt die Zivilgesellschaft? Über Möglichkeiten und Grenzen wirtschaftlicher Rationalität in NPOs' in I. Bode, A. Evers and A. Klein (eds) Bürgergesellschaft als Projekt, Wiesbaden: VS Verlag für Sozialwissenschaften, pp. 127–144.

National Audit Office (NAO). (2007). *Office of the third sector—Implementation of full cost recovery*. London: NAO.

Nickson, D., Warhurst, C., Dutton, E., and Hurrell, S. A. (2008). A job to believe in: Recruitment in the Scottish voluntary sector. *Human Resource Management Journal*, 18 (1), 8–33.

Parry, E., Kelliher, C., Mills, T., and Tyson, S. (2005), Comparing HRM in the voluntary and public sectors. *Personnel Review*, 34 (5), 588–602.

Parsons, E., and Broadbridge, A. (2006). Job motivation and satisfaction: Unpacking the key factors for charity shop managers. *Journal of Retailing and Consumer Services*, 13 (2), 121–131.

Scottish Council for Voluntary Organisations (SCVO). (2007a). *Quality through diversity: Emerging models for Scotland's public services*. Edinburgh: SCVO.

SCVO. (2010a). *Fair Funding for Voluntary Sector Services*, Available at http://www.scvo.org.uk/policy/local-resources/fair-funding-for-voluntary-sector-service. Accessed 10 November 2010.

SCVO. (2010b). *SCVO Scottish Voluntary Sector Statistics*. Edinburgh: SCVO. Available at http://www.scvo.org.uk/about-the-sector/sector-stats. Accessed 10 November 2010.

Scottish Government. (2008). *Students in higher education—Age participation index*. Scottish Government. Available at http://www.scotland.gov.uk/Topics/Statistics/Browse/Lifelong-learning/TrendAPI. Accessed 14 March 2008.

Scottish Funding Council (SFC). *Who we are*. SFC. Available at http://www.sfc.ac.uk/about/about_us.htm. Accessed 11 March 2008.

Shah, R. (2004a). *Voluntary sector: Scottish sector profile*. Glasgow: Futureskills Scotland/SCVO.

Shah, R. (2004b). *Labour market information report*. Edinburgh: SCVO.

Wainwright, S., Clark, J., Griffith, M., Jochum, V., and Wilding, K. (2006). *The UK voluntary sector almanac, 2006*. London: NCVO.

Wilding, K., Collis, B., Lacey, M., and McCullough, G. (2003). *Futureskills 2003—A skills foresight research report on the voluntary sector paid workforce*. London: Voluntary Sector National Training Organisation.

Wilson, M. I., and Larson, R. S. (2002). Non-profit management students: Who they are and why they enrol. *Non-profit and Voluntary Sector Quarterly*, 31 (2), 259–270.

Zebra Square. (2006). *Young people's perceptions and attitudes of working in the 'voluntary, community, & charity sector.'* London: NCVO.

7 Recruiting for Values in Charitable Organisations

A Comparative Perspective

Eleanor Burt and Dora Scholarios

INTRODUCTION

Grounded in exploratory research involving four UK-based charities, this chapter sets out a comparative perspective on the imperatives shaping recruitment processes. Our aim was to understand how, in the face of a shifting environment, charities use recruitment processes to achieve congruence between the values of potential recruits, whether staff or volunteers, and organisational needs.

The chapter begins by outlining the changing context for charitable organisations, which has seen the growing importance of a managerialist ethos and pressures to professionalise within the sector. We then consider the role which values play in these organisations. Of particular interest is whether and how the charities ensure that potential recruits reflect core organisational values in the face of sometimes conflicting imperatives shaping strategy and recruitment priorities.

The charities examined each reflected different degrees of engagement with public funding. Their fields of activity were welfare services (UK charity), humanitarian aid and development (big international charity), capacity-building and humanitarian support (medium-sized international charity), and educational development (small international charity). Whereas one of the charities was substantially engaged in the delivery of publicly funded services within the UK, the two international-facing charities significantly and consciously limited their receipt of government funding. Prior to 2009, the fourth UK-based international-facing charity had not been in receipt of government funding. However, as our fieldwork ended, this charity was in the process of submitting its first application for funding from the Department for International Development (DfID), with further applications anticipated.

CONTEXT

For some time, academic research and debate have centred on the growing relationship between the public sector and third sector organisations (Kramer and Grossman, 1987; Saidel, 1989; Kendall, 2009; Wolch, 1990;

Smerdon, 2009; Billis, 2010), with the nature and implications of the funding relationship being a preoccupying interest. Cast as pivotal in reshaping the environment in which charities provide services to the public and/or engage in public services delivery in the context of their defining characteristics, this relationship has tended to be conceptualised in the form of a 'resource-dependency' (Pfeffer, 1981), in which charities are understood to be less strongly positioned than public sector bodies from which, to varying degrees, their funding is drawn. Thus, dependence on public sector funding, and in particular the move from 'grants' to 'contracts' and other forms of 'earned income,' is seen to draw organisations that, historically, were strategically and operationally independent and autonomous into a relationship that is generally regarded as profoundly challenging in its potential to undermine the organisational characteristics and arrangements that are held to make charities uniquely valuable (Cunningham, 2008; Milofsky and Rothschild, 2006; Minear, 2002; Smillie and Minear, 2004).

Block grants have been largely superseded by tightly specified contracts, tied to specific services and performance levels. Voucher schemes that will more deeply embed the 'market mechanism' by enabling individual citizens to decide which services they will purchase, and from which providers, have been piloted (Department for Education and Science, 2006). As charities have drawn closer to government, so, too, there has been a trend toward formalisation (bureaucratisation) and professionalisation of staff and volunteers. Concepts and practices more commonly associated with for-profit businesses, strategic management and performance evaluation among them, are perceived to have become part of the landscape of modern charities. Further reinforcing what some charities have already experienced as a seismic shift toward embedding a managerialist ethos as well as business practices is the growing emphasis that government is placing on 'social enterprise,' a form of organisation that is held to reconcile social and business objectives (Department of Trade and Industry, 2002; Scottish Executive, 2003).

RECRUITING FOR VALUES

Charities are likely to attract people with an affinity to their cause (Light, 2002); thus they tend to have strong value systems built around members' shared purpose. Concepts such as 'perceived ethical-organisational fit' (Coldwell, Billsberry, van Meurs, and Marsh, 2008) and 'values-based' (Cunningham, 2010a) or 'ideologically-infused psychological contracts' (Thompson and Bunderson, 2003) have been used to describe this assumed value congruence. The values-driven nature of the nonprofit sector is thought to provide competitive advantage over the better resourced private sector (Frumkin and Andre-Clark, 2000), and organisations with high person-organisation fit generally have been shown to benefit from greater employee satisfaction, commitment and discretionary effort, and lower attrition (Bretz and Judge, 1994; Cable and Judge, 1996). The importance of mission attachment within voluntary organisations in this respect has been shown in studies by Brown and Yoshioka (2003) and Vigoda and Cohen (2003).

The drive for operational efficiency, however, directly challenges this value congruence. One possibility is that increasing pressures to professionalise, for example, recruiting to address skill shortages (Nickson, Warhurst, Dutton, and Hurrell, 2008), removes the need for congruence in the values of employees with the charity. In their study of American nonprofit organisations, Hwang and Powell (2009) link the adoption of business models for functions such as accounting or human resource management, aimed at improving efficiency and accountability, with an increase in the numbers of paid, professional staff. The employment relationship here is based less on shared values and more on instrumental exchange, as career employees seek other rewards, such as financial compensation or career prospects, and perhaps place less weight on what the organisation stands for or the 'fit' with their own values (for instance, Catano, Pond, and Kellaway, 2001).

Alternatively, voluntary sector organisations, especially given recruitment difficulties, could reap benefits from encouraging value congruence as part of the staffing process (see, for instance,- Hurrell, Warhurst, and Nickson, forthcoming, and Chapter 6 of this volume with respect to reorientating staffing strategy in order to attract more graduates to the sector). However, if ideology-infused psychological contracts are based on employees' beliefs that the organisation will remain committed to a cause or principle, any threat to this belief will damage the reputation of the organisation and violate these contracts. Cost pressures which drive decision making away from organisational mission toward administrative efficiency may therefore result in unfulfilled obligations and consequently loss of morale, low commitment, and a desire to leave (Akingbola, 2004; Cunningham, 2010a). The 'contract culture' also implies fewer permanent staff with accompanying adverse effects on pay, work intensification, and career development (Cunningham, 2008). Whereas some identify a more sophisticated approach to HRM within the sector focusing on nonfinancial means of maintaining a positive psychological contract (Parry and Kelliher, 2009), others warn of an under-resourced HR function constrained by political dynamics struggling to balance organisational mission with the need for strategic change (Cunningham, 2010b). In line with this last view, Ridder and McCandless (2010) have cautioned about potential threats to nonprofit organisations' value-laden strategic HRM orientation with respect to their employees.

How then is the shifting focus being managed by voluntary organisations, and to what extent are core values surviving as a unifying bond within the employment relationship? Recruitment and selection is the first point in the employment relationship where perceived value congruence can be established by both parties (Lievens and Highhouse, 2003; Ostroff and Judge, 2007). Our focus in this study, therefore, is on the recruitment strategies adopted by our four charities and how espoused values are surfaced, communicated, and used to guide decision-making. We were interested especially in the extent to which key imperatives were shaping these strategies and whether, in light of these external contingencies, values remained an important facet of attraction and selection.

RESEARCH METHODOLOGY

Reflecting the highly diverse nature of the organisations that inhabit it, the 'third sector' has been described as a 'loose and baggy monster' (Kendall and Knapp, 1995). A subset of the wider third sector, charities are no less diverse. The four organisations that we examined were selected on the basis that as charities providing 'human services,' they ought also to be manifestly philanthropic institutions. As such, in seeking to optimise 'person-organisation fit,' it could be expected that their recruitment processes would be pre-eminently geared toward ensuring congruence between their deeply held philanthropic philosophy and that of their staff and volunteer recruits. The organisations were also selected on the basis that they had a well-established human resource (HR) function and recruitment process in place. Thus, these organisations were well positioned to be recruiting strategically, in ways supportive of key organisational requirements.

In addition to being professionally-staffed, to varying extents the four charities were also volunteer-involving organisations. In two of the international charities, medium-sized international charity (MIC) and big international charity (BIC), volunteers were mainly involved in fundraising and administrative support capacities. In UK charity (UKC), staff and volunteers were engaged in frontline activities. In small international charity (SIC), volunteers were the frontline. UKC, MIC, and BIC each had professionally staffed, dedicated HR functions, with recruitment a key responsibility. In SIC, in contrast, the human resource management function was subsumed within the portfolios of the chief officers, with recruitment regarded as of especial importance. Of the four charities, SIC was also the only one that was still led and managed by its 'founding father.' When the size of the professional staff complement is employed as an indicator of the size of the organisation, SIC was also the smallest of the four charities with a professional staff complement numbering in single figures, relative to upward of fifty in UKC, and substantially higher numbers still in MIC and BIC. In examining the recruitment processes our focus was on the recruitment of frontline staff or volunteers, as it was here that the requirement for value congruence could be expected to be most acute.

UKC was a relatively small-scale charity providing welfare services in the UK. MIC was a UK-based charity, of international scope. SIC, an education and development charity, had an international orientation, drawing funding and volunteers from throughout the UK. BIC, the humanitarian aid and development charity, was a 'household name' organisation of international scope. The three international charities were faith-based, with multidenominational as well as secular staff and volunteer profiles.

The research methods involved analysis of in-house documentation including web-based information, and in-depth interviews with chief officers, directors of human resources, directors of volunteering, and senior operational staff. The interviews, which were typically of one to two hours duration, were either on a face-to-face basis or by telephone. With two exceptions, both members of the research team were present at each interview. Both engaged with each organisation in the course of the research. In the interests of confidentiality and anonymity the documentary sources are not referenced, and the times, precise dates, and locations of interviews together with the status of interviewees are not revealed.

FINDINGS

Key points of similarity and difference emerging from the case studies are set out below and in Table 7.1.

Case Study 1: United Kingdom Charity (UKC)

Established in the mid-19th century, UKC was a product of the visionary, pioneering, private philanthropy that was typical of the Victorian era (Williams, 1989; Prochaska, 2002). Today, though still receiving donative income, the organisation is substantially dependent upon public sector grants and contracts, with some flagship services 'owned' by public sector funders only available to their designated clients. Led by a chief officer with experience of the private and public sector as well as the charitable sector, the charity has undergone considerable structural and cultural change in recent years, as well as re-branding. Alongside this has been significant change in its staff profile, with only a very small number of original staff remaining in post, whereas a fivefold growth in appointments has occurred. The volunteer profile has also changed as the charity has sought to formalise and manage its volunteers more effectively. External imperatives for professional recognition have also influenced the volunteer profile, reinforced by the preference among professionals to deal with fellow professionals.

Whereas service users are represented at board level, ensuring that the charity has access to necessary skills and expertise is considered the priority at this level. Although the charity does not actively set out to recruit staff or volunteers from among its service users, its experience is that recruiting from among these stakeholders assists in sustaining and strengthening the values of the organisation. Clarity among staff and volunteers regarding the charity's values and their demonstrable empathy with them are regarded as of pivotal importance. However, here, too, external imperatives can lead to other criteria such as special expertise (in IT, for example) or skills (in monitoring and compliance, for example) taking precedence in recruitment and appointment. Frontline staff tend to migrate into the charity from the public services, bringing with them experience and skills from the social services arena in particular. In the main, the aim is to recruit staff and volunteers whose values align with those of the charity, and the recruitment process is substantially geared toward achieving this, whereas the subsequent induction and probation processes provide further opportunities for assessment.

The importance that the charity attaches to person-organisation fit is reflected in a robustly designed recruitment process, developed in-house, and employed when recruiting to permanent appointments. The process is designed with the aim of optimising opportunities for both the potential recruit and the charity to evaluate their mutual 'fit.' Sitting at the heart of the recruitment process are in-depth panel interviews and other assessment mechanisms, such as scenarios and tasks, through which the values held by the potential recruit are surfaced and made transparent. There are also opportunities for potential recruits to be observed by other staff members during the course of the day.

Analysis of interview and documentary materials, including recruitment materials, speaks to an organisation that is clearly committed to providing a 'high quality' of service to its clients, aiming both to 'empower' them and to deliver 'person-centred' services. Other underpinning values are, identifiably, 'transparency,' 'integrity,' 'respect,' 'conscientiousness,' and a commitment to 'workforce development.' Staff are expected to place greater emphasis on job satisfaction than on salary, while willingness on the part of staff and volunteers to provide 'value-added' is a related expectation. Whereas values such as person-centeredness and empowerment might be regarded as having philanthropic aspects, the values underpinning UKC are not, in essence, philanthropic. They are values that can be expected to exist in any organisation concerned with providing quality of service and good customer relationships, including public and private sector organisations.

Case Study 2: Medium-sized International Charity (MIC)

Established around the mid-20th century, MIC is a faith-based charity operating in more than twenty countries, across three continents. Irrespective of religious creed and working with partner organisations overseas, its small complement of professional staff and predominantly volunteer workforce provide support to empower and develop the capacity of individuals and communities numbering among the most vulnerable and deprived. As well as providing practical assistance in the form of skills and equipment, for example, the charity also delivers training to indigenous communities, while professional staff and volunteers provide specialist support to partner organisations and community projects. Practical support is also provided to organisations offering humanitarian relief missions. Receiving the majority of its multimillion pound income from individual donations, legacies, and investments, around a fifth comes from institutional sources including governmental bodies. Representative advocacy work and campaigning are both core activities.

Whereas the charity welcomes staff from across the faith and secular communities, tolerance of and respect for the denominational values that shape its philosophical and operational decisions are sought, and training is available to new employees whose roles and responsibilities require knowledge and understanding of the denominational teachings of the organisation's church. Related to this, whereas applicants are not asked about their religious affiliation, candidates are expected to be able to display a level of knowledge and understanding of the organisation germane to evaluating mutual fit. Additionally, the recruitment literature and the subsequent selection process both invite candidates explicitly to reflect on, first, what it means to work for a faith-based organisation, and, second, the extent of correspondence between their personal philanthropic values and those of the charity. This is the case for support posts as well as front-line posts, as the potential for philosophical tensions and conflict pervades both functions.

Thus, whereas demonstrable relevant experience and expertise are essential attributes for appointment on the part of MIC, philosophical congruence between recruit and organisation is also deeply important. The recruitment of volunteers bears broadly similar characteristics. Thus, with the exception of a small number of roles specific to the charity's faith community and for which applicants may be required to have the approval of their local religious leader before they can be considered for appointment, volunteers, too, are recruited irrespective of faith and mainly with regard to skills, experience, personality, and demonstrable philosophical empathy with the charity's defining values.

MIC's core values include respecting the dignity of others; working for the common good; seeking to improve the lives of others, particularly those in poverty; and showing solidarity with vulnerable communities. Underpinned by other associated values that are deeply embedded within the doctrinal philosophy that is the essence of the charity, and which inform *how* these desired outcomes are reached, is the potential for tensions and dilemmas to emerge. Thus, despite a shared commitment to alleviating poverty there may be deep divisions over how to achieve this (Whitman, 2008; Richardson, 1994; Vaux, 2001). The education of female children, allowing women to take up employment, and the use of contraceptive mechanisms and abortion, are illustrative of the types of issues centred around the *means* of alleviating poverty, that can be deeply divisive in faith-based philanthropic settings employing staff and volunteers whose philosophies and values, whether secular or faith-based, are not aligned with those of the charity. It is of considerable importance, therefore, that the recruitment process surfaces and invites reflection on the less visible philosophical positions of both applicants and charity. The philanthropic outcomes may be broadly shared irrespective of religious denomination or secular persuasion, but how they are achieved has the potential to be the subject of deep division. For MIC, the recruitment process is crucial in managing (and diminishing) this potential tension from the outset.

Case Study 3 Big International Charity (BIC)

BIC is also a faith-based organisation which was established in the mid-20th century and is engaged in international humanitarianism. Operating on a significantly larger scale than the other charities, in terms of geographical scope, income, and numbers of partner organisations and volunteers, its modus operandi mainly involves working through third sector partner organisations to develop the capacity-building and knowledge sharing capabilities that underpin long-term development, campaigning, and disaster relief. The emphasis, here, is on providing coaching and training within the indigenous community. With a view to safeguarding its operational independence, the majority of its income is generated through its faith communities as well as public fundraising, with government funding held at 30 percent of overall income.

The significance that BIC attaches to value congruence is expressed from the outset, being signalled explicitly in advertisements aimed at employee recruitment, irrespective of whether the advertised posts are of a type in which direct engagement with these expressed humanitarian values might be expected to be crucial and unavoidable (for example, frontline development worker) to those where their centrality to the post might be less obvious if surfacing at all (for instance, director of finance and accounts or construction engineer). Thus, during the time of our research, an advertisement for a professional fundraising manager whose primary role was to contribute to strengthening the independence of the charity through the delivery of a strategy for raising private funds stated that appointees should be 'committed to the aims of BIC to support the world's poorest people as they struggle for life and justice.' This was typical of advertisements for salaried professional positions, with others also signaling that candidates should share the humanitarian vision of the charity and have empathy with its aims. BIC, in similar vein to MIC (above) and SIC (following), was clearly seeking to weigh person-organisation congruence with its humanitarian principles against a growing need for technical skills and prior experience of working with NGOs. This was exemplified in its development of a database aimed at facilitating recruitment and performance management by profiling key values together with other requirements such as expertise and skills. Sensitive to the tensions that can emerge in practice around competing values, BIC also employed psychometric personality tests explicitly geared to evaluating the responses of potential recruits to value-based dilemmas.

With volunteer recruitment there was an assumption of 'self-selection' into the charity on the part of volunteers, who, it was perceived, would 'naturally' gravitate toward a charity whose values they shared. Consequently, the emphasis in the volunteer recruitment literature was on outlining skills and other attributes required for specialist volunteer positions such as those of youth worker, media liaison, teacher, or office administration.

'Impartiality,' 'neutrality,' and concern to bring about 'social justice' through ending poverty and disadvantage are among the core principles underpinning the philanthropic mission and operational activities of BIC, as well as shaping the strategic and day-to-day decisions and actions of staff, volunteers, and partner organisations. For BIC, in contrast to MIC, commitment to its humanitarian principles and mission on the part of staff and volunteers holds precedence over religious teachings and values. Instead, as with SIC (see below), tension has derived from managerialist and business imperatives associated with growth, regulation, audit and compliance, and resourcing large-scale international operations. Here, at the time of the research, BIC was seeking to manage this tension strategically by refocusing its corporate activities around robustly (re-) expressed humanitarian principles and re-branding.

Case Study 4: Small International Charity (SIC)

Established in the early 1990s, SIC is a multidenominational charity in the Christian tradition. Its complement of three permanent staff includes its chief officer of almost twenty years standing, a deputy director who came into post shortly after its inception, and an administrator who is also a long-standing member of the team. Other staff, including those who liaise with and provide support to volunteers, are engaged on a flexible basis as required, with appointees regularly drawn from the body of volunteers and partner organisations with which SIC has well-established relationships. The charity's income derives from a combination of sources that include a church-based block grant, trusts and foundations, individuals, and training courses. Partner organisations receiving volunteers provide supplementary resources. At the time of our research, there was a perception (and accompanying concern) that the charity must also seek income from government sources in the future, as its traditional sources had become considerably less certain. Also influencing strategic and operational change on the part of the charity is health and safety legislation that was seen to marry with a growing aversion to risk within society and an accompanying 'compensation culture' and to serve to make the charity more constrained regarding the locations and situations into which it places volunteers, making it difficult to meet the needs of some overseas partner organisations and communities. This, together with insufficient numbers of UK-generated volunteers available to meet the demands of overseas partners, has led SIC to begin to work with these partners to grow their indigenous volunteering capability supported by a community of 'virtual volunteers' providing on-line mentoring. At the same time, the charity is beginning to move away from sending volunteers overseas. Instead, it is beginning to place volunteers within deprived and vulnerable communities in the UK.

From the outset the charity has recruited its volunteers and governing board from within its ecumenical faith communities. It has also sought to secure its funding within its ecumenical community. These were considered pivotal strategies, the Christian communities significantly nurturing and anchoring the values that are fundamental to the work of the charity. Thus, as with UKC, strongly shared values were and remain of critical importance for SIC. At the same time, whereas SIC and UKC also share a growing requirement for volunteers with particular skills, in SIC it is the extent to which volunteers manifestly share the charity's values that remains the deciding factor in their selection to the volunteering programme. To this end, SIC has also developed and refined its own in-house recruitment and selection programme. Integral to this, the post-hire induction process presents a crucial opportunity for further substantive assessment on the part of the charity and the newly recruited volunteers, prior to the volunteers being received by partner organisations and indigenous communities.

The importance that SIC attaches to ensuring value congruence in person-organisation fit is reflected in the design and delivery of the recruitment process. Thus, at the heart of the process is a series of in-depth one-on-one interviews with the director, the deputy director, and one of the charity's experienced volunteers, in turn. The interview team then meets to share their evaluation of the candidate. Candidates who are successful at this stage are invited to attend the selection course, and, if they are successful at this stage, they will be invited to participate in the induction session. Scenarios, role playing, and reflective discussions are among the mechanisms used to surface and make visible the values held by potential volunteers. A residential dimension provides further transparency, with opportunities to observe candidates in more informal situations which are regarded as especially valuable and a key component of the selection process. The importance that the charity attaches to value congruence is also reflected in the decision that as there is a shift toward recruiting indigenous volunteers the charity will send experienced volunteers out to its partner organisations with a view to ensuring that the recruitment process remains robust, despite its geographical re-location and distance from SIC.

SIC is committed to developing 'bridging and bonding social capital' (Putnam, 2000), its volunteering activities intended to serve primarily as a two-way educational experience between the volunteer and the community into which the volunteer is received, with capacity-building secondary to this. Thus, volunteers are expected to live with local families, crossing geographical, economic, and faith boundaries, and to embrace and show demonstrable solidarity with their values and traditions. Alongside 'voluntarism' and 'solidarity,' other underpinning values embrace 'reflective learning,' 'partner-led' development, and 'responsible engagement.'

DISCUSSION AND CONCLUSIONS

Each of our four case studies illustrates an effort to define core values and achieve congruence with employees and volunteers through recruitment and selection. Several themes arise from the comparison. First, of the four charities that we examined UKC's values can be regarded as the least substantively philanthropic, more closely reflecting values that might be expected to colonise private sector firms and which have also become increasingly characteristic of governmental and public sector settings. Whereas UKC's considerable involvement in the provision of publicly funded services is undoubtedly influential, so, too, are other factors. The CEO of UKC came to the organisation from a background in the private and public sectors. We noted, too, the migration of professional staff in to UKC from the public sector. These staff could be expected to bring with them sets of shared values emanating from the social work profession and the public sector environment. UKC was also the only charity that was not faith-based. It is possible that the faith-based character of the other charities served to anchor their philanthropic mission and values more.

Second, each of the charities employed a robust selection process underpinned by multiple methods, including CVs, interviews, and role-play exercises, and in some cases, based on a competency or skills framework (see Table 7.1). This is in line with 'best practice' recommendations for staffing (Schmitt and Kim, 2007) and generally consistent with their size and professional HR presence (Ridder and McCandless, 2010). What is striking, though, is the intensely hands-on and robust scrutiny of applicants employed by UKC and SIC, neither of which had a professional HR unit, and which were small by comparison with MIC and BIC. Of the two, SIC was the most robust, with applicants undergoing a series of three one-on-one interviews with the staff team and an experienced volunteer who then came together to compare notes. This was followed by scenarios, role plays, and reflective discussions designed to surface values held by applicants. The most crucial element, designed to maximise transparency, was the several days of residential stay that enabled intimate observation of applicants in formal as well as informal settings 'off-guard' (interview with CEO, 2009). It was the need to ensure value fit that drove this process in SIC. Moreover, the imperative was stronger in SIC than in UKC, not because the values were philanthropic or faith-based, but, first, because they required particular tolerances to 'solidarism' and living, working, and worshiping with people of different cultures, circumstances, and faiths; and, second, because once recruited SIC's volunteers spent six months or more living in the homes of people whose circumstances may be unimaginably different as well as difficult and whose values and religious beliefs may be deeply challenging to the volunteers. SIC could only achieve its philanthropic aim of building bridging and bonding social capital if the volunteers that it sent to these communities overseas were able 'to go native' for the duration and did not require to be suddenly and unexpectedly extracted and brought home.

Thus, despite no professional HR capabilities and different funding structures, SIC and UKC emerged as the most proactive in managing value congruence through staffing, whether these represented professional values (as in UKC) or philanthropic values (as in SIC). Where the mission was in some part educational and aimed at building 'bonding capital' across faiths or cultures (SIC), value-based tensions were actively surfaced at the hiring stage. Using intensive two-way processes of information sharing, feedback, and transparency, SIC, and, to a lesser extent, UKC, exemplify a staffing strategy aimed at person-organisation fit and value congruence rather than fit with specific job or skill requirements (Ostroff and Judge, 2007). These charities designed in-house, 'socially valid' assessment processes (Schuler, Farr, and Smith, 1993) involving all staff to encourage the emergence of an ideologically infused psychological contract at the pre-entry stage of the employment relationship.

The larger charities, with professional HR functions, were more likely to have adopted skills-based assessment strategies and were less keenly concerned with identifying value-based issues or value congruence at the staffing stage. The adoption of psychometric testing and competency-based selection methods generally has been linked with greater organisational size and the professionalisation of HR functions (Wolf and Jenkins, 2006), both of which were features of these two charities. MIC and BIC may also have found greater need to recruit for specialist skills as a result of their increasing size. Yet, both also retained attraction strategies (Rynes and Barber, 1990), such as brand signaling, in order to attract an applicant pool with congruent values. These differences in staffing approach may reflect the influence of a professional HR presence which encouraged a conventionally defined notion of 'best practice' in selection rather than a response to specific external contingencies.

Although the degree of value congruence generated by these contrasting approaches could not be established in this study, it does raise the question of whether a professionalised HR function with more HR-led assessment processes represents an appropriate strategic shift (Ridder and McCandless, 2010). Will HR professionals have sufficient awareness and understanding of the value-based dilemmas faced by frontline staff and volunteers to screen for these? Is brand signaling as a means to self-selection on the part of applicants a sufficiently robust and reliable mechanism?

Table 7.1 Key Case Study Characteristics (Approaches to Staffing)

Case	HR function	Recruitment	Selection	Emphasis on value congruence
UKC	No professional unit	Draws from public sector and service users	• CV, assessment centres (task and scenario-based tests, interviews) • All staff engaged in observation and evaluation of the candidate in the work setting	Expertise may take precedence over values
MIC	Professional unit	Draws from faith community; slowly professionalising	• CV and interview-based • Emerging skills-based competency framework • HR-led, only key staff involved	Expertise may take precedence over values
BIC	Professional unit	Global reach; signals values in strategic, HR-led re-branding	• CV, interviews, psychometric testing • Global standardisation • HQ HR-led, only key staff involved	Expertise may take precedence over values
SIC	No professional unit	Draws from faith community	• CV, interview, scenarios, role-play, reflective discussion • Residential component enables intense scrutiny of applicant to evaluate value congruence over a period of days; involves formal and informal (leisure) settings • All staff and experienced volunteers involved	Values are primary

Finally, our comparative approach demonstrates the need to extend the analysis of recruitment and selection in charitable organisations beyond the nexus of government-third sector relationships, situating it against the context of embedded and emerging cultural and structural trajectories in the social, political, and economic seismology of contemporary society. The case studies ranged from one with substantial dependence on public sector funding, to two with limited levels of engagement, and one that operated independently of government funding (up to and including the period of the research). This allowed us to identify and draw out a number of additional imperatives at least as significant for MIC, BIC, and SIC as the funding relationship may be for UKC. These include the requirements of overseas partners; competition for funding, staff, and volunteers; concerns with organisational reputation and 'branding'; increasing momentum within contemporary society toward formalisation and professionalisation; and organisational missions and philosophies. Thus, in MIC and BIC growing demand for particular skills and expertise in combination with the trajectory of professionalisation characterising contemporary charities was associated with identifiable emphasis on skills-based assessment. Delivery of a clear brand 'identity' was believed to enable applicants to 'self-assess' the extent of their compatibility with the values of these charities. In SIC, the 'bridging and bonding' mission, combined with the lengthy immersion of volunteers in potentially very challenging overseas environments, meant that the recruitment and selection processes had to enable intense and deep scrutiny for value congruence. Thus, SIC's recruitment process was developed in-house, involved senior people within SIC and experienced volunteers, and took place on a residential basis involving formal and informal interactions over a number of days.

Clearly, this exploratory study raises a number of issues deserving further research with regard to the values-based nature of charities and the pressures for change. Our comparisons show that greater professionalisation of HR is linked to more skills-based assessment at the selection stages. Whether this threatens value congruence, perhaps by shifting the focus primarily to filling skills gaps or attracting staff with unrealistic expectations of philanthropic mission, requires further study, as does the issue of to what extent the influence of HR professionalisation is itself a product of wider environmentally informed strategic considerations, rather than a relatively 'independent' force for change.

BIBLIOGRAPHY

Akingbola, K. (2004). Staffing, retention, and government funding: A case study. *Nonprofit Management and Leadership*, 14 (4), 453–465.

Billis, D. (2010). *Hybrid organizations and the third sector: Challenges for practice, theory, and policy*. Basingstoke: Palgrave Macmillan.

Bretz, R. D., and Judge, T. A. (1994). Person-organisation fit and the theory of work adjustment: implications for satisfaction, tenure, and career success. *Journal of Vocational Behavior*, 44, 32–54.

Brown, W. A., and Yoshioka, C. F. (2003). Mission attachment and satisfaction as factors in employee retention. *Nonprofit Management and Leadership*, 14 (1), 5–18.

Cable, D. M., and Judge, T. A. (1996). Person-organisation fit, job choice decisions, and organisational entry. *Organisational Behavior and Human Decision Processes*, 67, 294–311.

Catano, V. M., Pond, M., and Kelloway, E. K. (2001). Exploring commitment and leadership in volunteer organizations. *Leadership & Organization Development Journal*, 22 (6), 256–263.

Coldwell, D. A., Billsberry, J., van Meurs, N., and Marsh, P. J. G. (2008). The effects of person–organization ethical fit on employee attraction and retention: Towards a testable explanatory model. *Journal of Business Ethics*, 78, 611–622.

Cunningham, I. (2010a). Drawing from a bottomless well: Exploring the resilience of value-based psychological contracts in voluntary organizations. *International Journal of Human Resource Management*, 21 (5), 700–720.

Cunningham, I. (2010b). The HR function in purchaser–provider relationships: Insights from the UK voluntary sector. Human Resource Management Journal, 20 (2), 189–205.

Cunningham, I. (2008). Race to the bottom? Exploring variations in employment conditions in the voluntary sector. *Public Administration*, 86 (4), 1033–1053.

Department for Education and Science. (2006). *Youth matters*. London: Green Paper.

Department of Trade and Industry. (2002). Social enterprise: A strategy for success. London.

Frumkin, P., and Andre-Clark, A. (2000). When missions, markets, and politics collide: Values and strategy in the nonprofit human services. *Nonprofit and Voluntary Sector Quarterly*, 29 (1), 141–164.

Hurrell, S. A., Warhurst, C., and Nickson, D. (forthcoming). Giving Miss Marple a makeover: Graduate recruitment, systems failure, and the Scottish voluntary sector. *Nonprofit and Voluntary Sector Quarterly*. Published online September 2009.

Hwang, H., and Powell, W. W. (2009). The rationalization of charity: The influences of professionalism in the nonprofit sector. *Administrative Science Quarterly*, 54, 268–298.

Kendall, J. (2009). 'The UK': Ingredients in a hyperactive horizontal policy environment. In J. Kendall (ed.), *Handbook on third sector policy in Europe: Multi-level processes and organized civil society* (pp. 67–94). Cheltenham: Edward Elgar.

Kendall, J., and Knapp, M. (1995). 'A loose and baggy monster': Boundaries and definitions in the voluntary sector. In J. Davis Smith, C. Rochester, and R. Hedley (eds.), *Introduction to the voluntary sector* (pp. 66–95). London: Routledge.

Kramer, R. M., and Grossman. B. (1987). Contracting for social services: Process management and resource dependencies. *Social Service Review*, 61, 32–55.

Lievens, F., and Highouse, S. (2003). The relation of instrumental and symbolic attributes to a company's attractiveness as an employer. *Personnel Psychology*, 56, 75–102.

Light, P. (2002). The content of their character: The state of the non-profit workforce. *The Nonprofit Quarterly*, 9 (3), 6–16.

Milofsky, C., and Rothschild, J. (2006). The centrality of values, passions, and ethics in the nonprofit sector. *Nonprofit Management and Leadership*, 17 (2), 137–143.

Minear, L. (2002). *The humanitarian enterprise: Dilemmas and discoveries.* Bloomfield, CT: Kumarian Press.

Nickson, D., Warhurst, C., Dutton, E., and Hurrell, S. (2008). A job to believe in: Recruitment in the Scottish voluntary sector. *Human Resource Management Journal*, 18 (1), 20–35.

Ostroff, C., and Judge T. A. (2007). *Perspectives on organizational fit.* New York: Lawrence Erlbaum Associates.

Parry, E., and Kelliher, C. (2009). Voluntary sector responses to increased resourcing challenges. *Employee Relations*, 31 (1), 9–24.

Pfeffer, J. (1981). *Power in organizations.* Pitman: Marshfield, MA:

Prochaska, F. (2002). *Schools of citizenship: Charity and civic virtue.* London: Civitas.

Putnam, R. D. (2000). *Bowling alone: The collapse and revival of American community.* New York: Simon and Schuster.

Richardson, H. S. (1994). *Practical reasoning about final ends.* Cambridge: Cambridge University Press.

Ridder, H., and McCandless, A. (2010). Influences on the architecture of human resource management in nonprofit organizations: An analytical framework. *Nonprofit Management and Leadership*, 39 (1), 124–141.

Rothschild, J., and Milofsky, C. (2006). The centrality of values, passions, and ethics in the nonprofit sector. *Nonprofit Management and Leadership*, 17 (2), 137–143.

Rynes, S. L., and Barber, A. E. (1990). Applicant attraction strategies: An organizational perspective. *Academy of Management Review*, 15 (2), 286–310.

Saidel, J. R. (1989). Dimensions of Interdependence: The State–Voluntary Sector Relationship. *Nonprofit and Voluntary Sector Quarterly*, 18 (4), 335–347.

Schmitt, N., and Kim, B. (2007). Selection decision-making. In P. F. Boxall, J. Purcell, and P. M. Wright (eds.), *The Oxford handbook of human resource management* (pp. 300–323). Oxford: Oxford University Press.

Schuler, H., Farr, J. L., and Smith, M. (1993). The individual and organizational sides of personnel selection and assessment. In H. Schuler, J. L. Farr, and M. Smith (eds.), Personal selection and assessment: Individual and organizational perspectives (pp. 1–6). Hillsdale, NJ: Lawrence Erlbaum Associates.

Scottish Executive. (2003). *A review of the Scottish Government's policies to promote the social economy.* Scottish Executive: Edinburgh.

Smerdon, M. (Ed.). (2009). *The first principle of voluntary action: Essays on the independence of the voluntary sector from government in Canada, England, Germany, Northern Ireland, Scotland, United States of America, and Wales.* London: The Baring Foundation.

Smillie, I., and Minear, L. (2004). *The charity of nations: Humanitarian action in a calculating world.* Bloomfield, CT: Kumarian Press.

Thompson, J. A., and Bunderson, J. S. (2003). Violations of principle: Ideological currency in the psychological contract. *Academy of Management Review*, 28 (4), 571–586.

Vaux, T. (2001). *The selfish altruist: Relief work in famine and war.* London: Earthscan.

Vigoda, E., and Cohen, A. (2003). Work congruence and excellence in human resource management. *Review of Public Personnel Administration*, 23 (3), 192–216.

Whitman, J. R. (2008). Evaluating philanthropic foundations according to their social values. *Nonprofit Management and Leadership*, 18 (4), 417–434.

Williams, I. (1989). *The alms trade: Charities, past, present, and future.* London: Unwin Hyman.

Wolch, J. R. (1990). *The shadow state: Government and the voluntary sector in transition.* New York: The Foundation Center.

Wolf, A., and Jenkins, A. (2006). Explaining greater test use for selection: The role of HR professionals in a world of expanding regulation. *Human Resource Management Journal,* 16 (3), 193–213.

Part IV

Work Experiences in an Era of Outsourcing

8 Outsourcing in British Social Care
Its Implications for Worker Security

Ian Cunningham and Philip James

INTRODUCTION

The outsourcing of public services has been a feature of government policy, under both Conservative and Labour Governments, for nearly three decades. Commencing under the Conservatives in the 1980s, its use has intensified in the period since the election of the first Blair Government in 1997. This process of intensification has, though, occurred against the backdrop of a rather different regulatory and policy context.

Initially, outsourcing was conducted via a focus on price-based competition, through the policy of compulsory competitive tendering (CCT). Since 1997, however, government policy has sought to address concerns regarding this focus by placing a greater emphasis on quality considerations in the award of contracts and by seeking to establish more collaborative, and longer term, contracting relationships (Kendall, 2003).

This shift of policy raises the question of whether the employment-related outcomes of outsourcing have also changed. In particular, it prompts the question of whether it has acted to challenge the tendency for the transfer of public service work to be associated with the creation of lower levels of worker security, including with respect to pay and other conditions of employment, job roles, and vulnerability to redundancy.

This chapter consequently seeks to shed light on this last issue by reference to the findings of a study on the outsourcing of social care services to voluntary organisations undertaken by the authors on behalf of the public-sector union UNISON. The chapter is divided into five main sections. First, the evolution and current nature of the British social care marketplace are examined, and attention is paid to how far this marketplace can be anticipated to generate employment-related outcomes different from those associated with the previous CCT regime. The next two sections detail the methodology of the UNISON-funded study and its key findings of relevance. Finally, a concluding section draws together the key themes emerging from the data and considers whether post-1997 Labour Governments have succeeded in preventing, through a social care marketplace embodying a 'third way' compromise, a further deterioration in worker employment security and terms and conditions.

THE BRITISH SOCIAL CARE MARKETPLACE

The development of the British welfare state in the immediate postwar era was organised around the principles of planning, centralism, direct control, and professionalism. As a result, it operated through large, complex organizations providing uniformity of service and embodying strong producer control (Walsh, 1995).

This model of service delivery came under challenge in the 1980s following the election of the Thatcher Government and the related acceptance by it of 'New Right' critiques that the welfare state was poorly managed, unaccountable, professionally dominated, and lacking client involvement because of an absence of market incentives and pressures (Walsh, 1995; Osborne, 1997). This paradigmatic shift also occurred in other countries, such as New Zealand, Canada and the USA, and acted to support programmes of restructuring aimed at securing the delivery of social services via market-based mechanisms (Evans, Richmond, and Shields, 2005: Evans and Shields, 2002).

In line with this critique and support for market-based delivery, successive Conservative Governments during the period to 1997 consequently sought to create a mixed economy of welfare under which local and health authorities changed from being monopoly providers of care to becoming the planners, commissioners, and monitors of services contracted out to nonstatutory providers in the private and voluntary sectors (Harris, Rochester, and Halfpenny, 2001).

This emphasis on the 'enabling' role of local and health authorities has not only continued but increased in the period from the election of the Blair Government in 1997. It has done so alongside governmentally advanced arguments that 'third sector' organisations possess a number of virtues or attributes that make it desirable to accord them a greater role in the delivery of public services. These virtues are, notably, seen to include their greater closeness to service users, specialist skills and expertise, and capacity for innovation (Davies, 2007). As a consequence the voluntary sector has experienced year-to-year increases in statutory income, up by 5 percent over the last year of analysis, 2006–07 (National Council for Voluntary Organisations [NCVO], 2009).

Unsurprisingly, when combined with a substantial increase in government expenditure on social care services, this policy context has led to a significant increase in the role that private and voluntary bodies play in their delivery (NCVO, 2009). The highest proportion of income to the voluntary sector is received by social care organizations; an income which totaled £4.2 billion in 2006–07 and includes funding from high-profile government programmes. For example, it has been estimated that more than 65 percent of the services funded under the government's flagship Supporting People programme, which provides housing-related support to vulnerable groups, are now being delivered by the third sector (Davies, 2007). Meanwhile, more generally, numbers employed in the sector as whole increased from 408,000 in 1995 to 608, 000 in 2004, thereby coming to represent 2.2 percent of the total UK workforce (Wainwright, Clark, Griffith, Jochum, and Wilding, 2006). Moreover, between 1997 and 2006 there was a 58 percent rise, from 220,000 to 350,000, in the number of voluntary sector workers employed in social work activities, an increase that has been seen as reflecting the transfer of social care services from the public sector (NCVO, 2009).

At the same time, this growth in externalised service delivery has been further accompanied by a rhetoric that has placed more emphasis on 'obligational' rather than arms length, transactional relationships with voluntary sector providers which are less underpinned by price-based competition (Sako, 1992; Marchington, Grimshaw, Rubery, and Willmott, 2005). In turn, a number of regulatory changes have been utilised to achieve these objectives. Following its election in 1997, for example, the first Blair Government moved quickly to create a framework aimed at facilitating 'partnership working' between government departments and the voluntary and community sectors. Thus, drawing on the 1996 report of the Deakin Commission on the future of the voluntary sector, in 1998 it published a 'Compact' which detailed a series of principles intended to inform how government and the sector should work together and went on to produce a series of supporting Codes of Good Practice (Home Office, 1998). One of these Codes, initially published in 2000 and later amended and reissued in 2005, addressed the issue of funding (Home Office, 2005).

In its present form, this Code covers not just levels of funding but also the process of procuring services from voluntary organisations. In doing so, its content reflects the analysis and recommendations of a 2002 Treasury Cost-Cutting Review on 'The Role of the Voluntary and Community Sector in Service Delivery'—in particular, the commitment given in this review to 'implement longer term funding arrangements where these represent good value for money' and to accord recognition to the fact that 'it is legitimate for voluntary and community organisations to include the relevant element of overhead costs in their estimates for providing a particular service' (HM Treasury, 2002).

Meanwhile in local government, this encouragement of longer contracts and 'full cost recovery' has occurred against the backdrop of the replacement of CCT with a best value regime. This change, in theory, although not necessarily in practice, enables local authorities to accord greater weight to quality issues in the award of contracts and provides them with an option of pursuing such value in ways other than via market competition (Geddes, 2001; Higgins, James, and Roper, 2005; Roper, James, and Higgins, 2005).

These policy developments, by placing less focus on price-based competition and encouraging the establishment of longer term, more collaborative contracting relationships, seem, logically, to carry with them the potential to create a social care marketplace marked by a reduced tendency to drive down the job security, and terms and conditions, of those employed by contracting voluntary organisations. This is particularly the case given that these policy initiatives have occurred alongside the promulgation by the government, in response to union concerns about the way in which market competition was acting to drive down the terms and conditions of contractor staff, of a *Code of Practice on Workplace Matters*. This code requires most types of public bodies to ensure that staff employed to work on outsourced contracts alongside transferees from the public sector receive terms and conditions that are no less favourable than those of the transferees.

The validity of this anticipated outcome cannot, however, be straightforwardly accepted. Government regulations and policy exhortations cannot be viewed as completely determining the market-orientated behaviours of 'buyers' and 'sellers.' Indeed, if they did so, it would be difficult to see how a 'market' could be said to exist.

Relationships between social care service 'buyers' and 'sellers' must, ultimately, therefore be viewed as being shaped, albeit on a to-some-extent constrained basis, by the nature of the wider marketplace within which outsourcing contracts are concluded, as well as by their own policy objectives and market positions. As a result, it cannot be assumed that these relationships will, in practice, echo those desired by government. For example, notwithstanding government preferences, financial constraints may in reality act to push public sector service commissioners to continue to adopt a 'cost-minimisation' approach to commissioning. In addition, imbalances of power between service commissioners and providers may, in turn, be supportive of the successful pursuit of such an approach, with all that this entails for the feasibility of establishing obligational-type contracting relationships incorporating high levels of fairness and mutuality based collaboration (Sako, 1992; Marchington et al., 2005; Rainnie, 1992; Grimshaw, Willmott, and Rubery, 2005).

THE STUDY

The UNISON-funded study drawn upon was conducted in two phases. In the first, the impact of the emerging contract culture in social care was explored through the obtaining of employer and union perspectives on its implications. In the case of the employer perspectives, these were gained from twelve voluntary organisations in which UNISON either was recognised for the purposes of collective bargaining (six cases) or had some membership presence but not full recognition. These covered a variety of services ranging from children's services (two cases), housing associations (two cases), community health (one case), adults with learning difficulties (two cases), mental health problems (one case), the elderly (one case), advisory centres for a range of vulnerable groups (one case), the homeless (one case), and services for disabled people (one case).

This employer-based data was drawn from two sources. The first involved contacting senior managers in each organisation, usually chief executives or senior directors, with a request to complete a short questionnaire asking for background information on areas such as income, funding sources, duration of contracts, and the management of funding applications, as well as various types of workforce data. Face-to-face interviews were then conducted using a series of prepared questions but also probing for information as a result of the data supplied in the initial questionnaire.

As regards the obtaining of union perspectives, qualitative interviews were held with one national official and four regional activists based, respectively, in England, Wales, Scotland, and Northern Ireland, who were selected on the basis of their specialist roles in servicing and organising within the voluntary sector, and further ones undertaken with five workplace activists and three branch officials. These interviews focussed on perceived trends in the extent and costs of contracting and their links with forms of workforce insecurity and the quality of care. They also, it should be noted, were supplemented by the holding of parallel interviews with representatives from several employer bodies.

The aim of the second phase of research was to gain a more direct impression of the impact of the insecure funding environment on employees. To this end, we conducted interviews with lay activists in three of the above organisations and held focus groups containing between six and twelve union and nonunion members of staff (one in each case study). The specific themes explored during the course of these groups were developments in pay, job security and roles, working time and health, and safety protection; the way in which such developments were impacting worker morale; and views concerning the effectiveness of union representation.

The first of these organisations was a small voluntary organisation working in the area of children's services, given the name Astro, which had nineteen staff and one or two UNISON members. The second was a large provider of services to adults with learning difficulties, referred to as Merlin here, which had 600 staff, union recognition, approximately 40 percent membership density, a shop-steward committee structure, and a consultative forum which also contained nonunion representatives. The last, a user-led small-to-medium-sized organisation specialising in services promoting inclusive living for disabled people, which is given the name Telstar for present purposes, had thirty staff, union recognition, with 70 percent membership density and one shop steward. All data from the interviews and focus groups from the two phases of research were taped and fully transcribed.

WHITHER WORKER (IN-)SECURITY?

The notion of worker insecurity can be viewed as a multidimensional one, and to be amenable to analysis at both the 'macro' and 'micro' organisational levels, as well as the individual one, and from 'objective' and 'subjective' perspectives (see, for instance, Heery and Salmon, 2000; Dibben, 2007). For example, the notion of worker insecurity can potentially be assessed in relation to such matters as the reliability and predictability of income from employment, the stability of job roles, functions, and workloads, the availability of financial (and other) support during periods of ill health, and vulnerability, both actual and perceived, to job loss (Standing, 1990; Burchell, 2002).

Ideally, therefore, how the dynamics of the social care contracting marketplace have impacted the security of voluntary sector workers should be investigated on a correspondingly wide-ranging basis. Here, however, in part for reasons of space and in part because of limitations in the data collected, these dynamics are explored more narrowly through a consideration of how they have affected the pay and conditions, and job roles and employment security of such staff.

Job Roles and Security

In relation to these issues, a remarkably consistent picture emerged from both phases of the research concerning how the current contract culture in social care had given rise to increased levels of insecurity. Virtually all the employer respondents, for example, indicated that in recent years they had made redundancies. In a similar vein, without exception the regional organisers interviewed were able to cite examples of organisations where, as a result of the loss of contracts, redundancies had been made.

Whereas redeployment appeared to be commonly used to mitigate the consequences of such insecurity, it was reported in some cases that this had acted, in turn, to create other, sometimes broader, forms of insecurity. In one organisation, for example, a union activist reported how workers had been temporarily redeployed into less skilled posts, albeit on their existing pay, and went on to observe that this had left them facing the dilemma of whether to stay with, or leave, the organisation:

> People are saying 'Do I hang on here at the end of this three-year contract in the hope that I can continue working here if another piece of work comes up, or do I jump ship because I don't know what is going to be around the corner.'

He further observed that if those concerned did chose to look for work, there was a question of how potential alternative employers would regard their experience of prolonged employment at a lower grade.

It was also highlighted that the use of redeployment was, in fact, leading on occasion to an increase in the degree of flexibility expected of staff. This was most apparent in several larger organisations where there had been moves toward creating 'generic' care workers, who were equipped with core competencies and expected to provide housing support to a variety of different client groups ranging from adults to young people.

Yet a further dimension to this insecurity in job roles included cases where management were issuing new 'Martini contracts' designed to deliver 'anything, anywhere, anytime' (UNISON activist) in accordance with what the demands of particular funders required. Reportedly, if they signed these contracts, employees would be expected to work a thirty-seven hour week, over seven days, with little notice being given of the need to work weekends or other unsocial hours.

One of the representatives of the umbrella organisations in the sector meanwhile made some interesting, although speculative, points regarding the future vulnerability of staff to interorganisational transfers following re-tendering exercises, with all the risks that they entail. In particular, this individual reported how a recent contract issued by a local authority stipulated that in the last year of a three year contract voluntary organisations would not be allowed to redeploy staff to other parts of the organisation. The argument advanced by the local authority to support this approach was that it protected quality of care by preventing organisations from 'asset stripping' prior to tendering through removing the best staff from the project and replacing them with less skilled employees. However, an obvious implication of this type of contract for staff was that they could find themselves undergoing a change of employer, along with concomitant anxiety and disruption, and could be employed in an organisation that might not have the commitment or capacity to deliver the level of service they were used to delivering.

For the smaller organisations in the study, however, it was usually not possible to redeploy staff when funding was cut. They had to react instead with more draconian measures. For example, when one of the two previously mentioned small organisations, which provided an advice centre, had its core funding threatened, all staff were informed that they might be made redundant at the end of the six-month notice period provided by the funder and were additionally placed on a four-day week for a four-month period and paid accordingly. Similarly, in the other earlier-mentioned small respite care provider, the senior manager felt that continuing attacks on its core funding in the forthcoming year could lead to the partial or complete closure of its services.

Management's perceptions of the reaction of employees to the range of situations outlined above were mixed. Thus, some respondents reported how there was a remarkable degree of loyalty among their employees as illustrated by their willingness to stay on through periods of uncertainty. However, others revealed that employees experienced significant anxiety in such situations and chose to leave their employment before they were made redundant or went through a transfer to another employer.

For their part, activist and employee interviewees were more likely to emphasise the aforementioned anxieties. In particular, a number of the latter expressed profound unease among staff with regard to what one described as the 'sword of Damocles' hanging over them and reported that it was usually the case that they had to wait right up until the last minute before they found out that they *definitely* were able to remain in employment. In addition, they also reported that this insecurity could have serious implications for their work-life balance.

> There is nothing worse than sitting on the end of a phone at the end of a contract with three months work and your friends ring and say we are going to the cinema and then going for a drink, come and join us. You sit there thinking well actually I don't know whether I can or not, or if there is a night school class you want to go to and you think that is another £55.00 and think can I afford it? Well actually no because I don't know what is going to happen. (Female support worker, Astro)

Many of these respondents, it should also be noted, were either single women, who highlighted that if they are thrown out of work there was no partner or family to sustain mortgage or rent payments, or older and disabled workers, who felt that their prospects of obtaining other employment were relatively limited.

Such insecurity also had potentially significant implications for service quality to vulnerable clients, as the following quote illustrates:

> One of my colleagues is currently thinking about her future job. She has had two or three years of job insecurity and is sort of thinking I want more sustainable security in the future . . . and that is going to impact on the delivery of the service, because it might be one member of staff who has really good skills, good experience, and is really competent in what she does. (Project manager, Telstar)

Pay and Conditions

A common feature of at least larger voluntary organisations has historically been the linking of their pay arrangements in some way to nationally negotiated local authority terms and conditions agreements. Such linkages were still apparent in eight of the organisations studied. It was, however, clear that their maintenance was becoming problematic, particularly because of cuts to such programmes as Supporting People and as a result of local authorities refusing to pass on inflationary uplifts to annual funding arrangements.

Several of the smaller organisations, for example, felt that the continuation of linking pay to local authority scales was essential to retain competitiveness in the labour market, but also pointed out that its maintenance was dangerous because the annual funding uplift usually did not cover the full cost of local authority increases, with the result that several of them needed, on occasion, to draw from donated voluntary income and reserves to cover annual pay rises. Yet, this last option was itself not always available, as the following comments of a senior manager from one of our case studies (Telstar) regarding his organisation's financial situation illustrates:

> We have been desperately trying to build reserves, we can't do that. We just don't have any security, and year after year it looks like we may be projecting a deficit and we just get by through the skin of our teeth.

Similar dynamics also appeared to be at work in larger organisations. Indeed, more generally, a respondent from UNISON's housing association branch expressed the fear that moves to sever a linkage with local authority terms and conditions would become a common feature of this subsector, given the ongoing funding cuts that organisations in it were facing. In fact, this severing of the local authority linkage was beginning to in effect emerge in several of the case study organisations through the implementation of pay freezes and the recruitment of new staff on non-NJC rates.

Other larger adult organisations were, meanwhile, reducing other staff terms and conditions. In the case of a provider of services for children, adults, and families with learning disabilities, for example, cuts in Supporting People funding had led to reductions in employees' mileage allowance and a capping of sleepover allowances. Similarly, at Telstar, the management respondent reported that the organisation had recently cut sickness benefits in response to financial pressures, and several other organisations mentioned that they had changed the rules regarding access to their occupational pension schemes because local authorities did not help fund this benefit.

Overall, there were concerns relating to the sustainability of employee morale in these conditions of income insecurity. The chief executive in the aforementioned organisation which had implemented a pay freeze and changes to sleepover allowances, for example, stated:

> Up to that point we had goodwill with the shop stewards and generally with the staff which allowed us to get that kind of agreement, without any serious objections. My feeling now is that, that is not a bottomless well that we can go back to and draw on, and we already know that if we have to make other efficiencies of that kind . . . we will not find the same goodwill.

The three focus groups conducted lent weight to this concern. Thus, the opening response to a question on pay to the group at Merlin was one of lots of ironic laughter by all participants, before the mood turned more sombre. A support worker, who was a union member, then went on to state how he believed there to be 'a feeling of helplessness among staff' as a result of a lack of real influence over external funders and a lack of established collective bargaining which was able to deliver a workable 'going rate' for the sector. This same individual also additionally observed that there was increasing frustration with an environment in which those that worked in the voluntary sector never received the same cost-of-living increases as their local authority counterparts.

In a similar vein, those who took part in the focus group in Telstar expressed frustration regarding the constant uncertainty over whether staff would receive any pay increase in the current funding environment, and participants in Astro spoke of how even when they were given rises, they failed to maintain their living standards, a view captured in the following response:

> You never get a raise, apart from the 1.9 percent. . . . I have been here for four and a half years, and you know the cost of living has gone up a lot more than the yearly two percent. You may not be taking cuts, but in real terms you are taking a cut because everything has moved on but your salary hasn't.

More generally, participants in the focus group also commented that salaries were not keeping pace with rising mortgage costs, higher fuel bills, and so on. Most alarmingly for management, in Merlin (whose current turnover level was estimated at 25 percent), when respondents were asked whether, if they had a choice, they would be in their roles next year, the majority outlined that for various reasons, including redeployment, retirement, and dissatisfaction over the balance between pay and effort, they had serious doubts.

CONCLUSION

This chapter has sought to shed light on how the current social care market is affecting the security of those working in voluntary organisations through a consideration of the market's impacts on pay and conditions, and the stability of job roles and ongoing employment. In doing so, it has further sought to identify whether attempts by post-1997 Labour Governments to engender a social care marketplace marked by longer term collaborative contracting, and a greater degree of financial stability and security for voluntary organisations participating in it, have acted to challenge the tendency for the transfer of public service work to be associated with the creation of lower levels of worker security.

Its findings, taken together, suggest that any such challenge has been relatively limited. Thus, they suggest that actual and threatened redundancies have been common, that similar adverse dynamics have been frequently at work in relation to staff terms and conditions, and that moves toward greater flexibility in work roles have also been apparent.

Such findings, which it should be noted echo those of earlier studies (Cunningham, 2008; Knapp, Hardy, and Forder, 2001; Barnard, Broach, and Wakefield, 2004), inevitably raise the question of why so little change appears to have occurred. Broadly, there seem three, somewhat related, potential explanations.

One is that government attempts to change the contracting behaviour of service commissioners, as well as voluntary organisations, are taking time to have an effect; a view that can be found to receive some support in the work of the Audit Commission (2007). A second is that the action which the government has so far taken is simply insufficient to challenge countervailing pressures in the social care market stemming from the needs of service commissioners to prioritise short-term cost reductions in a competitive context in which they often have the power to achieve them. Finally, a third is that, notwithstanding the attempts that have been made to shape social care contracting practice, government policy remains, albeit largely implicitly, centred on the use of market mechanisms to gain 'price' benefits while protecting service quality.

In reality, all three of these explanations may have some leverage. The first two, for example, can potentially be seen to receive support from evidence that the provision of full-cost recovery and longer term funding remain very much minority pursuits on the part of service commissioners (Alcock, Brannelly, and Ross, 2004; Cunningham and James, 2009; Charity Commission, 2007a). Meanwhile, a striking feature of government pronouncements and policy statements relating to the expansion of the role of the voluntary sector in the delivery of social care has been the limited and narrow references made to the working conditions, and related interests, of staff. In particular, it is noticeable in this regard that whereas the introduction of full-cost recovery and longer term funding arrangements has been partly advocated on the grounds that these actions can support skills development and staff recruitment and retention, the potential benefits have been invariably highlighted because of their implications for service quality.

Whereas the reasons for the lack of change in the nature of the social care marketplace are therefore open to debate, it must be observed that the prospects for a marked shift in the direction of espoused government policy cannot in the current environment be viewed as good. For in a context where there is a broad political consensus concerning the need to cut public expenditure, it is difficult to see how service commissioners will not feel under increased pressure to drive a 'hard bargain' and seek reductions in contract prices.

Insofar as this prognosis is correct, it seems reasonable to suggest that voluntary organisations may well face an increasing dilemma with regard to their continued participation in a marketplace that is likely to be marked by increasing tensions between the contract terms effectively 'on offer' and their beliefs concerning how services should be delivered and what constitutes 'a good service.' It may be, of course, that many organisations will conclude on financial grounds that they have no choice but to learn to live with these tensions. In doing so, however, there seems a real risk that the concerns which have been expressed by the Charity Commission (2007b) about the potential for 'mission drift' to occur among charities engaged in public-sector contracting will prove to be well founded. This risk, ironically, carries with it the further one that the dynamics of the social care marketplace will act to undermine the very attributes that the government has identified as supporting the greater involvement of voluntary organisations in the delivery of services.

BIBLIOGRAPHY

Alcock, P., Brannelly, T., and Ross, L. (2004). *Formality or flexibility? Voluntary sector contracting in social care and health.* London: NCVO.

Audit Commission. (2007). *Hearts and minds: Commissioning from the voluntary sector.* London: Audit Commission.

Barnard, J., Broach, S., and Wakefield, V. (2004). *Social care: The growing crisis.* London: Social Care Employers Consortium.

Burchell, B. (2002). The prevalence and redistribution of job insecurity and work intensification. In B. Burchell, D. Ladipo, and F. Wilkinson (eds.), *Job insecurity and work intensification* (pp. 61–76). London: Routledge.

Charity Commission. (2007a). *Stand and deliver: The future for charities providing public services.* London: Charity Commission.

Charity Commission. (2007b). *Charities and public service delivery: An introduction and overview.* Liverpool: Charity Commission.

Cunningham, I. (2008). *Employment relations in the voluntary sector.* London: Routledge.

Cunningham. I. (2001). 'Sweet charity!' Managing employee commitment in the UK voluntary sector. *Employee Relations Journal*, 23 (3), 226–240.

Cunningham, I., and James, P. (2009). The outsourcing of social care in Britain: What does it mean for voluntary sector workers? *Work, Employment, & Society*, 23 (2), 363–375.

Davies, S. (2007). *Third sector provision of local government and health services.* London: UNISON.

Dibben, P. (2007). Employment security and job insecurity in public services: Two sides of the same coin? In P. Dibben, P. James, I. Roper, and G. Wood (eds.), *Modernising work in public services: Redefining roles and relationships in Britain's changing workplace* (pp. 121–136). Houndmills, Basingstoke, Hampshire: Palgrave Macmillan.

Evans, B., Richmond, T., and Shields, J. (2005). Structuring neoliberal governance: The nonprofit sector, emerging new modes of control, and the marketisation of service delivery. *Policy and Society*, 24 (1), 73–97.

Evans, B. and Shields, J. (2002). The third sector: Neo-Liberal restructuring, governance, and the rethinking of state-civil society relationships. In C. Dunn (ed.), *The handbook of Canadian public administration* (pp. 139–158). Oxford: Oxford University Press.

Geddes, M. (2001). What about the workers? Best value, work. and employment in public services. *Policy & Politics*, 29 (4), 497–508.

Grimshaw, D., Willmott, H., and Rubery, J. (2005). Inter-organizational networks: Trust, power, and the employment relationship. In M. Marchington, D. Grimshaw, J. Rubery, and H. Wilmott (eds.), *Fragmenting work: Blurring organizational boundaries and disordering hierarchies* (pp. 39–68). Oxford: Oxford University Press.

Harris. M., Rochester, C., and Halfpenny. P. (2001). Voluntary organisations and social policy: Twenty years of change. In M. Harris and C. Rochester (eds.), *Voluntary organisations and social policy in Britain: Perspectives on change and choice* (pp. 1–20). Basingstoke: Palgrave.

Heery, E., and Salmon, J., eds. (2000). *The insecure workforce.* London: Routledge.

Higgins, P., James, P., and Roper, I. (2005). The role of competition in best value: How far does it differ to CCT? *Local Government Studies,* 31 (2), 219–235.

HM Treasury. (2002). *The role of the community and voluntary sector in service delivery: A cross cutting review.* London: HM Treasury

Home Office. (2005). *Funding and procurement: Compact Code of Good Practice.* London: Home Office.

Home Office. (1998). *The Compact on Relations between the Government and the Voluntary and Community Sector.* London: Home Office.

Kendall, J. (2003). *The voluntary sector.* London: Routledge.

Knapp. M., Hardy. B., and Forder. J. (2001). Commissioning for quality: Ten years of social care markets in England. *Journal of Social Policy,* 30 (2), 283–306.

Marchington, M., Grimshaw, D., Rubery, J., and Willmott, H. (Eds.). (2005). *Fragmenting work: Blurring organizational boundaries and disordering hierarchies.* Oxford: Oxford University Press.

Mirvis, P. (1992). The quality of employment in the nonprofit sector: An update on employee attitudes in nonprofits versus business and government. *Nonprofit Management & Leadership,* 3 (1), 23–41.

National Audit Office. (2005a). *Supporting people.* Wetherby: Audit Commission Publications.

National Audit Office. (2005b). *Working with the third sector.* London: NAO.

National Council for Voluntary Organisations (NCVO). (2009). *The state and the voluntary sector: Recent trends in government funding and public service delivery.* London: NCVO.

Osborne, S. P. (1997). Managing the coordination of social services in the mixed economy of welfare: Competition, cooperation, or common cause?' *British Journal of Management,* 8, 317–328.

Rainnie, A. (1992). The reorganization of large firm contracting: Myth and reality. *Capital and Class,* 49, 53–75.

Roper, I., James, P., and. Higgins, P. (2005). Workplace partnership and public service provision: The case of the 'best value' regime in British local government. *Work, Employment, and Society,* 19 (3), 639–649.

Sako, M. (1992). *Prices, quality, and trust: Inter-firm relations in Britain and Japan.* Cambridge: Cambridge University Press.

Standing, G. (1999). *Global labour flexibility: Seeking distributive justice.* Basingstoke: Macmillan.

Wainwright, S., Clark, J., Griffith, M., Jochum, V., and Wilding, K. (2006). *The UK voluntary sector almanac, 2006.* London: NCVO.

Walsh, K. (1995). *Public services and market mechanisms.* Basingstoke: Macmillan.

9 Taking the Strain?
The Psychological Contract of Voluntary Sector Employees Following Transfers of Employment

Ian Cunningham

INTRODUCTION

Our knowledge of the way in which different contexts act to sustain or undermine the psychological contracts of employees in the voluntary sector remains incomplete. Studies exploring this theme in the era of outsourcing reveal a complex, multifaceted set of worker orientations underpinned by a strong commitment to organisational cause/mission. At the same time, the psychological contract of employees has been seen to be vulnerable to violations when their organisation's relationship with funding bodies undermines their sense of mission attachment or terms and conditions of employment (Cunningham, 2008; Nickson, Warhurst, Dutton, and Hurrell, 2008). One crucial unexplored context in terms of the changes to worker psychological contracts concerns the impact of transfers of employment across organisations in the voluntary sector as a consequence of re-tendering exercises undertaken by state funders.

This is an important area of study for several reasons. First, transfers of staff between voluntary organisations are anticipated to increase as funders in the UK, and probably other parts of the EU, abide by the EU Public Contracts Regulations (2006) (Community Care Providers Scotland [CCPS], 2008). Second, the sector relies extensively on the high commitment of its staff to deliver quality services, but studies have found that transfers of employment across and within other sectors through tendering and re-tendering exercises have led to problems with employee motivation and commitment as a consequence of perceptions among workers of declining commitment to service quality by their new employer, feelings of betrayal, loss of job security, and changes to working conditions (Lee Cooke, Hebson, and Carroll, 2005; Hebson, Grimshaw, Marchington, and Cooke, 2003).

This chapter explores these issues through an exploratory study of the impact of re-tendering and transfers of employment and services on the psychological contract of voluntary sector workers. The chapter begins by outlining a framework that helps us understand the psychological contract of voluntary sector workers. This is followed by an overview of the explicit threat to the psychological contract from re-tendering as well as a series of factors that may offset that threat, including employment regulation, management interventions, and union activity. It then presents findings from the aforementioned study of the consequences of transfers of employment from re-tendering on worker psychological contracts and explores whether breaches and violations are offset by various moderating factors. The final section presents a conclusion and discussion.

UNDERSTANDING PSYCHOLOGICAL
CONTRACTS IN THE VOLUNTARY SECTOR

Research exploring the employment relationship in voluntary organisations reveals a multitude of factors influencing people's choices for taking up, retaining, and leaving employment in the sector (Mirvis and Hackett, 1983; Mirvis, 1992; Alatrista and Arrowsmith, 2004). In the light of this, despite concerns regarding its uniqueness, content validity, and construct validity (see Arnold, 1996; Guest, 1998; Lester, Turnley, Bloodgood, and Bolino, 2002; Shore and Tetrick, 1994), for present purposes the psychological contract construct is seen as a source of help in understanding these multifaceted orientations to work in voluntary organisations and exploring how instrumental, relational, and value-based factors interact to shape employment choices.

A definition of the term 'psychological contract' is an individual's belief that a reciprocal exchange agreement has occurred between the employee and the employer (Rousseau, 1990; Robinson and Rousseau, 1994).[1] In turn, the complexity of these reciprocal obligations between the parties in the employment relationship is illustrated through utilising the transactional and relational continuum of the construct (Rousseau, 1990). Here, transactional contracts are based on short-term monetary exchanges, where individuals are expected to return a suitable level of performance to the employer, but invest little emotional attachment or commitment to the organisation (Rousseau, 1995). In contrast, relational contracts assume a more mutual, open-ended employment relationship involving a degree of reciprocal investment by employees and employer. The terms of such contracts would include emotional involvement, as well as economic exchange, a commitment to personal growth and development and trust (Rousseau, 1995). The construct is seen as fluid in nature in that it can be revised and reassessed throughout an employee's tenure, and it can also lead to employee perceptions changing over time (Rousseau and Parks, 1993).

It is also the case, however, that the relational aspect of the psychological contract's continuum does not fully account for employees who commit to an organisation in exchange for being able to serve a social cause/mission. In recognition of this, studies have developed the notion of a *voluntary sector ethos* (VSE) to analyse value-infused psychological contracts in voluntary organisations (Cunningham, 2008). Here, employee orientations include identification with the needs and interests of a wider client group/community and workers perceiving the nature of the job to be more important than pay. The VSE also incorporates orientations to work peculiar to the sector, such as a philosophical or religious commitment to promote social change and a desire to have autonomy in work and participation in decision-making (Paton and Cornforth, 1992). Here, employees will commit to their employer in order to work toward achieving certain religious, ethical, or philosophical goals. Moreover, in line with established work (Millward and Hopkins, 1998; Shore and Tetrick, 1994), this approach accepts that individual psychological contracts in the voluntary sector are combinational and to varying degrees embrace orientations which are transactional, relational, or based on a VSE.

The psychological contract is also useful because of its capacity to evaluate the causes and consequences of tensions in the voluntary sector employment relationship. This is through utilising the notions of breach and violation and their subsequent impact on commitment and organisational citizenship behaviour (OCB). Breaches occur when employees perceive the organisation has failed to meet some obligation. Violations are distinct emotional responses to such breaches (Morrison and Robinson, 1997) and occur when 'a failure to keep a commitment injures or causes damages that the contract was designed to avoid' (Rousseau, 1995, 112).

If violations to any aspect of the psychological contract occur, then employee commitment will be undermined, and, at worst, individuals may then choose to quit or exhibit an unwillingness to undertake other forms of OCB, including those aspects of behaviour which are positive for the employer beyond the literal contractual obligations of workers, and not explicitly recognised by any reward structure—for instance, unpaid overtime (Robinson and Morrison, 1995; Coyle-Shapiro, 2002; Hui, Lee, and Rousseau, 2004). Employees can also express negative satisfaction through poor performance, sabotage, theft, aggressive behaviour, and quitting (Morrison and Robinson, 1997;: Robinson and Rousseau, 1994; Robinson, Kraatz, and Rousseau, 1994; Robinson 1996; Podsakoff, Mackenzie, Paine, and Bachrach, 2000). The undermining of OCB would have significant consequences for a sector that relies heavily on its employees working beyond contract.

As previously mentioned, there have been studies exploring the resilience of the psychological contract in voluntary organisations in the context of its relationship with the state (Cunningham, 2008). There has not, however, been an exploration of psychological contract breach/violation for employees in the sector who have experienced a transfer of their employment to another employer, because of re-tendering of services. This is a significant gap in the era of contracting when re-tendering is increasingly occurring between the state and the third sector in the UK. The paper has wider relevance across the EU as procurement regulations are implemented in different contexts across member states. The next section explores the potential for violations as a consequence of re-tendering.

THE UK VOLUNTARY SECTOR AND RE-TENDERING

Re-tendering has increased through the implementation of the Public Contracts Regulations 2006 (Public Contracts [Scotland] Regulations 2006), which were introduced as a consequence of the Public Contracts Directive 2004/18/EC. Recent research highlights a number of concerns from the providers' perspectives on how re-tendering exercises have been taken forward, including the costs associated with transfers of staff and quality of service and levels of administrative and management time, expense, and effort (CCPS, 2008). It is also clear that the transference of services to different employers as a consequence of re-tendering has the potential for undermining people's psychological contracts and ultimately their commitment to work in the voluntary sector.

A useful concept in understanding the nature of such violations is 'value interpenetration' (Thompson and Bunderson, 2003). Here, employees become increasingly wary and sensitive as relationships with state funding bodies lead to them encountering agents from the state or other bodies that are not committed to their particular cause or they espouse a different set of values altogether. Here, it is predicted that employees will become alienated as the original organisational mission drifts from its objectives (Thompson and Bunderson, 2003). Such mission drift subsequently challenges the traditional altruistic motivations and activities of staff that are displaced by new commitments to increasing capacity and performance (Carmel and Harlock, 2008).

The process of re-tendering and the subsequent transference of a service to another organisation could lead to several such sources of breach and violation through value interpenetration. The first concerns employee responses to the principles of re-tendering itself. Here the voluntary organisation's relationship with state funders through re-tendering is reshaped so that concepts of value for money, cost saving, and competition are the dominant criteria for determining who provides a service rather than the quality of that provision and the needs of the client group. This could be further aggravated if re-tendering of services becomes the norm in the sector and there is a gradual corrosion of quality standards following regular, periodic re-tendering exercises. In such circumstances, employees who are focused on an organisation's mission may experience a breach to the VSE aspect of their psychological contracts and experience violation through an undermining of their morale and commitment.

The second source of psychological contract breach through value interpenetration concerns the transfer of employment and services as a consequence of re-tendering. Here, a breach could occur if employees are transferred to an organisation that has different values from their original employer, and the new employer makes changes to the service so that quality of provision is again perceived to be detrimentally affected.

Sources of breach and violation to the transactional aspect of the psychological contract can also emerge from re-tendering and transference. In particular, transference of employment between agencies can undermine a workers' sense of employment security. There may also be concerns relating to the impact on the pay and working conditions of employees in the voluntary sector after a transfer of employment. Changes to conditions of employment through work intensification could be an additional source of breach or violation because the competitive nature of re-tendering could lead to employers seeking to cut costs by doing more with less as a condition of securing a re-tendered service.

It must also be recognised, however, that violations to the psychological contract do not necessarily follow breaches and that even when violations occur, this does not necessarily mean the end of the contract (Morrison and Robinson, 1997; Rousseau, 1995). This suggests the influence of moderating factors. Examples of such moderators include acknowledgment that value interpenetration, for example, may be offset if employees perceive that the situation is temporary, or if it is recognised that the breach is 'the norm' across all similar organisations because of the wider political, social, and competitive context. It is also the case that if employees perceive that a violation is not the fault of their employer, but instead of some outside agency, then this can, again, offset violation (Graham, 1986; Thompson and Bunderson, 2003; Sparrow, 1996). Certainly, if re-tendering does become more common, then employees may come to see the consequences of such exercises as part of being employed in the sector. There is also a question of whether transfers between nonprofit organisations will lead to 'value interpenetration' among staff if these organisations broadly share the same values.

In addition, there are potential moderating influences on breaches and violations caused by changes to pay and conditions. Commentators have stressed the need to consider how the economic, socioemotional, and ideological (VSE) currencies of the psychological contract interact. Specifically, a strong VSE among employees may compensate for unfulfilled obligations on the transactional/relational components of the continuum. There is also the degree to which employees, despite disenchantment with a particular employer over working conditions, focus their commitment on service users, again offsetting violation (Alatrista and Arrowsmith, 2004).

Furthermore, there needs to be consideration as to whether management interventions to restore employee commitment such as organisational procedural justice mechanisms, efforts to overturn temporary causes of discontent, and restoring management oversights (Morrison and Robinson, 1997) can mollify the impact of breaches. In addition, more research is needed concerning whether collective action through trade unions can redress the effects of psychological contract breach. Here, successful collective resistance to management changes to terms and conditions have been seen to act as a moderator to violations (Turnley, Bolino, Scott, and Bloodgood, 2004).

Another potentially significant moderator in the context of this study concerns employment protection legislation, specifically the legal protection offered by the Transfer of Undertakings (Protection of Employment) Regulations 2006 (TUPE). TUPE is seen to continue to provide important legal safeguards for workers' terms and conditions, but there remains some latitude for employers to take advantage of legal loopholes to cut pay and conditions. This is particularly the case with the 'ETO' reason, where an employer can vary terms and conditions on the basis of issues arising because of economic, technical, or organisational reasons. Employers can also dismiss an employee if the issue is principally due to the 'ETO' reason. Other issues which are commonly problematic for organisations include the greater emphasis placed on information and consultation during the transfer, the release of workforce information from transferor to transferee, and its timing. If there is a lack of information and consultation, both the old and new employer can be jointly liable and subject to a claim from a trade union or employee representative. It is also noteworthy that under TUPE there is no right after the transfer for employees to participate in the same occupational pension, and there is only limited protection for employees under the Pensions Act 2004. Where there is a collective agreement with a trade union, this will be transferred, as will union recognition, 'when the group of employees who transfer retain a distinct identity' (Cavalier and Arthur, 2006).

In utilising the above framework, the present chapter explores the following questions:

- What happens to the psychological contract of workers whose services and employment are transferred to another employer after a retender?
- To what extent do a variety of moderators offset the impact of breaches and violations to the psychological contract of employees who are subject to a transfer of their employment as a consequence of re-tendering?

METHOD

The findings presented below are exploratory and drawn from a wider, ongoing study (see Cunningham and Nickson, 2009) exploring the impact of re-tendering on the voluntary sector. This wider study was undertaken in three Scottish case study organisations that had recently been involved in re-tendering exercises with local authorities. This included a provider that had lost several re-tendering exercises (Sapphire); one that had won several re-tendering exercises (Emerald); and another that had won and also lost services through re-tendering exercises (Diamond). In total interviews were held with twenty-eight line managers and non-management employees employed directly in services that were outsourced to the three voluntary organisations and had been put up for re-tender by local authorities in the previous year. Further interviews were also held with six senior managers across the organisations.

However, for current purposes, the focus of analysis will be on those respondents transferred to another employer as a consequence of a re-tendering exercise (nine respondents). Six of these were now employed in Diamond, but were previously employed in Sapphire, and three were employed in Emerald, but had previously worked in an organisation which did not participate in this study, but had been subject to re-tendering. In addition, the paper will utilise findings from interviews with the senior managers across the three organisations participating in this study.

Interviews asked about employment history; orientations to work; the nature of care work; employee experiences of the tendering process and its impact on service users; their reactions once re-tendering decisions were made; the impact on their terms and conditions and service quality; and intentions to quit. Interviews were transcribed verbatim, and the data analysis utilised the general analytical procedure favoured by Miles and Huberman (1994).

FINDINGS

Reactions to Re-Tendering Decisions

Before exploring employee reactions to the re-tendering decisions, it is useful to note how respondents did exhibit the aforementioned multifaceted orientations to work that included factors such as attraction to decent terms and conditions of employment, training, and career development.

> I was really impressed with the support and development and the fact that they were quite willing to further your career within the organisation. (Support worker, Sapphire, transferred to Diamond)

At the same time, all employees joined the sector because of a strong VSE.

> It began with an altruistic wish to help and makes things better for folk . . . and that was the kind of area I wanted to go into . . . it's a kind of underpinning motive over the years. (Area manager, Sapphire, transferred to Diamond)

Initial reactions to the news that services were to be re-tendered revealed a degree of surprise among staff, largely because each of the projects had previously successfully passed regular local authority and central government quality audits. Breaches to the psychological contract of these workers were clearly in evidence and led to several respondents reporting an undermining of their sense of employment security to the point where they were looking for alternative work even before the final re-tendering decision was made.

Once their respective contracts were lost to another employer, breaches to employee psychological contracts through value interpenetration were also evident, with respondents expressing significant dissatisfaction that the principles of cost saving and value for money were the deciding factor in re-tendering decisions.

> The overriding thing was pure anger that came across higher than anything, they were judging us on value. (Team leader, transferred to Emerald)

and

> Money saving, just to save money, really because I don't think they took account of the kind of people that we were looking after. (Support worker, transferred to Emerald)

This was linked to profound concerns for the fate of service users if the service was diminished or altered in any significant way because of cost savings.

> The main concern, I think was, were they still going to be able to offer the support to the people, you know, was it going to affect them. (Support worker, Sapphire, transferred to Diamond)

and

> I just felt it for the people we were supporting. You know your first instinct is 'oh my God what's going to happen to them you know.' We were horrified, horrified! (Support worker, transferred to Emerald)

In terms of how the loss of the contract made individuals feel about their own personal situation and their employment, expressions such as 'disempowerment' and 'disenfranchisement' were common, with the majority expressing disappointment at transferring to another employer.

> Obviously I was sad because I chose to work for Sapphire. I applied to their advert, so I was sad because I had spent time getting used to Sapphire, used to their policies, I had been through their training, so I was a bit disappointed. (Support worker, Sapphire)

and

> There was so much anger against what had happened and their lack of choice. (Team leader transferred to Emerald)

Such feelings of loss were shared by senior managers from Sapphire.

> We build, instil the values with the training we give them, the way we want them, and then we say 'well sorry, you're going elsewhere.' I mean it's absolutely tragic . . . Ethos, that's what it is and that in my view, in HR terms, is the most difficult to instil, to get people on board with that, and therefore it's one of the greatest losses, when we lose our people. There's the tangible investment in terms of training that adds stuff, but there's also that unquantifiable aspect. (HR manager, Sapphire)

There were also breaches to the transactional aspect of employee psychological contracts through an undermining of workers' sense of employment security.

> I think there was a bit of apprehension. Will we keep our jobs? Will everything progress as normal? Will they restructure our workplace? (Support worker, Sapphire transferred to Diamond)

and

> The people that got it [*the contract*] maybe paid a lot less for the tendering so they would have to claw back some of that money somewhere and we thought that we were all going to be out of a job. (Support coordinator, transferred to Emerald)

Among employees eventually transferred to Emerald, these feelings were exacerbated by initial uncertainty regarding whether they would be transferred to a voluntary or private sector provider. Here, perceptions of insecurity also mixed with feelings of apprehension with regard to the threat of value interpenetration as employees feared the consequences for service quality in a profit-making organisation. Discontent continued after transfer as the decisions regarding the final destination were seen to be arbitrary, with some former colleagues going to a private sector provider. At the same time, there was considerable relief among employees who transferred into Emerald because they remained in the voluntary sector.

The retention of existing pay and conditions were also a significant issue among respondents.

> People are saying, so when is it that Emerald are going to start doing us over? When are they going to change our terms and conditions? (Support worker, transferred to Emerald)

Transferees to Diamond had additional difficulties relating to alterations to the dates they were paid and the subsequent implications for their monthly budgeting and payment of direct debits. Other concerns included differences in holiday entitlement between Sapphire and Diamond and the loss of payments for subsistence to employees who accompanied service users on social events.

Despite the above, it appeared that the transfers did not lead to any significant violations to people's psychological contracts either on the transactional or VSE related parts of the spectrum. Employees reported that since transfer they continued to undertake the aforementioned aspects of OCB. As a consequence, the majority of front-line staff expressed no desire to quit. The following section outlines explanations for this phenomenon.

SUSTAINING HIGH COMMITMENT AMONG TRANSFEREES

Protection through TUPE

Despite some evidence of initial problems with the dissemination of information by management regarding their employment rights once transferred to a new employer, respondents indicated that the protection offered through TUPE regulations went some way to allay their anxiety concerning changes to pay and conditions. A transferee into Emerald stated: '*I think a lot of people thought well, you still get your pay.*'

It was also the case that after transfer there were no widespread changes to the organisation of work among front-line non-management workers, such as work intensification and changes to hours or shift patterns. The only example of work intensification appeared to be targeted on existing line managers within Diamond. Senior managers revealed that the taking on of additional services led to significant increases to workloads, leading to reports of stress and difficulties finding time to continue with new accreditation standards for front-line managers.

However, following transfers into Emerald, the organisation made several incoming managers redundant through the ETO provisions under TUPE, leading to some concern among the other transferees about their job security. Indeed, management in Emerald spoke of ongoing problems ensuring continued staff motivation.

> The more difficult side of it is, you know, the motivational aspect for staff who are transferring over . . . they didn't trust us. I think they were still worried about their terms and conditions when they transferred over. I think there was anxiety and it took us months to try and reassure people what we were all about, what our values were, what

was going to happen to them, and what was not going to happen to them. (HR manager, Emerald)

It is now useful to look at how other moderators intervened to maintain commitment among transferred employees.

Sustaining Quality of Service

A key factor in maintaining staff commitment related to how transfers to Diamond and Emerald did not involve any detrimental change to the provision of services. Employees expressed relief that they could continue to provide continuity of service to their clients, and that this was because their new employers largely shared the value base of their old organisation—thus avoiding the threat of violation through 'value interpenetration.' Employees were not passive in this regard. On being notified of transfer, individuals reported that they engaged in detailed scrutiny (through Internet and contacts in the sector) of the values of their new employer to see whether they matched their own and that of their previous employers in their commitment to service quality. This persuaded respondents to not search for alternative employment.

> You've got to give your new employers the chance . . . I was aware of the new organisation anyway. Quite a good reputation as well. Just had a better idea about the organisation, and as I say I've been quite impressed with them so far. (Service manager, Sapphire transferred to Diamond)

and

> I was quite confident in Emerald as an organisation. I would say that their aims are the same. You know their services weren't going to change. We could still support our people. (Support Worker, Transferred to Diamond)

Most transferees subsequently expressed commitment to their new employers and its values, to the goals of their projects and the individual well-being of service users.

Management Interventions

Related to the above, management within Diamond and Emerald positively intervened to sustain people's psychological contract. Several respondents reported that proactive management interventions during critical incidents involving care of clients or their own workloads were crucial in forming a positive view of their new employer. One line manager, for example, expressed relief at Diamond's decision to recruit more front-line workers into the service to cover existing staff.

They're recruiting for male relief staff and they're recruiting for two thirty hour posts for my services which badly need it so that's a positive side of it . . . Because I have been struggling for a long time . . . I think they'd already themselves seen the way I was running about like a headless chicken.

A further key to this building of trust appeared to be continued reassurance from management with regard to continuity in terms and conditions of employment. Transferees to Emerald favourably reported how their new management team joined representatives from their previous organisation on a joint 'Roadshow' to reassure staff that nothing would fundamentally change with regard to their employment conditions or service provision.

I mean we're still in a job eighteen months later and the people we support are still receiving that support. (Support worker transferred to Emerald)

The maintenance of employment security and terms and conditions of employment among transferred staff did not, however, come without a cost to Diamond and Emerald. These organisations had to retain different terms and conditions of employment for various groups of staff, and any future changes to this were predicted to be long-term and a consequence of natural employee turnover, with new starts hired on the organisation's own terms and conditions. Management also expressed concern over the long-term implications for ever having organisation-wide terms and conditions for staff if such transfers and re-tendering became the norm.

Union Interventions

Union interventions also made some contribution to sustaining employees' psychological contracts, but this was not without difficulties. Transfers of staff between Sapphire and Diamond, for example, were complicated by the fact that each organisation recognised a different union. For transfers into Emerald this involved staff coming into the organisation from a non-unionised to a unionised environment.

The value of unions in sustaining morale among transferred employees was most keenly felt with regard to information dissemination about employee rights upon transfer, whether as a single union or in partnership with other unions and/or the employer.

The management from our old providers and the union, I think they all liaised regularly, to keep us in the picture with what stage it was. So I was certainly happy with that. And obviously I received letters and that on the decision as well, and this kept us up to date. (Support worker, Sapphire)

Employees also reported, moreover, how the union UNITE contributed to easing tensions during the transfer of staff from Sapphire to Diamond by consulting with management on how to minimise the disruption caused by different payment dates for salaries and cuts to budgets that subsidised social events for service users.

Perceptions of Powerlessness

Despite acknowledging that the contributions of the above factors to ensuring transfers to another employer were undertaken relatively smoothly, several employees also remarked that they had little choice and used expressions such as 'powerlessness' or 'disenfranchisement.' Employees also remarked that re-tendering was becoming a characteristic of working in the sector and that they could do little to change it. This also helped management in the three organisations as it was clear that blame for the transfer was ultimately placed with the local authority.

> I was disgusted, really appalled by it, you know that they could do that to vulnerable people and this was after they were saying, get them into the community, where was the community care when they did that? (Support coordinator transferred to Emerald)

Long-Term Prospects for Psychological Contracts in the Era of Re-Tendering

It was also the case that some employees perceived threats to their psychological contracts in the future. Here, there appeared to be a 'wait and see' attitude among employees who were transferred, because of ongoing anxieties over terms and conditions, the organisation of work, job security, and service provision. Similarly, other transferees revealed that they were aware that although things were stable for the time being, a next round of re-tendering in the forthcoming years could undermine services, and that filled them with a strong sense of anxiety.

> Prices are cut, and I think people know the tender process, we know that what gets cut is the quality of the service provision. They've pared down management to the bare minimum, so what comes next? What is going to get cut, you know in the next round? (Support worker transferred to Emerald)

and

> We may well be in this situation next year or the year after or maybe the year after, which I think is absolutely appalling if they're going

to do this again, so we're all going through the same emotions and feelings again. (Support worker, Sapphire)

DISCUSSION

The aim of this chapter has been to answer two related questions, namely:

What happens to the psychological contract of workers in the voluntary sector where services and employment are transferred to another employer after a retender?

and

To what extent do moderating factors offset the impact of breaches and violations to the psychological contract of employees experiencing transfers to another employer?

In answering these questions, the study reported here revealed a significant degree of resilience with regard to worker psychological contracts. This is in spite of the initial shock of transference, alongside flawed and incomplete information provided by employers regarding worker rights. Workers continued to display high levels of commitment to their client group and even their new employer by exhibiting OCB and not quitting.

In explaining this continued commitment, it was clear that a variety of factors outlined in the literature section combined to sustain the transactional and VSE aspects of the psychological contract among respondents. These factors included the protection offered to terms and conditions through the TUPE regulations, management interventions, and, to a limited degree, union activity. There was also an element of resignation and powerlessness among voluntary sector employees because of a lack of choice over their own destiny in this climate.

The study did, however, reveal some cautionary points with regard to the future of the psychological contract in the context of increased re-tendering of services across and outside the sector. It was clear that where the ETO provisions of TUPE were used by management, this led to a heightened sense of anxiety by staff. Employees revealed that they paid a great deal of attention to the type of organisation they were being transferred into and that voluntary sector providers with similar values were viewed favourably. The question remains as to how resilient the psychological contract of transferred workers would be if they were moved on to a private sector organisation that was solely concerned with profit, rather than service users' needs or the employment conditions of workers. It is noticeable in other studies that transfers of staff and services from public to private organisations reveal far more problems in terms of sustaining staff morale and commitment (Hebson et al., 2003). It could also arguably be the case that not all transfers within the sector would be between organisations with similar values—a transfer of staff and services from a secular to a faith-based organisation, for example, may lead to tensions.

In the long term, the data also raises concerns regarding the impact of regular re-tendering exercises. If successive re-tendering consistently prioritises cost-saving and value for money, then this is likely to eventually affect pay, working practices, and service quality. This outcome is even more likely given the current political and economic climate in the UK, where cuts to public service provision are favoured by all political parties as a solution to burgeoning budget deficits caused by the 'credit crunch.' Such a combination of circumstances will surely have detrimental consequences for the psychological contract in the voluntary sector and subsequent implications for the well being of staff and service users.

NOTES

1. The author recognises that this is but one definition of the psychological contract construct and that there is a rich debate that has led to new interpretations and refinements, for example, Wellin's (2007) notion of the 'personal deal.'

ACKNOWLEDGMENT

The author would like to thank Judith Midgeley and Caroline Sturgeon from the Voluntary Sector Social Services Workforce Unit for their assistance in data collection.

BIBLIOGRAPHY

Alatrista, J., and Arrowsmith, J. (2004). Managing employee commitment in the not-for-profit sector. *Personnel Review*, 33 (5), 536–548.
Arnold, J. (1996). The psychological contract: A concept in need of closer scrutiny? *European Journal of Work and Organisational Psychology*, 5 (4), 511–520.
Carmel, E., and Harlock, J. (2008). Instituting the 'third sector' as a governable terrain: Partnership, procurement, and performance in the UK. *Policy and Politics*, 36 (2), 155–171.
Cavalier, S., and Arthur, R. (2006). *Providing a service? The new TUPE regulations*. Liverpool: The Institute of Employment Rights.
Community Care Providers Scotland (CCPS). (2008). *Re-tendering of social care services: Service providers perspective*. Edinburgh.
Coyle-Shapiro, J. (2002). A psychological contract perspective on organisational citizenship behaviour. *Journal of Organisational Behaviour*, 23 (8), 927–946.
Cunningham, I. (2008). *Employment relations in the voluntary sector*. London: Routledge.

Cunningham, I., and Nickson, D. (2009). *A gathering storm? Procurement, re-tendering and the voluntary sector social care workforce.* Stirling: Voluntary Sector Social Services Workforce Unit.

Graham, J. W. (1986). Principled organisational dissent: A theoretical essay. *Research in Organisational Behaviour,* 8, 1–52.

Guest, D. E. (1998). Is the psychological contract worth taking seriously. *Journal of Organisational Behaviour,* 19 (7), 649–664.

Hebson, G., Grimshaw. D., Marchington, M., and Cooke, F. (2003). PPPs and the changing public sector ethos: Case study evidence from the health and local authority sectors. *Work, Employment, and Society,* 17 (3), 481–501.

Hui, C., Lee, C., and Rousseau, D. (2004). Psychological contract and organisational citizenship behaviour in China: Investigating generalisability and instrumentality. *Journal of Applied* Psychology, 89 (2), 311–321.

Lee Cooke, F., Hebson, G., and Carroll, M. (2005). Commitment and identity across organisational boundaries. In M. Marchington, D. Grimshaw, J. Rubery, and H. Willmott (eds.), *Fragmenting work: Blurring organisational boundaries and disordering hierarchies* (pp. 179–198). Oxford: Oxford University Press.

Lester, S. W., Turnley, W. H., Bloodgood, J. M., and Bolino, M. (2002). Not seeing eye to eye: Differences in supervisor and subordinate perceptions of and attributions for psychological contract breach. *Journal of Organisational Behaviour,* 23 (1), 39–56.

Miles, M. B., and Huberman, A. M. (1994). *Qualitative data analysis.* 2nd ed. London: Sage.

Millward, L. J., and Hopkins, L. J. (1998). Psychological contracts, organisational and job commitment. *Journal of Applied Psychology,* 28 (16), 1560–1556.

Mirvis, P. (1992). The quality of employment in the nonprofit sector: An update on employee attitudes in nonprofits versus business and government. *Nonprofit Management & Leadership,* 3 (1), 23–41.

Mirvis, P., and Hackett, J. (1983). Work and workforce characteristics in the nonprofit sector. *Monthly Labour Review* (April), 3–12.

Morrison, E. W., and Robinson, S. L. (1997). When employees feel betrayed: A model of how psychological contract violation develops. *Academy of Management Review,* 22 (1), 226–256.

Nickson, D., Warhurst, C., Dutton, E., and Hurrell, S. (2008). A job to believe in: Recruitment in the Scottish voluntary sector. *Human Resource Management Journal,* 18 (1), 20–35.

Onyx, J., and Maclean, M. (1996). Careers in the third sector. *Nonprofit Management & Leadership,* 6 (4), 331–345.

Paton. R., and Cornforth. C. (1992). What's different about managing in voluntary and non-profit organisations. In J. Batsleer, C. Cornforth, R. and Paton (eds.), *Issues in Voluntary and Non-Profit Management* (pp. 1–12). Wokingham: Addison Wesley.

Podsakoff, P., Mackenzie, S. B., Paine, J. B., and Bachrach, D. G. (2000). Organisational citizenship behaviours: A critical review of the theoretical and empirical literature and suggestions for future research. *Journal of Management,* 26 (3), 513–563.

Robinson, S. L. (1996). Trust and breach of the psychological contract. *Administrative Science Quarterly,* 41 (4), 574–599.

Robinson, S. L., and Morrison, E. W. (1995). Psychological contracts and OCB: The effect of unfulfilled obligations on civic virtue behaviour. *Journal of Organisational Behaviour,* 16 (3), 289–298.

Robinson, S. L., and Rousseau, D. M. (1994). Violating the psychological contract: Not the exception but the norm. *Journal of Organisational Behaviour,* 15 (3), 245–259.

Robinson, S. L., Kraatz, M. S., and Rousseau, D. M. (1994). Changing obligations and the psychological contract: A longitudinal study. *Academy of Management Journal*, 37 (1), 137–152.

Rousseau, D. M. (1995). *Psychological contracts in organisations: Understanding written and unwritten agreements*. London: Sage.

Rousseau, D. M. (1990). New hire perceptions of their own and their employer's obligations: A study of psychological contracts. *Journal of Organisational Behaviour*, 11 (5), 389–400.

Rousseau, D. M., and Parks, (1993). The contracts of individuals and organisations. In L. L. Cummings and B. M. Staw (eds.), *Research in Organisational Behaviour* (pp. 15–143). Greenwich, CT: JAI Press.

Robinson, S. L., and Morrison, E. W. (1995). The psychological contract as an explanatory framework in the employment relationship. In C. L. Cooper and D. M. Rousseau (eds.), *Trends in Organisational Behaviour* (pp. 91–109).

Sparrow, P. (1996). Transitions in the psychological contract: Some evidence from the banking sector. *Human Resource Management Journal*, 6 (4), 75–92.

Thompson, J. A., and Bunderson, P. (2003). Violations of principle: Ideological currency in the psychological contract. *Academy of Management Review*, 28 (4), 571–586.

Turnley, W. H., Bolino, M. C., Scott, W. L., and Bloodgood, J. M. (2004). The effects of psychological contract breach on union commitment. *Journal of Occupational and Organisational Psychology*, 77 (3), 421–428.

Wellin, R. (2007). *Managing the psychological contract. Using the personal deal to increase business performance*. Aldershot: Gower Publishing.

10 Beyond National 'Varieties'

Public-Service Contracting in Comparative Perspective

Ian Greer, Ian Greenwood, and Mark Stuart

INTRODUCTION

In this chapter, we will explore how work in contracted-out public services, including that in the voluntary sector, maps onto the broader international political economy of work. Comparative scholars often write about society correcting the excesses of the market, and it is hard to imagine a phenomenon more relevant to this than the voluntary sector. Yet this sector is itself subject to market forces, ironically perhaps, because of its ever-closer relationship with the state. Our study of employment in welfare-to-work services in the UK and Germany, whose findings are summarised below, shows how this relationship works and what its effects on workers are.

Comparative employment relations theory tends to rely on a static 'varieties of capitalism' view (Hall and Soskice, 2001) or more dynamic accounts of institutional change (Streeck and Thelen, 2005). Like us, these theorists are interested in the interplay between state, society, and market; unlike us, they are primarily focused on export-oriented manufacturing and comparisons at the national level. We are building therefore on literature that looks at the political process of market making and the within-country inequalities it creates (Lillie, 2010), especially in the service industries, public and private, that account for most work (Bosch and Weinkopf, 2008; Doellgast, Batt, and Sørensen, 2009).

Our argument is that as market logic becomes pervasive in the governance of public services, it is increasingly the funding regimes, rather than the industrial relations systems, that determine the course of labour-management relations. Where this has manifested itself as increasingly cost- and target-driven commissioning behaviour, we see a shift toward more precarious forms of work and an erosion of trade union power. Statutory protections, such as transfer of undertakings legislation, and institutions of worker representation are not well placed to compensate for these trends, either in the UK or Germany. More important, instead, seems to be the success or failure of organisations to manage relations with their funders to avoid or succeed in cutthroat competition.

We begin by introducing our argument in light of the literature on public-service governance and standard accounts of comparative political economy. Second, we compare employment relations in welfare-to-work services in the UK and Germany. Finally, we conclude with a discussion of marketisation in these two countries, its limits, and its social effects.

MARKETISATION AND THE PUBLIC-SERVICE WORKPLACE

Much theorising on international-comparative employment relations is derived from the Anglo-German comparison. Whereas Britain rolled back its worker protections in the 1980s, Germany retained a strong regime of collective bargaining, workplace-level co-determination, and employment-protection legislation. These institutional divergences produced in Germany higher levels of equality and a manufacturing economy that performed better in world markets. Meanwhile, German public services resisted UK-style 'new public management' reforms, partly because of a complex federal government structure protected by a written constitution (Knuth, 2009) and partly because of an entrenched tradition of 'subsidiarity' that ensured a strong role for the voluntary sector (Seibel, 1990).

In several ways, however, Germany is becoming like the UK. Under the red-green government after 1998, market mechanisms emerged governing a wide range of public services (Hipp and Warner, 2008; Keune, Leshche, and Watt, 2008). In postal, telecommunications, and health care services, new competitors emerged that only rarely adhered to public-sector pay deals. Incumbent firms—such as the privatised Deutsche Telekom or the municipal hospitals—created new subsidiaries, which outsourced services with lower pay (Doellgast, Batt, and Sørenson, 2009; Böhlke, Greer, and Schulten, 2010). As the agencies that remained in the public sector gained more autonomy and began to derecognise collective bargaining, the states (*Länder*) withdrew from centralised bargaining, and a new collective agreement introduced low-wage groups and 'escape clauses.' This coincided with the Hartz Reforms, which deregulated low-wage precarious work in the private sector, expanded means testing in the welfare state, and introduced new work-for-benefit schemes that subsidised low-wage work in the voluntary sector. Without a statutory minimum wage, these reforms led to a massive increase in inequality; between 1995 and 2005, the share of low-wage work increasing from 15 to 22 percent, similar to the British level (Bosch and Weinkopf, 2008).

The causes of these inequalities can be seen in the dynamics of the voluntary sector, where much of Germany's low-wage workforce is employed. Germany's voluntary sector is rooted in a centuries-old tradition of subsidiarity that was reinforced in the 20th century by the rise of the social-democratic movement and neighbourhood-based nonprofits often connected to the 'new social movements' (Bode, 2003; Eick, Grell, Mayer, and Sambale,

2004). The introduction of market mechanisms regulating the flow of resources to them, however, has changed what they need to do in order to survive, including in relation to their employment policies. Looking at marketisation allows us to use resource dependence—an underused concept in comparative employment relations research—for leverage in explaining why market-based change has led to greater inequality in Germany.

For managers of nonprofits, funding is of central importance, and a recurring theme in the academic literature on this subject is resource dependence. Of course, funding is not everything. Organisations have to be close to the neighbourhoods that supply clients, staff, and political support, and often they are put in this position by a history of place-based advocacy work that creates a sense of purpose or mission (Marwell, 2004; Galaskiewicz, Bielefeld, and Dowell, 2006). But funding does matter, because nonprofits depend on it (Smith and Lipsky, 1993). Contracting undermines some organisations; for others, it creates incentives to adapt, through new administrative functions and a change in focus and culture. As a result, many organisations—especially (former) social movements of the poor and unemployed—struggle to avoid 'losing their soul' in the process (Sanger, 2004; Eick et al., 2004).

Usually in public-services contracting there is one buyer (the commissioning body) and many sellers (providers). Under these conditions, power relations are asymmetrical in favour of the buyer, but the latter is not omnipotent. The buyers of services need providers to deliver in order to hit their own targets, and they are therefore as interested in providers' ability to do the work as they are in extracting 'value for money.' This problem can be acute for the buyer when there is one provider that fulfils a unique function, fostering a kind of 'resource interdependence' (Saidel, 1991). One way that buyers of services can address this is through 'relational contracting,' in which the buyer of the services communicates with providers throughout the process of devising programmes, procuring the work, carrying out projects, and evaluating them (Cunningham, 2008).

This power relation has implications for employment relations. Whereas reducing costs is not the only reason for contracting, it is a common and important one, with implications for wage setting. In areas subject to intense cost-based contracting, employers who pay according to collective bargaining may lose bids to lower-paying competitors (Enggruber and Mergner, 2007). Even in a strong system of industrial relations like that of Germany, privatisation can disrupt collective bargaining and lead to the creation of low-pay groups, especially among new hires (Böhlke, Greer, and Schulten, 2010). Contracting can bring into public service groups of workers who have no access to union representation, and even solidarity within the same union can be difficult if workers have different employers (Marchington, Grimshaw, Rubery, and Willmott, 2005).

Contracting can affect job security and tenure in at least two ways. On the one hand, make-work schemes can create financial incentives for voluntary organisations to augment the workforce through subsidised temporary low-wage positions (Eick et al., 2004). On the other hand, the starting and stopping of funding streams can make it difficult to employ people over long periods; in some especially volatile areas the vast majority of staff are employed on a freelance basis (Enggruber and Mergner, 2007). That both of these previously quoted studies are from Germany shows that many of these employers have found ways around employment protection legislation.

The effect of contracting on the employment relationship seems not only to affect employees' well-being; contracting seems also to affect workers' worldviews, their loyalty to their employer, and their views about their occupations. A 'contracting culture' often emerges that affects the motivations and attitudes of those previously employed in charitable and public-sector work. For some workers, this may lead to dissatisfaction (Cunningham, 2008) and for others new financial inducements for creativity or entrepreneurship (Considine, 2001). Hebson, Grimshaw, and Marchington, (2003) argue that, whereas 'working in the public interest' remains important to the overall workforce, conflicts engendered by the contracting process are undermining this ethos among managers. In the public-private partnerships they studied, the former premise of the labour-management relationship—an exchange of working conditions for worker commitment—were eroding, along with employers' ability to maintain those conditions. The importance of money, combined with job insecurity and inequality, are consequently important features of the culture of this 'welfare market' (Bode, 2008).

To summarise, this literature allows us to hypothesize that contracting has exacerbated inequality in the workforce, made work increasingly precarious, and eroded traditional notions of 'public-service' work.

THE WELFARE-TO-WORK SECTOR
IN THE UK AND GERMANY

In 2007–2008 we spoke to around 150 people involved in the welfare-to-work sector, as policymakers, civil servants, managers, front-line workers, trade-union representatives, community activists, or clients. Our goal was to examine welfare-to-work, not in terms of individual policies or the ideologies or rationales behind them, but in terms of the working conditions of front-line staff and the possible effects on client outcomes. We began by speaking with the organisers of small trade union and voluntary sector projects aiming to make people in poor communities—mainly South Wales, East Germany, and parts of Leeds and Cologne—more 'employable.' As it became clear that we were looking at a sector, we began speaking to the civil servants responsible for designing programmes and managing contracts, as well as to front-line staff and managers in larger public-sector and for-profit providers.

Below we discuss preliminary findings from this study. Because it is unusual to discuss welfare-to-work as a sector, we will say what it is, including the basic structure of funding and provision, followed by a brief description of employment relations within it.

Funding and Provision

We define the sector functionally as a diverse group of organisations that work with people on welfare benefits to put them in, or bring them closer to, work. Almost all of these organisations' income comes from the state, and the main commissioning bodies are the public employment services. The sums involved are considerable. In 2006–2007 the UK's Department for Work and Pensions (DWP) spent £2.8 billion on personnel and £1.1 billion on contracted-out provision; the comparable figures for 2006 at the German *Bundesagentur für Arbeit* (BA) were €4.2 and €2.2 billion, respectively.

The German phrase for this policy is *fördern und fordern*: placing demands on, and providing supports to, recipients of welfare benefits. In both countries, the policy includes a mixture of punitive policies (new conditions for receiving benefits and sanctions for not meeting those conditions) and supports (spending on 'activation' programmes, such as the British New Deals and Pathways programmes, and Future Jobs Fund). In addition to central government spending, further funding comes from a range of other agencies at the local, regional, and European levels. In recognition of the rootedness of unemployment and poverty in the social dynamics of specific neighbourhoods, welfare-to-work policies funded at any of these levels can have a strong local dimension (Finn, 2000), with funding often targeted at local government and charities with a 'track record' in serving specific communities. These funding streams pay providers to undertake the following tasks:

- Job placement, along with the payment of benefits, is the most traditional area of activity. Under the 2003 Hartz reforms in Germany, the BA is responsible for the short-term unemployed, whereas most locales have Arbeitsgemeinschaften, ARGEs, that are joint ventures between the locally run Sozialämter (benefits offices) and BA-run Arbeitsämter (employment offices) for the long-term unemployed. The UK has a simpler structure, because of the recent restructuring of employment services in which DWP placed in-house front-line provision in the hands of Job Centre Plus (JCP). In addition, temporary staffing agencies and local nonprofits have carved out various niches for themselves as contractors for the BA or JCP.
- *Training* includes everything from basic literacy and numeracy to apprenticeships and formal qualifications. Whereas the DWP and BA fund some of this work, the larger funders are the education min-

istries (in the UK via the Learning and Skills Councils). Upgrading the skills of the unemployed is done in further education colleges (in Germany, the *Volkshochschulen*) and by a wide range of private and voluntary sector providers, many of whom in the UK have special units dedicated to advising the unemployed and reaching out to 'hard-to-reach communities.'

- *Advice, counseling, and guidance* is a second area linked explicitly with employability and involves helping people overcome barriers to work such as debt, lack of transportation, or access to public services, and drug or alcohol abuse or mental illness. Often this work overlaps with advocacy, with some of the providers concerned also, for example, with representing the unemployed when there is a disagreement with the BA or JCP. This area of work in both countries is dominated by the nonprofit sector: trade union unemployed workers' centres, associations of Muslim women, and neighbourhood-based legal aid services, for example, are all found in both countries.
- *Small-business startups* can involve advice, business incubators, or other supports for new activity, or the conversion of existing under-the-table work into legitimate small businesses. In Germany, the most famous example was the 'Ich-AG' initiative in the Hartz reforms, and similar thinking is behind the UK government's Local Economic Growth Initiative (LEGI). These programmes are often run by business chambers and companies that span the private and nonprofit sectors, such as social enterprises. The spectrum of public funding bodies in this area is extremely broad in both countries.
- *Make-work schemes*, such as the New Deals and one-euro jobs[1], are politically very visible and involve massive amounts of money. Subsidised by the state, providers find or create job placements, organise training and counseling for participants, and pay some sort of compensation. In Germany, the notion of subsidising short-term low-wage work in the private sector is opposed by the business community as an illegitimate form of market manipulation. As a result, the law requires of all projects additionality (*Zusätlichkeit*–projects may not replace work already planned) and social benefit (*Gemeinnützigkeit*—the work cannot be for-profit), making them the preserve of the voluntary sector. In Britain, where there are fewer objections to subsidising low-wage work, analogous schemes enjoy political support across the political spectrum and are delivered by for-profit, non-profit, and public sector organisations.

The largest providers do not specialise in one or another of the services mentioned above. Some organisations, such as the Yorkshire-based multinational A4e, have grown up specifically to deliver welfare-to-work programmes within a broad service offering aimed specifically at the outcome of job placements. Other organisations, not established to deliver employment-related services, have built employability into a broader pre-existing offering of social services. For example, Germany's nationwide 'welfare associations,' the Catholic *Caritas*, Protestant *Diakonie*, and the Social-Democratic *Arbeiterwohlfahrt*, are among Germany's largest employers. Social workers within these organisations may provide counseling to the unemployed and place them in schemes in affiliated hospitals. In the UK, smaller organisations with access to those deemed by job centres 'hard-to-reach,' such as homeless shelters or ethnic associations in deprived neighbourhoods, tend to receive money to pay for more specialised work such as counseling, child care, training, or job placements. These functions are then linked to the public sector through client referrals.

The BA and DWP are not the only bodies that fund services to put specific kinds of people to work. The EU also funds, through the European Regional Development (or Structural) Fund, Social Fund, and Globalization Adjustment Fund, 'active' measures for the unemployed. State and local government are similarly involved because of their role in neighbourhood regeneration or poor relief. Finally, many other public bodies view 'activating' the unemployed as complementary to their remit, for example, to prevent released prisoners from re-offending, to reduce antisocial behaviour in housing estates, or to bring women or minorities into occupations where they are under-represented. Large providers draw on several of these funding streams simultaneously, whereas small providers may be dependent exclusively on one.

These funding streams are managed in different ways. One approach can be labelled 'co-production.' This is common with pilot projects, in which local government targets a specific neighbourhood or client group, but with little indication of which goals are realistic. Rather than subjecting a project to proscriptive bidding according to standard criteria, the project is developed jointly by a government agency and one or more charities. Many German make-work schemes fit this description. In Cologne (pop. 970,000), for example, there are thirty agencies organising make-work projects, organised within fifteen consortia. Whereas the funding decision has to be made objectively according to fixed criteria, these criteria are developed by local government staff based on their knowledge of the local providers. Whereas competition has to be advertised EU-wide, the 'public benefit' criterion creates clear advantages for nonprofits. In the UK, similar arrangements are common in local government, where nonprofits carry out some of the work that, for whatever reason, cannot be carried out in-house. In extreme cases, the charity's staff is entirely seconded by the local authority.

Other bodies use more formalised market-based procurement arrangements. The DWP, for example, governs provision in a way that is simultaneously centralised and marketised (Wiggan, 2009). Bidding is based on relatively clear and objective criteria that can be replicated on a wide scale, and payment is subject to standardised measures of performance. For many of their large New Deal programmes and (more recently) Pathways to Work Programmes for the Disabled, JCP has been centralising its procurement procedures and moving to larger contracts. A typical large contract covers a 'sub-region' such as West Yorkshire (population 2.1 million) and is one of a few delivering the same programme across the whole country. This procurement process is centralised, and DWP staff assess bids from around the country in a process designed to be objective and not susceptible to local political influence. A variation on this theme is the dominant practice at the BA, which has a similarly sealed-off decision-making process at the 'regional' level (that is, one or more *Länder*), a focus on objective outcomes (mainly cost), but shorter running times of programmes (as short as six months).

The latter set of contracting relations has several features that distinguish them from 'co-production.' The first is its cyclical nature. After a given contract runs its course, the work goes back out to bid, and a well-performing organisation can lose the contract if a competitor writes a better bid. The second is payment by results. For job-placement services, organisations are usually paid once when a client finds a job and again once the client has been employed for some time. A third is the process through which the funding decision is made. Set objective criteria such as cost dominate, and informal influence and local knowledge are inadmissible. Finally, the latter pattern of contracting is complex and therefore favours firms and charities with specialised grant-writing and contract-management functions.

Employment Relations

Institutionalised worker protections were not devised for a world of contracting, and the workings of some funding streams make them ineffective. Looking across the welfare-to-work sector, we see organisations with very different employment arrangements sometimes being pit against one another in intense price-based competition. Whereas both the UK and Germany have well-organised representative structures in the public sector, neither has structures that encompass the whole range of welfare-to-work providers.

Trade unions have influence in the organisations where they have large numbers of members. Elsewhere they are either completely absent or their role comes down to influencing government policy and using the courts to enforce workers' individual employment rights. In both countries there are separate union structures for the public employment service (PCS and ver.di FB04), charities (UNITE, UNISON, FB03, and FB05), local government (UNISON and FB07), and training (for instance, UCU, NUT, GEW, and FB05)[2], and employer organisation is similarly fragmented. As a result, the picture of workplace-level worker participation, pay determination, and worker turnover reflects a disorganised pattern of employment relations.

This can be seen in Germany, which is well known for its strong worker participation rights in the workplace. Germany has four separate legal frameworks that govern within-workplace participation in welfare-to-work provision. Worker representatives have different rights, depending on whether they work for churches, state and local government, the central government (for instance, the BA), and the private sector. For example, variations exist in terms of which areas are subject to mandatory co-determination: the private-sector framework gives works councillors the most rights, and the church framework the fewest; the public sector frameworks are in between. Within the ARGEs, there are two separate frameworks in a single organisation, state and central government *Personalvertretungsgesetze*. Moreover, in practice, issues that according to law should be approved locally are in fact decided centrally by the BA's works council and management and implemented with little local consultation. Outside the public sector, works councils in the organisations that we visited were present in the welfare associations, but—as in the rest of the economy—absent from smaller nonprofit and for-profit providers, as well as those employing large numbers of freelancers.

In the UK, the situation is similarly unequal, with very little in the way of lay trade union structures outside the public sector and full-time officials in these situations appearing primarily to sort out conflicts that could end in an employment tribunal case. Indeed, here, statutory rights for individuals are probably even more decisive in regulating the workplace. Most providers emerged when unions were already in sharp decline and so never had strong in-workplace structures; with the passage of new antidiscrimination, minimum wage, working time, and other laws, employment tribunals consequently became a more important forum. In fact, in interviews in Leeds, trade unionists indicated that they had their hands full dealing with derecognition threats and employment tribunals, especially concerning discrimination and transfers of undertakings. They did not, in contrast, play much of a role in the day-to-day handling of issues like work intensity or workforce skills development, and we did not hear of any organisations that had invoked the recent 'works council' regulations on the provision of information and consultation to employees.

Without encompassing collective bargaining to maintain standards across the various employers, a huge diversity has emerged in the terms and conditions of employment. The most obvious gulf is between the public sector and its contractors. The former have strong collective bargaining, whereas the latter have weak or no collective bargaining. However, although this situation regarding contractors could facilitate a 'race to the bottom,' it need not: depending on the performance of organisations and the character of the funding regimes, wages can be as high as, or higher than, in the public sector.

Perhaps the clearest example of a 'race to the bottom' in either country is Germany's further education system. Providers here operate in a harsh contracting regime managed at the national and regional levels. In some areas, the BA promotes intense, cost-based competition, and in others it dictates reductions in payments per trainee; in one extreme case, in Cologne, a provider won a bid by offering €15 per contact-hour. Specialised training organisations, in turn, cope with the uncertainty associated with contracting by relying heavily on freelancers.

Some of the contractors with local government that we interviewed in Cologne did follow the national public-sector collective agreement. Because of recent reforms to public sector bargaining, however, they reported increasing difficulty in following these guidelines. There are also increasing points of divergence in public sector collective agreements, driven by states and sectors that have made separate deals and by 'opening clauses' allowing lower wage groups in the event of economic hardship. Furthermore, one-euro jobs have created a vast reservoir of low-wage work for the German voluntary sector not covered by collective agreements or other employment protections. Thus, for political, economic, and institutional reasons, German nonprofits are moving rapidly away from their tradition of recognising the public-sector pay framework.

In the UK the picture in this area is rather mixed. Although the country has an analogous split between the public sector and its contractors, commentators have painted a more complex picture of bargaining in the voluntary sector (for example, Cunningham, 2008). Despite competitive pressures, overall wages in Britain in recent years have been pushed up by the tight labour market of the past decade and the rapid expansion of welfare-to-work as a sector. This does not mean, though, that in all occupations comparable pay with the public sector has been maintained, there may therefore have been a rise in inequality between different occupations, depending on the level of demand in the labour market and the role of performance-related pay. Those organisations that still use public sector collective agreements tend to be local nonprofits that are closely tied into local government and operating under stable funding regimes. Regarding the situation in the for-profit sector, none of the organisations we visited recognised unions, and they tended to have lower base pay than the public sector. We also saw instances of performance-based pay, based on client job outcomes, reflecting the criteria for payment set by the commissioning bodies.

Given the uncertainty generated by contracting, the most important statutory worker protection is that governing transfers of undertakings. If contracting inevitably forces providers to hire and fire as contracts and contractors come and go, it is worth asking how workers are protected when they switch employers.

In Germany, whereas transfers are regulated by the *Bürgerliches Gesetzbuch*, these protections expire a year after a transfer, and we have yet to see a case in our research where these rules have been invoked. Part of the reason for this is that those organisations that need to hire and fire the most—training providers subject to the short-term cost-based contracting of the

BA's central contracting arm—use freelance workers not covered by the law. However, this situation also reflects the fact that other nonprofits use employment arrangements, such as fixed-term contracts and one-euro jobs.

In the UK, the TUPE regulations, which confer rights to workers in cases where work is transferred to another organisation, are similar to those in German law and are often invoked when one organisation loses its contract and another organisation gets the work. However, the application of these regulations can be open to question in situations when it is unclear whether the new contracted programme is the same as the old one and whose job was funded by the old contract. In the case of the loss of Leeds City Council's New Deal contract, for example, the council recommended forty-five employees for transfer, whereas the new contractor said it only had work for thirteen of them. Despite their protected status, most of the transferred workers, it should be noted, left soon afterward because they disapproved of the profit-driven model of provision.

Finally, there is a question about the emerging culture in the sector. This is probably where there is the clearest divide between public, private, and voluntary sectors, a divide that is not just a function of worker representation, but also of organisational size and origins. Large public sector bodies that have evolved continuously over the postwar era, for example, have a different feel from nonprofits set up by local community activists. There is considerable evidence from our interviews that individuals in these sectors are motivated by different things—some prefer security, others flexibility, whereas some are motivated by wealth accumulation. These differences reflect different biographies, as unionised public sector workers, as activists agitating against local redevelopment, or as entrepreneurs seeking to make a profit. These people often distrust their counterparts in other sectors, and people who have moved between sectors tend to strongly prefer one to the other. There is also some evidence of change within the voluntary sector, as exemplified by the numerous charities in our UK sample creating trading arms, and the shift in German welfare associations away from hiring law graduates, toward hiring entry-level managers with business degrees (*Betriebswirtschaftslehre*). However, there is still little evidence that these sectoral differences translate into more or less of an orientation toward the quality of service, as opposed to following directives or chasing money.

Despite the 'varieties' story standard in comparative institutional research, what emerges from the above analysis is that these two national landscapes of provision have developed a similarly high degree of variation and inequality. There is no worker or employer organisation covering welfare-to-work provision as a whole, and outside the public sector it is largely up to workers and managers within individual organisations to work out how to cope with the sector's developments. It would be a mistake to say that workers are passive in coping with the changes taking place or that strong worker participation within an organisation does not make a difference. However, it is equally untrue to say that workers have participation mechanisms that can counter the uncertainty created by contracting. Insofar as national variations do exist, these are primarily the product, not of collective worker and employer organisations, but of the details of statutory regulation and individual employer strategies. While many German employers, especially in the public sector, accept institutionalised norms, such as co-determination, employment protection, and collective bargaining, others find ways to avoid them, for example, by using freelancers.

THE MARKETISATION OF THE VOLUNTARY SECTOR: EFFECTS AND LIMITS

Above we sketched the different institutions of public-service governance and their effects in the workplace. Despite differences, neither the UK nor Germany had unions or statutory worker protections that protected the workforce as a whole from intensified competition and the restructuring that resulted. Consequently, new forms of competition built into the evolving funding rules put intense pressures on employers to reduce costs, the cyclical nature of bidding undermined job security, and the bureaucratic, money-driven nature of contracting affected the culture of organisations.

One result of trends in contracting seems to be the concentration of provision in the hands of ever fewer for-profit organisations; for workers, this will have a mixed effect. Large organisations are more likely to have professional human resource management and are better able to transfer employees internally in response to lost contracts. The problem of regulating between-organisation transfers of workers could be further reduced if large contractors managed fluctuations in the volume of work by subcontracting with incumbent providers, rather than forcing their competitors out of business by shifting the services in house. Larger contracts could also lead to more relational contracting: in recognition of the problems of contract management, JobCentre Plus recently has restructured its procurement unit to assign officers to the thirty largest contractors.

On the other hand, these shifts will in some ways heighten the uncertainty. Because local organisations and governments find it harder to win regional or subregional contracts than do the big, national players, they will be increasingly dependent on large for-profit firms for contracts. Given the complexity of contracting, there is consequently no guarantee that even small providers who perform well will survive the intense pressures of contracting. The different models of provision and cultures of management at successful organisations could also make it difficult for employees to transfer between sectors, as seen in the case of the New Deal provision in Leeds mentioned earlier.

A question that arises from our research is therefore how to prevent contracting from wiping out local nonprofit provision and pushing skilled workers out of the sector. In the UK, especially, there is a lucrative market for large organisations capable of operating across large swathes of country; these organisations are also winning contracts in Germany, France, and elsewhere.

One option here is to get around the fundraising savvy of large providers by creating loopholes in procurement legislation, such as the German *Gemeinnützigkeit* principle in the make-work schemes or the old British practice of giving grants rather than contracts. Turning down the intensity of competition by making contracting subject to the judgment of local actors would undoubtedly have a stabilising effect in the workplace. With more secure sources of funding and solid relationships with commissioning bodies, small voluntary sector organisations would be more likely to recognise trade unions and invest in training. Removing the existential threat to effective projects would also have obvious advantages for clients.

Bottling up competition after years of privatisation and contracting will be difficult and open to legal and political challenge. This structure has been created more for political reasons than for those arising from evidence of its effectiveness (Davies, 2008), and change will be divisive in the provider camp. Local protection violates the intent of EU contracting laws to open all large contracts from member states to service providers from across the EU. Local protection also runs contrary to the interests of large providers, who can argue that they are best placed to provide the low-cost, standardised provision needed for large-scale national labour-market programmes.

A more politically feasible response would be to build institutions to compensate for this market-based tendency to marginalise small providers. In the UK, the government created an Office for the Third Sector in 2006 to 'build capacity' and 'rationalise' the supports that already existed. In practice, this created funding streams for organisations responsible for back office support, including fundraising, accounting, and human resources, as well as bodies responsible for representing the sector's interests at the national and local levels. The idea here was to help organisations adapt to the market and to make small organisations fit for competition through the upgrading or carrying out of their accounting and human resource functions. These enhanced infrastructures, however, are themselves subject to the pressures on other contracted out services. For example, the funding regime has made infrastructure bodies quite timid in the area of employment relations and has forced some community-based worker representatives to re-brand themselves as voluntary-sector human resource consultancies. A more effective model consequently may be the cluster or consortium, a body narrowly focused on managing the relationships between a commissioning body and small providers for a given programme, as in the case of the Cologne consortium mentioned above.

After more than two decades of increased public-services contracting, the landscape of contracted-out welfare-to-work provision is, then, highly unstable, and funders, providers, and unions have only begun to develop responses. The workforce faces considerable uncertainty compared to that of the public sector. In the voluntary and private sector organisations we have studied, large and small, British and German, trade unions are barely present; where they do appear, it is in cases where the employer may have broken the law.

These problems are not unique to the voluntary sector welfare-to-work provision, or to 'liberal' countries like the UK. In most countries and sectors, it is probably the case that contracting is disruptive and a bad thing for workers. However, not all contracts are created equal. In order to really understand the effects of marketisation, policy-relevant social science needs to continue the search for those features of contracts that make the most difference in the workplace.

NOTES

1. The 'one-euro job' was created by the Hartz reforms. It is the commonly used designation for 'work opportunities' (*Arbeitsgelegeheiten [AGH]*) attached to a benefit top-up (*Mehraufwandsentschädigung*) of 1–2 euros per hour. Before these reforms, most make-work schemes (*Arbeitsbeschaffungsmassnahmen*) lasted longer and were paid according to collective agreements. In 2006 the BA reported 805,000 entries into such schemes, of which about 90 percent were AGH; these numbers have remained stable since.
2. PCS stands for Public and Commercial Services Union, UCU stands for the Universities and Colleges Union, GEW stands for *Gewerkschaft Erziehung und Wissenschaft*, and ver.di's stands for *vereinte Dienstleistungen*. The latter is broken into autonomous numbered Fachbereiche (FB). UNITE and UNISON are not short for anything.

BIBLIOGRAPHY

Bode, I. (2008). *The culture of welfare ,markets: The international recasting of pension and care systems*. London: Routledge.
Bode, I. (2003). Flexible response in changing environments: The German third sector model in transition. *Nonprofit and Voluntary Sector Quarterly*, 32 (2), 190–210.
Bosch, G., and Weinkopf, C. (Eds.). (2008). *Low-wage work in Germany*. New York: Russell Sage Foundation.
Considine, M. (2001). *Enterprising states: The public management of welfare-to-work*. Cambridge: Cambridge University Press.
Cunningham, I. (2008). A race to the bottom?—Exploring variations in employment conditions in the voluntary sector. *Public Administration*, 86 (4), 1033–1053.
Davies, S. (2008). Contracting out employment services to the third and private sectors: A critique. *Critical Policy Studies*, 28 (2), 136–164.
Doellgast, V. (2009). Still a coordinated model? Market liberalization and the transformation of employment relations in the German telecommunications industry. *Industrial and Labor Relations Review*, 63 (1), 3–23.

Doellgast, V., Batt, R., and Sørensen, O. (2009). Institutional change and labour market segmentation in European call centres. *European Journal of Industrial Relations*, 15 (4), 347–371.

Eick, V., Grell, B., Mayer, M., and Sambale, J. (2004). *Nonprofit-Organisationen und die Transformation lokaler Beschäftigungspolitik*. Munster: Verlag Westfälisches Dampfboot.

Enggruber, R., and Mergner, U. (Eds.). (2007). *Lohndumping und neue Beschaeftigungsbedingungen in der Sozialen Arbeit*. Berlin: Frank & Timme.

Finn, D. (2000). Welfare to work: The local dimension. *Journal of European Social Policy*, 10 (1), 43–57.

Galaskiewicz, J., Bielefeld, W., and Dowell, M. (2006). Networks and organizational growth: A study of community based nonprofits. *Administrative Science Quarterly*, 51 (3), 337–380.

Greer, I, Böhlke, N., and Schulten, T. (2010). '*Deutsche Gründlichkeit: Liberalization and Local Industrial Relations in German Hospitals.*' CERIC Working Paper 9. February. Leeds: Leeds University.

Hall, P., and Soskice, D. (Eds.). (2001). *Varieties of capitalism*. Oxford: Oxford University Press.

Hebson, G., Grimshaw, D., and Marchington, M. (2003). PPPs and the changing public sector ethos: Case-study evidence from the health and local authority sectors. *Work, Employment, and Society*, 17 (3), 481–501.

Hipp, L., and Warner, M. (2008). Market forces for the unemployed? Training vouchers in Germany and the USA. *Social Policy & Administration*, 42 (1), 77–101.

Keune, M., Leshcke, J., and Watt, A. (Eds.). (2008). *Privatisation and marketisation of services—Social and economic impacts on employment, labour markets, and trade unions*. Brussels: European Trade Union Institute.

Knuth, M. (2009). Path shifting and path dependence: Labour market policy under German federalism. *International Journal of Public Administration*, 32 (12), 1048–1069.

Lillie, N. (2010). Bringing the off-shore on shore: Transnational production, industrial relations, and the reconfiguration of sovereignty, *International Studies Quarterly*. 54(3), 685–706..

Marchington, M., Grimshaw, D., Rubery, J., and Willmott, H. (2005). *Fragmenting work*. Oxford: Oxford University Press.

Marwell, N. (2004). Privatizing the welfare state: Nonprofit community-based organizations as political actors. *American Sociological Review*, 69 (2), 265–291.

Saidel, J. (1991). Resource interdependence: The relationship between state agencies and nonprofit organizations. *Public Administration Review*, 51 (6), 543–553.

Sanger, B. (2004). *The welfare marketplace*. Washington, D.C.: Brookings Institution.

Seibel, W. (1990). Government/third sector relationship in comparative perspective. *Voluntas*, 1 (1), 42–60.

Smith, S., and Lipsky, M. (1993). *Nonprofits for hire*. Cambridge: Harvard University Press.

Streeck, W., and Thelen, K., Eds. (2005). *Beyond continuity*. Oxford: Oxford University Press.

Wiggan, J. (2009). Mapping the governance reform of welfare to work under New Labour. *International Journal of Public Administration*, 32, 1026–1047.

11 Restructuring and Labour Processes under Marketisation

A Canadian Perspective

Donna Baines

INTRODUCTION

Like connecting a cut-rate pair of second-hand stereo speakers to a shiny new IPod, the voluntary sector in Canada deals with high volume demand in a context of inappropriate mechanics and inadequate capacity. As such it reflects and amplifies the downward thrust of neoliberal, minimalist, welfare provision, legitimising the private market as a credible solution to social ills and muting calls for public care and service. Priding itself on its roots in civil society and advocacy, the Canadian voluntary sector has been called upon not only to provide services to people who increasingly have nowhere else to turn, but also to take on this role equipped with very few resources and provided with very little voice in terms of how services are delivered, at what level, and with what goals in mind.

Neoliberal and globalisation projects tend to work hand-in-glove promoting global capitalism and the centrality of market relations, undermining other strategies for social well-being and discrediting social participation that is not aimed at maximising profit and individual achievement (Teeple, 2000; Leonard, 1997). With its emphasis on participatory relations and shared responsibility for social care, the voluntary sector is often at odds with neoliberal, managerial agendas, though in other ways the sector awkwardly or enthusiastically reflects and extends globalised themes. For example, in tandem with international migration and globalisation, the workforce in the Canadian voluntary sector is increasingly racialised. In Canada's most populous province, Ontario, more than a third of voluntary sector employees identify as people of colour (Clutterbuck and Howarth, 2007, 19) with an overall majority of the workforce in Toronto, Canada's largest city, identifying as a 'visible minority' and/or speaking a language other than English in the home (City of Toronto, 2009). Though the links between the racialised workforce and the sector is under-researched, Indigenous people[1] and workers of colour often find themselves employed in ethno-specific services and programmes which are among the least securely funded and most vulnerable to closure (Richmond and Shields, 2004; Baines, 2008).

Similar to the global labour force, the work and workforce in the Canadian voluntary sector are highly gendered. The Canadian Policy Research Network puts female workforce participation in the voluntary sector at 73 percent (Saunders, 2003), with subsectors such as social services at closer to 85 percent. The gendered nature of the sector pivots on the assumption that providing care and services for others is just something women do 'naturally' as an extension of their roles as mothers, sisters, and daughters (Baines, Evans, and Neysmith, 1998; Baines, 2004a). This delegitimises the skills and knowledge required for voluntary sector jobs, making it hard to improve terms of employment or wages and benefits (Aronson and Neysmith, 1996). It also makes it easier to replace full-time, permanent employees with short-term, part-time, contract and casual employees, or even volunteers, as it is assumed that anyone, or at least any woman, can do the job under any conditions (Baines, 2004a). Indeed, as neoliberal restructuring produces growing populations of poor and desperate people in need of services (Teeple, 2000; Cornia 2004), increasingly insecure paid and unpaid workers absorb the overflow in demand through self-exploitation and the elasticity of their labour, temporarily restabilising an inherently unstable and unsustainable sector.

This chapter begins with a look at forces shaping voluntary sector restructuring in Canada and the general neoliberal drift in the system, including the way that Canada's division of responsibilities between the provincial and federal governments contributes to chronic underfunding and overburdening in this sector. Whereas marked differences exist between the Canadian provinces and territories in terms of service provision and entitlements, marketisation and managerialism are shown to provide threads of consistency and continuity across the country. An additional thread of constancy identified is the resistance to agendas of social uncaring and injustice on the parts of workers in the voluntary sector. Though this resistance appears to be self-exploitation in the form of working longer hours for no increase in pay and subsidising the workplace in a variety of ways, it is noted to simultaneously represent a means through which workers can express many of the values and missions excluded from the managerialised workplace. Following this analysis, the chapter moves on to explore aspects of voluntary sector restructuring and ways that decreased protections for workers and rapid changes in labour processes translate into challenges for front-line employees. It then concludes by drawing out some of the more unique aspects of the Canadian experience.

THE BACKDROP TO VOLUNTARY
SECTOR RESTRUCTURING

In previous work, the author has argued that there are three forces providing the backdrop to the contemporary voluntary sector restructuring in Canada, namely: (1) deinstitutionalisation; (2) discourses of client and human rights, and 3) market-oriented restructuring of the welfare state (Baines, 2004a). Below, these three forces will be reviewed and the third factor, market oriented restructuring, will be analysed through the lens of the federal-provincial distribution of powers in Canada.

Deinstitutionalisation

Throughout the postwar period, Canada has had a mixed economy of care (Valverde, 1995) in which the voluntary sector grew in tandem with the public sector to extend and personalise services beyond the more formal, bureaucratic provision provided by the state (Evans, Richmond, and Shields, 2005). By the 1970s, the care of many individuals had been transferred from large state-run institutions into the community to be provided by nonprofit organisations in smaller, more informal, flexible, home, or home-like, environments. This process of de-institutionalisation included: people of all ages with physical, mental health, and intellectual challenges; people with addictions; people in conflict with the law; and frail elderly people. Inadequate funding from governments generally meant, however, that rather than full integration into caring, inclusive communities, many previously housed in institutions continued to be isolated and marginalised within the community (Taylor and Bogdan, 1989; Braddock and Hemp, 1997). In addition, de-institutionalisation permitted governments to substantially cut costs by moving work away from the highly unionised Canadian public sector into the low wage, low benefit, and more flexible nonprofit environment.

In the voluntary sector, it is widely assumed that employee commitment to the mission and population served by the agency at least partially compensates for poor conditions of employment, notably through the willingness of the predominantly female workforce to self-exploit (Nickson Warhust, Dutton, and Hurrell, 2008; Cunningham, 2008). Some have consequently argued that the 'home-like' context of de-institutionalised service provision and its dependence on a low or unwaged female labour force mirror the exploitation of women's unpaid labour in the home and assumptions about women's endless care regardless of conditions of work, up to and including violence and abuse (Baines, 2004b; Baines and Cunningham, under review: also see Kosny and MacEachen, 2009, on other health and safety issues).

Discourses of Client and Human Rights

De-institutionalisation initially formed part of a wider cultural and political philosophical shift from 'patient' to 'person' (Traustadottir, 2000; Michalko, 2002), reflecting the empowerment of numerous groups within the liberalisation of Canadian society in the postwar period and their growing sense of entitlement and democratic participation during the height of the welfare state (Leonard, 1997; Lightman, 2003). As part of a larger discourse of human rights, clients' and patients' rights gained some formal recognition, making it more difficult for service providers and governments to ignore demands for less rigid and oppressive services to be delivered within models of mutual respect and care (Carniol, 2005).

These discourses resurfaced again in the early 2000s to be used by third-way politicians claiming the same ground in the name of social inclusion and diversity. However, rather than providing care that meets the needs of service users and employees in ways that reflect dignity and equity, in both cases, these popular discourses were instead used to move services from the public to the voluntary sector as a means of cutting costs and introducing changes to the labour process, while providing very little in the way of consistently improved service and pitting various groups in the sector against one another in terms of rights and interests (Baines, 2006).

Market-Oriented Restructuring

In order to understand restructuring in the Canadian voluntary sector, it is important to first understand the division of responsibilities and powers between the federal and provincial governments and territories. As one of the most decentralised federated states, power in Canada is divided between the central government and the ten provinces and three territories. Each is considered to have sovereignty in a number of important areas, some of which have been renegotiated from time to time (Rocher and Smith. 2003).

Though the provinces retain the responsibility for the delivery of most social services (with notable and important exceptions including employment insurance and the Canada Pension Plan), the federal government has more resources available and a cross-Canada mandate from which to establish national visions and standards for human service provision. In 1995, the federal government's commitment to national standards was, however, terminated with the establishment of new funding arrangements for human services (Lightman, 2003). Under these new arrangements, provinces were provided with far greater autonomy in how they spent federal human service dollars alongside a decrease in the overall monies transferred to them. In addition, the removal of dollar matching from the federal government meant the removal of the capacity to track whether provinces spent all transferred monies on social services, and the removal of national standards further meant that service provision and entitlement could and did become increasingly disparate across the country. Thus, embracing neoliberal economic policies emphasising the importance of low tax regimes in the global competition to attract investment, provinces and territories cut their taxes levels and capacity to fund social programmes. Claiming to embrace decentralisation and the importance of local control, they also downloaded the costs and responsibilities for many social programmes onto municipalities who were and continue to be unable to meet the need and demand for social provision (Meinhard and Foster, 1998).

Following the marked change in funding arrangements, decreases in funding were immediately evident at all levels. For example, the provincial government in Ontario, Canada's most populous province, passed a 22 percent cut onto municipalities, resulting in a 7.5 percent cut to voluntary agencies across the board (Clutterbuck and Howarth, 2007, 37) and a shift from core to contract funding. Contract funding will be discussed in more detail later in this section.

Given the autonomy of provinces and municipalities to provide services in whatever way and at whatever level they choose, authors attempting to map the similarities and differences in the voluntary sector across Canada (Brock and Banting, 2001) have generally produced highly complicated compilations that confirm a patchwork of entitlements and provisions. The most consistent pattern over the last couple of decades is that the highest level of social provision is found in Quebec, whereas Alberta has the lowest (Graham, Swift, and Delaney, 2003; Westhues, 2003). Building the broadest possible support for separatism by occupying the centre-left, the Parti Quebecoise in Quebec has consistently provided more comprehensive funding, innovative programming, and social entitlements than provinces in English-speaking Canada (Lightman, 2003). In contrast, long an individualist, pro-business province seen nationally and internationally as a leader in new public management (NPM) and public sector downsizing (Mukherjee, 2000; Gendron, Cooper, and Townley, 2001), Alberta fosters charitable and self-help solutions to social inequities and exclusion (Harrison, 2005).

Across Canada, meanwhile, there has been a general shift to contract funding for individual programmes and projects rather than core funding aimed at supporting infrastructure and the offering of integrated, holistic bundles of programmes and projects by any given voluntary agency (Hall and Reed, 1998). Drawing again on the Ontario example, currently less than 17 percent of funding in the voluntary sector is core funding, with 75 percent being directed to time-limited projects and 8 percent to seed funding (Clutterbuck and Howarth, 2007).

Clutterbuck and Howarth (2007) claim that contract relationships are transforming the voluntary sector away from its mission of care and social justice by commercialising operations and compromising autonomy. In a similar vein, Evans, Richmond and Shields (2005, 74) argue that through contracting services *'the state has introduced quasi-markets or at minimum required voluntary agencies to engage in more competitive practices, with negative consequences for nonprofit mission, culture, and labour-management practices.'* Indeed, competition between and among voluntary agencies for funding has disrupted normal patterns of cooperation and mutual support that characterised the sector prior to contracting out. Representing an additional downside to contracting services, funding is rarely adequate to cover the costs of providing services, let alone those associated with infrastructure, research and development, human resources development, advocacy, or policy work. The reduction or removal of these aspects of voluntary agencies has thereby reshaped their capacity and role in society, while pushing them into new kinds of relationships with the public and government.

In two separate studies, Eakin (2002 and 2004) found that even among the most competitive voluntary agencies, state contract funding generally fell at least 7 to 15 percent short of real costs, compelling voluntary agencies to return to charity and individual fundraising to make up shortfalls. Against this background, an earlier study, undertaken by the author of restructuring in three Canadian provinces, showed that most voluntary sector employees are involved in numerous kinds of fundraising for their employers, ranging from selling raffle tickets to organising charitable auctions, running social events and fundraising parties, making cash donations, and so forth (Baines, 2004d). Moreover, although larger agencies often have fundraising staff, front-line, even here it appears that employees are also expected to contribute to this work, making little or no use of the skills for which they were hired, extending their working days, adding to already heavy workloads, and reinforcing the sense that funding, like employment, is increasingly precarious and not to be taken for granted.

Because of its time-limited nature and in the name of taxpayer accountability, contract funding increases the documentation required of managers and front-line workers, shifting much of the focus of work from hands-on service provision to completion of paperwork. Though models like NPM exhort the virtues of public accountability through quantitative metrics, Evans, Richmond and Shields (2005) have argued that there is very little that is *public* about the narrow *administrative* accountability measures that dominate the voluntary sector. Rather, they assert that most metrics are used to deflect responsibility and blame for deteriorating services from government onto voluntary sector providers (p. 87). This argument highlights the neoliberal trend to push risk and accountability downward (see also Taylor, 2002), fostering relationships of control rather than partnerships between governments and voluntary agencies (Ford, 1998, 37).

An additional aspect of neoliberal welfare state restructuring has been an increased emphasis on disaggregating services or providing direct payments to individuals in order for them to contract directly with individual service providers rather than to work with multiservice agencies. Direct payments drain much-needed resources from established agencies and service providers, while inconsistent or reduced demand for services from individual service users, who may prefer to 'shop around,' makes it difficult for agencies to provide dependable programming and service levels and curbs the development of new or innovative programming. In the name of 'empowerment' and 'individual choice,' direct payment systems also download statutory employer obligations and human resources functions onto service users, effectively turning them into small businesses but without training, regulating, or supporting service users in the complex tasks of labour relations and employer obligations (Baines and Perlmuttter, 2008). Against this backdrop, research unsurprisingly shows a deterioration in working conditions under direct payment systems, pitting employees' rights to fair pay, pensions, and reasonable working hours against service users' demands for flexibility, autonomy, and choice (Aronson, Denton, and Zeytinoglu, 2004; Leece, 2008). Wages are often well below the sector, especially when unpaid care work is factored in, and benefits, such as holiday pay and sick time, are rarely provided, though individual employers are legally required to provide them or pay in lieu of benefits (Dale, Brown, Phillips, and Carlson, 2003).

Benefits of direct payments or voucher systems accrue mostly to those who feel able to hire, fire, instruct, monitor, trouble-shoot, and problem-solve for those they employ, arguably a very small minority of service users in the voluntary sector. Some service users therefore find they have reduced control under a voucher system as they have no way to screen those they employ, find it hard to reprimand or dismiss staff, and sometimes feel they are being exploited, misused, or harmed by their own employees (Aronson, 2006). Though direct payment schemes can mean that family and friends can potentially receive a wage for some of the care work they undertake for loved ones, they often find that demand for care expands once pay cheques start to flow, resulting in workers providing increased hours of both paid and unpaid care (see Ungerson, 1999; Leece, 2008).

THE EROSION OF LABOUR RIGHTS AND PROTECTIONS

Provinces and territories retain the major responsibility for labour regulations and protections with a few exceptions that have no relevance to this sector (Thompson and Taras, 2004). In Canada, collective bargaining agents (usually unions) must prove that they have the support of the majority of those employed in a particular work unit, thereafter known as the bargaining unit, in order to be certified by government-appointed Labour Relations Boards. Known as the closed shop system, certified bargaining agents represent all the workers in a given unit and collect all dues regardless of whether the workers voted for or against the union. They also negotiate workplace collective agreements with individual employers and operate within a set of regulations interpreted and adjudicated by provincial Labor Relations Boards. Individual collective agreements reflect the priorities and relative strength of the local and the parent union, as well as the ideological leanings of each Labour Relations Board.

Again resembling a patchwork of different rights and regulations, whereas a minority of provincial governments left their postwar system largely intact, most provincial and territorial governments in Canada introduced restrictions on union rights and rolled back substantial gains made in the last sixty years. Changes include the repeal of restrictions or bans on the use of replacement workers during strikes (colloquially known as scabs); making supervised votes necessary in all workplaces rather than card checks for union certification drives; and expanded opportunities for employers to encourage employees to decertify (leave the union). The impact of these changes makes it harder for unions to organise and represent workers (Fudge and Vosko, 2001; Yates, 2002), as is reflected in declining density, though overall numbers, particularly in the nonprofit sector, continue to grow (Statistics Canada, 2003 and 2007).

This system of union representation can mean that some workers in a given workplace are represented whereas others working alongside them are not (for example, full versus part-time, or front office staff in a large agency versus front-line service staff). It can and does therefore result in some categories of workers in the same workplace receiving greater protection and better wage packets than others, while also disaggregating the workforce and undermining workplace solidarity. Increased dependence on temporary, casual, contract, part-time, and flex-time workers has exacerbated these differences, as most categories of precarious workers have not been included in union bargaining units. In the neoliberal vernacular, some employees are shaped as part of the new economy of entrepreneurialism and self-reliance rather than dependence on old-fashioned impediments to efficiency such as unions, whereas other workers remain somewhat cocooned from neoliberalism within the relative protection of the bargaining unit.

IMPACTS AT THE FRONT-LINES

In the Canadian voluntary sector, the dispersion of neoliberal policies operates through two main mechanisms, which, while *pro-market* in that they extend and legitimise commercialism and corporatism within sectors previously thought to be antithetical to these practices, simultaneously remain nominally *nonmarket*. This occurs because (most) Canadian nonprofits do not engage in commercial activities and thus, while under pressure to generate cost savings, do not generally generate profits (Baines, 2004b). First, the downloading and privatising of state services, concomitant with calls for cost savings and efficiencies, has meant that the voluntary sector has acquired new, often poorly funded services, at the same time that it has experienced increased service demands and budget cuts to existing services (McDonald, 2005). Second, newly introduced budget cuts, state standards, and accreditation requirements have provided the impetus for agencies to adopt private-sector-like managerial models, such as NPM, that track costs and impose efficiencies (Cunningham, 2001; Meager and Healy, 2003).

Purporting to coach employees in 'best practices' and 'competencies,' NPM standardised practices, removed activities that were seen to be

repetitive or wasteful, and directed employees to adopt new, closely monitored, highly routinised interventions (Baines, 2006; Dominelli, 2004).
NPM has, as a consequence, simultaneously reduced employee discretion
and control, replacing intuitive, interactive relationship-building activities
with standardised check-box assessment forms and tightly scripted intervention plans (Aronson and Sammon, 2001).

One of the author's earlier studies confirmed that front-line workers are
very aware that their work has been standardised and felt that it represented
both a loss of decision-making power and control as well as a decline in
the quality of care they could provide. As the following observations from
a long-term front-line worker demonstrate (Baines, 2004a):

> The identifying issue might be the same but every person and family
> is different. We can't treat them all like little chocolates on an assem-
> bly line. Each person needs a different level of care and I, as a social
> worker, should get to decide that level in conjunction with the client
> rather than a stupid form telling me how I have to work with each per-
> son. (Community mental health worker, Nova Scotia)

Front-line workers were also acutely aware that increased documentation
had not only robbed them of discretionary decision making and planning,
but also deskilled their work, making it easier for them to be replaced by
lower paid workers and volunteers. For example (Baines, 2004a), as one
front-line supervisor noted, the assessment forms her agency used *'can be
completed by anybody, they don't need a social worker in this job'* (Coun-
selling, Nova Scotia).

Though never the mantra of public or voluntary services in the past, market-based discourses of NPM efficiency are now widely used to emphasise
the need for 'flexible workforces' and cost cutting. This has resulted in the
erosion of permanent, full-time employment and the rapid expansion of the
precarious forms of employment mentioned earlier in this chapter. Moreover, the standardisation characteristic of NPM has not only facilitated this
change in the workforce, but made it easier to increase the pace and volume
of work, as well as extending the reliance placed on the unpaid work of volunteers and family members (Gilroy, 2000; Baines, 2004b). Working lean,
that is, alone or with only one or two other staff on shift, who are sometimes available only by beeper or phone, has therefore become the norm in
many voluntary work sites, leaving many workers isolated, working largely
on their own, undertaking repetitive, often bureaucratic tasks, documenting and processing individual clients (Baines 2004a and 2007).

An increased incidence of client violence against workers has been linked
to this growth of flexible and leaned-out workforces (Baines 2004d and
2006; Cunningham 2008) because the constantly changing parade of flexible workers often exacerbates stress among clients desperately in need
of predictability and constancy. Veteran workers in the voluntary sector

generally have an array of interventions in their skill sets and tend to know a great deal about the particularities of their clients' challenging behaviors as well as strategies to detect, deflect, and diffuse stress. Precarious workers, and those working on their own, have few, if any, opportunities to work with or learn from veteran workers (where they still exist) and few ways of finding out the particularities of each case, let alone what might trigger client outbursts, the best ways to distract or diffuse outbursts when they seem about to occur, or the best ways to de-brief and de-escalate violence once it does take place. The leaned-out labour process and ongoing transfer of discretion and control to management through NPM standardisation and scripting can, for these reasons, be indicted for increasing the likelihood of occupational violence and reducing strategies for preventing, diffusing, and resolving it.

In many ways, the restructured workplace resembles the care environment found in many homes where women provide ongoing affection and support to those who abuse them, receiving little or nothing in the way of official response or recognition that a problem even exists, let alone that violence can and should be prevented. Muted or nonexistent responses from employers similarly normalise violence as just part of the job that must be tolerated and endured in ways that reflect and reproduce its wider acceptance in care-based relationships in the home and family. Work intensification is another common aspect of the restructured voluntary sector workplace. This takes the form of increased caseloads (volume of work) as well as intensity (complexity of the cases as clients seek services for increasingly desperate situations).

Computer-based technology has sped up the work of documenting and processing cases in larger agencies, thereby justifying increases in caseloads (Sawchuk, 2003), notably by prompting workers with electronic messages to complete work within various preset timeframes and benchmarks, as well as providing e-supervision and electronic permission to move on to the next preset task and timeframe. When smaller nonprofit agencies are unable to afford these computerised packages, the content of daily work in many such agencies has also, meanwhile, been sped up in various ways, including shortening the number and length of interactions with clients; making extensive use of irregular shifts such as the aforementioned lean and solo shifts; and paying workers by the client rather than through a salary or by the hour (transferring the cost of 'no shows' to the worker).

This intensification takes place in the context of endless messages reminding staff that the sector and agency have few and very tenuous resources and that everyone must constantly think of ways to do more with less. Some staff have responded to these messages and work intensification by undertaking an expanded number of unpaid overtime hours including working through their lunch breaks and coffee breaks; staying late at work and arriving early; working during holiday breaks; taking work and clients home with them; answering voice mail and email while commuting; and subsidising the workplace with goods from home and the unpaid labour of family members (Baines, 2006).

Many worksites encourage their staff to take on unpaid work, including extending their hours of work with no increase in pay, in effect volunteering at their own place of work. Precarious workers, who are often workers of colour and Indigenous people, are particularly vulnerable to these demands as they attempt to position themselves favourably for increased hours or more secure job opportunities. Thus, in an earlier study of changes in non-profit workplaces, a worker of colour reported that she worked twenty hours for pay and was expected by her manager and co-workers to put in another twenty hours of volunteer work every week, in effect cutting her pay in half (Baines, 2004a). These contributions are expected by, though not recorded by, management; hence they remain an undocumented and largely invisible subsidy to the voluntary sector and its clients (Baines, 2006). Whereas many workers resent this imposition, others simultaneously feel that their work pushes back the boundaries of neoliberalism, resisting social disintegration and a larger uncaring society (Baines, 2004c). Ironically, though, whereas many employers depend on their predominantly female staff's boundless capacity for care work, the same employees find deep meaning in the care they provide for others and the opportunities it provides to 'make a difference' in a system that produces a seemingly endless stream of people in need.

NPM-like restructuring has also eliminated many of the collective forums for staff participation in agency-level and wider community decision making. Unlike the private sector, which claims to have recently discovered that increased staff participation in decision making can pay off in increased productivity, the voluntary sector has long prided itself on its more horizontal structures in which staff, service users, and community members are encouraged to participate in all levels of decision making (Van Til, 2000). This participatory aspect, like the missions of many agencies, has, however, unraveled under neo-liberal restructuring (Bush, 1992; Brainard and Siplon, 2004), being removed entirely or remade as professional input into performance improvement and outcome measures. In addition, internal, agency forums for shared decision making, such as agency and staff meetings, peer supervision models, community councils, and town hall meetings, have been largely been removed, replaced by standardised surveys aimed at quality control and other forms of tightly standardised feedback. Similarly, despite the fact that work content involving community participation such as advocacy, community organizing, and activism often attracts staff to the voluntary sector, most of this work has also been removed or dramatically cut back in order to stretch tight budgets and eliminate tasks that do not contribute directly to 'core functions' (Smith, 2007).

Given the curtailment of opportunities for shared decision making and their sense that participation in social issues has never been more important, some voluntary sector workers have unionised their workplaces or increased their participation in their unions. Using unions as vehicles for participation in agency- and community-level decision making, these workers claim that they are explicitly seeking to replace and expand the 'voice' that they feel has been lost under managerialism and restructuring (Baines, 2010). Linking the needs of clients and the community with workplace concerns, the local president in a mid-sized, multiservice agency, for example, argued that:

> Wages and working conditions are always important to our members, but people really want a voice in how decisions get made. We have expertise in our programme areas, we know our clients and communities. and we want some say in how things get done. (Baines, 2009)

Participation in the unions active in the voluntary sector cuts a wide swath, ranging from demanding union input into agency-level operations and planning to organising coalitions on major social issues such as the war in Iraq and the growth of poverty, and joining community networks addressing homelessness, issues facing immigrants and refugees, and violence against queer people.

A recent study that the author undertook of unions in the nonprofit sector showed that union activists very consciously focused on making the union local a place where workers could develop ties of friendship and mutual support, build skills and undertake some of the advocacy and community development work now excluded from their increasingly narrowed job descriptions. These approaches continue a Canadian tradition of social unionism in which unions mobilise not just around workplace issues, but adopt the priorities of the communities in which their members live and work (Black, 2005; Ross, 2007).

Yates (2002) argues that predominantly female workplaces are more likely to adopt new models of social or community unionism, pursuing issues beyond the boundaries of the workplace, such as campaigns for universal health care, increased funding for human services, fair wages, universal child care, anti-violence, and overall social development. At the same time, human service unions are also likely to use workplace actions and bargaining to lower caseloads and waiting lists and to improve quality of service (Baines 1999; Rosenburg and Rosenburg, 2006). Indeed, some claim that social unionism is a form of community development in which the global and the local come together and the interests of those within and those outside the union meld into activist campaigns that revitalise civil society, meet growing social needs, and experiment with new forms of democratic participation (Tufts,1998; Black, 2005). Certainly, this approach has been found to hold particular appeal among the predominantly female and significantly non-white voluntary sector work force, who tend to favour collective solutions to social problems and see social participation as the best way to build healthy, productive communities.

CONCLUSION

Managerialism is a well-recognised mechanism of neoliberalism, and its impacts have been widely felt in the voluntary sector (Teeple, 2000; Evans, Richmond, and Shields, 2005). The standardising influence of performance management strategies have been widely documented as a force that, in the name of efficiency, accountability, and cost savings, strips voluntary sector work of its participatory, holistic, and innovative character, generally replacing it with narrow, alienating, and routinised practices (Baines, 2004a and 2006; Cunningham, 2008). The discussion in this chapter suggests that the predominantly female workforce in the voluntary sector resists marketisation and managerialism in the ways available to them in the constrained and gendered contexts of their work lives. The constraints include underfunding and neoliberal ideologies, which facilitate the adoption of performance management models of work organisation where the intensification and standardisation of work and flexiblised, precarious workforces have become the norm. Leaned-out staffing patterns result in increased workloads and workplace violence, at the same time as employee voice is silenced through the removal of participatory practices at the level of the agency and across the larger community in the name of efficiency and accountability.

Worker resistance in the restructured voluntary sector includes various forms of self-exploitation, such as voluntary overtime, volunteering in their places of employment, bringing goods from home and taking clients home with them, as well as more formal mechanisms such as unionisation and social union mobilisation to claim back space for participation and demand adequate social care for the marginalised communities they serve. In all cases, workers use their unpaid labour to challenge practices and discourses that detract from their commitment to caring for and about client groups and larger community issues.

The changing labour process under NPM managerial models and workers' resistance to it remains the constant between and among Canada's diverse and divergent provinces and territories. The removal of federal standards and dollar matching in Canadian social service funding has meant that social entitlements and service levels vary significantly across the ten provinces and three territories, providing numerous opportunities for the various levels of government to point blame at one another, though in reality, responsibility and risk have been downloaded to voluntary sector agencies and their front-line staff.

Whereas the labour force in Canada's voluntary sector may be more racialised than in the UK, EU, and Australia (outside particular major cities), and the tradition of social unionism may not have the same roots or may not taken hold to the same degree, the chapters in this book show that these debates and struggles exist in similar forms across the industrial world. Just as managerialism and marketisation shape the voluntary sector across the highly decentralised landscape of Canada's social provision, these same forces impact voluntary and social provision globally. Similarly, just as workers' resistance and the voluntary spirit of social care and mutuality assumed unique forms in Canada, the same spirit of care and struggles can be found wherever voluntary and public provision occurs.

NOTES

1. The use of language to label and define is highly political. The struggle for First Nations' self determination uses language and labels in strategic ways to name 'problems' and their 'solutions' and to reclaim sovereignty in the lives of First Nations people. Though likely not familiar to Europeans, most First Nations' people in Canada interchangeably use the terms 'Indigenous,' 'Aboriginal,' 'Native,' or 'First Nations' (Freeman, 2007).

BIBLIOGRAPHY

Aronson, J. (2006) 'Just fed and watered": Women's experiences of the gutting of home care in Ontario. In K. Grant, C. Amaratunga, P. Armstrong, M. Boscoe, and A. Pederson (eds.), *Caring Possibilities: Women's Work, Women's Care* ( ). Aurora: Garamond.

Aronson, J., Denton, M., and Zeytinoglu, I. (2004). Market-modeled home care in Ontario: Deteriorating working conditions and dwindling community capacity. *Canadian Public Policy*, 30 (1), 111–125.

Aronson, J. and Sammon, S. (2001). Practice amid social service cuts and restructuring: Working with the contradictions of small victories. *Canadian Social Work Review*, 17 (2), 167–187.

Aronson, J., and Neysmith, S. (1996). You're not just in there to do the work': Depersonalizing policies and the exploitation of home care workers' labour. *Gender and Society*, 10 (1), 59–77.

Baines, D. (2010). Neoliberal restructuring, participation, and social unionism in the nonprofit social services. *Nonprofit and Voluntary Sector Quarterly*, 39 (1), 10–28.

Baines, D. (2008). Race, resistance, and restructuring: Emerging skills in the new social services. *Social Work* 53 (2), 123–132.

Baines, D. (2004a). Caring for nothing. Work organization and unwaged labour in social services. *Work, Employment, and Society*, 18 (2), 267–295.

Baines, D. (2004b). Pro-market, non-market: The dual nature of organizational change in social services delivery. *Critical Social Policy*, 24 (1), 5–29.

Baines, D. (2004c). Seven kinds of work—Only one paid: Raced, gendered, and restructured care work in the social services sector. *Atlantis: A Women's Studies Journal*, 28 (2) (Spring), 19–28.

Baines, D. (2004d). Case studies in women's occupational health in the new labour market: Social services, stress, violence, and workload. *Canadian Woman Studies*, 23 (3), 157–164.

Baines, D. (1999). Strike frequency, gender, and social caring'. *Canadian Review of Social Policy*, 43 (Fall), 114–115.

Baines, D., and Perlmutter, G. (2008). *Funding voluntary sector services: A question of fair funding and balancing rights*. Toronto: Ontario Federation of Labour, Social Services Council.

182 *Donna Baines*

Baines, C., Evans, P., and Neysmith, S. (1998). *Women's caring: Feminist perspectives on social welfare.* Toronto: Oxford Press.

Baines, D., and Cunningham, I. (Under review). 'White knuckle care work: Working on the edge with the most excluded. *Work Employment and Society.*

Black, S. (2005). Community unionism: Strategy for organizing in the new economy. *New Labor Forum*, 14 (3), 24–32.

Braddock, D., and Hemp, R. (1997). Towards family and community: Mental retardation services in Massachusetts, New England, and the United States. *Mental Retardation*, 34 (4), 241–256.

Brainard, L., and Siplon, P. (2004). Toward nonprofit organization reform in the voluntary spirit: Lessons from the Internet. *Nonprofit and Voluntary Sector Quarterly*, 33 (3), 435–457.

Brock, K., and Banting, K. (2001). The Nonprofit sector and government in a new century: An introduction. In K. Brock and and K. Banting (eds.), *The Nonprofit Sector and Government in a New Century* (pp. 1–20). Montreal and Kingston: McGill-Queens University Press.

Bush, R. (1992). Survival of the nonprofit spirit in a for-profit world. *Nonprofit and Voluntary Sector Quarterly*, 21 (4), 391–410.

Carniol, B. (2005). *Case critical. The dilemma of social work in Canada.* 5th ed. Toronto: Between the Lines.

City of Toronto. (2009). Toronto facts: Toronto's racial diversity. City of Toronto. Available at www.toronto.ca/toronto_facts/diversity.htm. Accessed 4 February 2010.

Clutterbuck, P., and Howarth, R. (2007). *Heads up Ontario! Current conditions and promising reforms to strengthen Ontario's nonprofit Ccmmunity services sector: Final report.* Toronto: Community Social Planning Council of Toronto.

Cornia, G. (2004). *Inequality growth and poverty in an era of liberalization and globalization.* Oxford: Oxford University Press.

Cunningham, I. (2008). *Employment relations in the voluntary sector.* London: Routledge.

Cunningham, I. (2001). Sweet charity! Managing employee commitment in the UK voluntary sector. *Employee Relations*, 23 (3), 192–206.

Dale S., Brown R., Phillips, B., and Carlson, B. (2003). *The experiences of workers hired under consumer direction in Arkansas.* Princeton: Mathemetica Policy Research Inc.

Dominelli, L. (2004). *Social work: Theory and practice for a changing profession.* Cambridge: Polity Press.

Eakin, L. (2004). *Capacity draining: The impact of current funding practices on non-profit community organizations.* Toronto: Community Social Planning Council of Toronto.

Eakin, L. (2002). *Supporting organizational infrastructure in the voluntary sector.* Ottawa: Voluntary Sector Initiative Secretariat.

Evans B., Richmond, T., and Shields, J. (2005). Structuring neoliberal governance: The nonprofit sector, emerging new modes of control, and the marketization of service delivery. *Policy and Society*, 24 (1), 73–97.

Ford, R. (1998). *Trends and issues in governance and accountability*, Upublished manuscript, Ryerson University, Toronto.

Fudge, J., and Vosko, L. (2001). By whose standards? Re-regulating the Canadian labour market. *Economic and Industrial Democracy*, 22 (2), 327–356.

Gendron, Y., Cooper, D., and Townley, B. (2001). In the name of accountability: State auditing, independence, and new public management. *Accounting, Auditing, and Accountability Journal*, 14 (3), 278–310.

Gilroy, J. (2000). Critical issues in child welfare. Perspectives from the field. In M. Callahan and S. Hessle (eds.), *Valuing the Field: International Child Welfare* (pp.). London: Ashgate.

Graham, J., Swift, K., and Delaney, R. (2000). *Canadian social policy: An iintroduction*. Scarborough, ON: Prentice Hall Allyn and Bacon Canada.

Hall, M., and Reed, P. (1998). Shifting the burden: How much can government download to the non-profit sector? *Canadian Public Administration*, 41 (Spring), 1–20.

Harrison, T. (2005). Introduction. In T. Harrison (ed.), *The Return of the Trojan Horse. Alberta and the New World Disorder*, (pp. 1–23). Montreal: Black Rose Books.

Kosny, A., and MacEachen, E. (2009). Gendered, invisible work in non-profit social service organizations: Implications for worker health and safety. *Gender, Work, and Organization*. Early view available 10.1111/j.1468–0432.2009.00460. Accessed

Leece, J. (2008).Paying the piper and calling the tune: Power and the direct payment relationship. *British Journal of Social Work*, 12(4), 1–19.

Leonard, P. (1997). *Post modernist welfare: Reconstructing an emancipatory project*. Thousand Oaks, CA: Sage.

Lightman, E. (2003). *Social policy in Canada*. Toronto: Oxford University Press.

Lightman, E., and Baines, D. (1996). White men in *blue* suits: Women's policy in conservative Ontario. *Canadian Review of Social Policy*, 38 (Fall), 145–152.

McDonald, C. (2005). *Challenging social work: The institutional context of practice*. Basingstoke: Palgrave Macmillan.

Meagher, G., and Healy, K. (2003). Caring, controlling, contracting, and counting: Governments and non-profits in community services. *Australian Journal of Public Administration*, 62 (3), 40–51.

Meinhard, A., and Foster, M. (1998). *Response of Canada's voluntary organizations to shift in social policy: A provincial perspective*. Working Paper No. 19, Ryerson University, ON, Centre for Voluntary Studies, Working Paper Series.

Michalko, R. (2002). *The difference that disability makes*. Philadelphia: Temple University Press.

Mukherjee, R. (2000). *Administrative and civil service reform*. Washington, D.C. World Bank Group.

Nickson, D., Warhust, C., Dutton, E., and Hurrell, S. (2008). A job to believe in: Recruitment in the Scottish voluntary sector. *Human Resource Management Journal*, 18 (1), 20–35.

Richmond, T., and Shields, J. (2004). NGO restructuring: Constraints and consequences. *Canadian Review of Social Policy*, 53 (Spring/Summer), 53–67.

Rocher, F., and Smith, M. (2003). *New trends in Canadian federalism*. 2nd ed. Peterborough, ON: Broadview Press.

Rosenberg, J., and Rosenberg, S. (2006). Do unions matter? An examination of the historical and contemporary role of labour unions in the social work profession. *Social Work*, 51(4), 295–302.

Ross, S. (2007). Varieties of social unionism: Towards a framework for comparison. *Just Labour: A Canadian Journal of Work and Society*, 11 (Autumn), 16–34.

Saunders, R. (2003). *Human resources in the non-profit sector: A synthesis of CPRN's research findings*. Ottawa: Canadian Policy Research Centres.

Sawchuk, P. (2003). Worker responses to technological change in the Canadian public sector: Issues of learning and labour process. *Journal of Workplace Learning*, 15 (7), 28–43.

Smith, K. (2007). Social work, restructuring, and resistance: 'Best practices' gone underground. In D. Baines (ed.), *Doing Anti-oppressive Practice. Building*

Transformative, Politicized Social Work (pp. 145–159). Halifax: Fernwood Books.

Statistics Canada. (2003). *Perspectives on labour and income*. Ottawa: Statistics Canada.

Statistics Canada. (2007). *Perspectives on labour and income*. Ottawa: Statistics Canada.

Taylor, M. (2002). Government, the third sector, and the contract culture: The UK experience so far. In U. Ascoli and C. Ranci (eds.), *Dilemmas of the Welfare Mix: The New Structures of Welfare in an Era of Privatization* (pp. 77–108). New York: Kluwaer Academic/Plenum Publishers.

Taylor, S. and Bogdan, R. (1989). On accepting relationships between people with mental retardation and nondisabled people: Towards an understanding of acceptance. *Disability, Handicap, and Society*, 4 (1), 21–36.

Teeple, G. (2000). *Globalization and the decline of social reform*. 2nd ed. Toronto: Garamond Press.

Thompson, M., and Taras, D. (2004). Employment relations in Canada. On G. Bamber, R. Lansbury, and N. Wailes (eds.), *International and Comparative Employment Relations* (pp.)., 4th ed. Sydney: Allen & Unwin.

Traustadottir, R. (2000). Disability reform and women's caring work. In M. H. Meyer (ed.), *Care Work. Gender, Labour, and the Welfare State* (pp. 249–269). London: Routledge.

Tufts, S. (1998). Community unionism in Canada and labor's (re)organization of space. *Antipode*, 30 (3), 227–250.

Ungerson, C. (1999).'Personal assistants and disabled people: An examination of a hybrid form of work and care. *Work, Employment, and Society*, 12 (4), 583–600.

Valverde, M. (1995). The mixed economy as a Canadian tradition. *Studies in Political Economy*, 47 (Summer), 33–60.

Van Til, J. (2000). *Growing civil society: From nonprofit sector to third space*. Bloomington: Indiana University Press.

Westhues, A. (2003). *Canadian social policy. Issues and perspectives*. Waterloo, ON: Wilfred Laurier Press.

Yates, C. (2002). Expanding labour's horizons: Union organizing and strategic change in Canada. *Just Labour*, 1 (Winter), 31–40.

12 Outsourcing and the Australian Nonprofit Sector

Catherine McDonald
and Sara Charlesworth

INTRODUCTION

Australia has always had a mixed economy of welfare. As a consequence, it is easy to assume that recent developments in the relationship between the nonprofit personal social services sector (or as it is known in this country—the community sector) and the state are little more than a continuation of a well-established theme. This, however, is not really the case. A more accurate reading suggests that the impact of new public management (NPM)-inspired government policies and procedures on the sector has undercut what we here conceive of as its organising rationality. As we will demonstrate, this has led to a situation in which long-held sectoral beliefs in, and commitments to, fairness and justice have come into an uneasy alliance with imperatives to operate in a 'business-like fashion.' We characterise this as an example of a clash in institutional orders—between that of the traditional community sector and that of the emergent NPM-inspired community sector. It is a context where the relationships between organisations and their employees, although superficially constituted within discourses acceptable to the sector, are in reality now constituted in a manner more like the relations between capital and labour traditionally found in the for-profit manufacturing sector. However unlike employment in the manufacturing sector, wages and conditions in the community services sector are poorer and more precarious.

In this chapter we proceed as follows. First, we sketch the history of state-community sector relations, particularly the role the community sector plays in the delivery of personal social services in the Australian mixed economy of welfare. We illustrate how, with the breakdown of the Australian version of the Keynesian post–World War II welfare state, the role of the community sector has grown in significance, but not necessarily in substance. By this, we mean that whereas the levels of service delivery remain relatively unchanged, their significance in terms of the overall system of transfers from capital to labour developed in Australia has dramatically increased as other forms of transfer have weakened. Following this, we describe the impact of the application of the principles of

NPM. Specifically, we illustrate how the organisational rationalities that have emerged in the new 'business-like' community sector agencies clash with older rationalities informing their orientation, practices, and culture. Finally, we examine in some detail the impact of these developments on the working conditions of employees.

THE 'AUSTRALIAN WAY' AND INSTITUTIONAL CHANGE

Except for a brief three-year flurry of welfare state-building by the Whitlam Labour Government in the 1970s, Australian governments have rarely displayed much enthusiasm for welfare, preferring generally that people look after themselves or seek market solutions to needs they might have or difficulties they might experience. Instead, along with New Zealand, Australia adopted a unique model of redistribution which minimised government's institutional role. Specifically, through the three-pronged model of centralised wage fixing, tariff controls (protecting Australian industry), and an immigration policy that supplied a steady stream of labour, Australian wages generally were kept artificially high. This was symbolised in a particular Conciliation and Arbitration Court ruling in 1907 known as the Harvester judgment, in which Justice Higgins intoned that wages should be kept at a level to keep a man, his wife, and three children in *'a condition of frugal comfort by human standards'* (Rickard, 1984, 172). In this way the Australian system of redistribution via the wage system afforded government a minimalist role in providing income support to those (few) groups excluded from the labour market deemed worthy of support. Similarly, since colonisation Australia has relied on the nonprofit and charitable sector to provide a range of community or personal social services that elsewhere were and are provided by the state. In particular, although there are variations between the Australian states, the community sector has always worked collaboratively with governments to provide, for example, child welfare services, disability services, and aged services. In summary the 'Australian way' (Smyth and Cass, 1998) was, since the early years of colonisation, an institutional model wherein states relied on the private and nonprofit sectors in the economy to service the needs and maintain the well-being of the population.

That said, the retrenchment of the Australian version of the Keynesian welfare state over the last thirty years provides one of the starkest examples of the institutional re-configuration of the role of community services in the new regimes of welfare in liberal democratic states. As suggested above, Australia's labourist traditions of welfare expansion were dominated by the construction of the (male) wage earners' welfare state (Castles, 1983), representing a particular and quite specific version of the Keynesian welfare state. Within that regime, the enactment of an exclusionary form of social citizenship was operationalised through selected forms of redistribution and social protection that were located within the ambit of economic and industrial policy as opposed to social policy. Wearing (1994) goes so far as to describe the Australian style as one of industrial citizenship, in which associated benefits of social citizenship were institutionally distributed via predominantly male labour market participation. As a consequence, women's labour market participation with significantly lower levels of remuneration accorded women a lesser form of social citizenship, reliant in no small degree on services provided by the community or nonprofit sector; itself relying, in part, on governments for support.

THE GROWTH IN NONPROFIT COMMUNITY SERVICES

In 2007, the Australian Institute of Health and Welfare (AIHW) noted that the nonprofit community welfare sector provided services to the homeless and inadequately housed, to children and young people, to families, the aged, the disabled, refugees, and migrants. Both Commonwealth and State[1] governments have been significant in funding the growth of community services, particularly those delivered by the nonprofit sector. In 2006, the sector spent A$20.3 billion in service delivery (Australian Institute of Health and Welfare [AIHW], 2007, 315)—of which 62 percent came from governments, 25 percent from client fees, and 13 percent ($2.6 billion) from the sector itself. The expansion of nonprofit community organisations was over time progressively driven and, as shown above, partially funded by governmental programmatic responses to local needs, as was witnessed in the 1970s through the Australian Assistance Plan and the Community Health Programme. Similarly, responses to the housing and support needs of homeless people, reflected in the establishment of community based refuges and support services throughout Australia, has been possible because of the Commonwealth Government-funded Supported Accommodation Assistance Program introduced in the 1980s. At the same time, the Home and Community Care (HACC) Program was established, which provides a range of nonresidential support services to the aged and to people with disabilities. Both of these large programmes are jointly funded by the Commonwealth and the States, managed by the States, and delivered in the main by the nonprofit sector, with some for-profit provision.[2] These developments consequently highlight that the role of the state in community services is articulated within funding relationships between governments and service providers. They also illustrate the complexity of the mixed economy of service provision.

Furthermore, services funded under the HACC programme, as well as other aged care residential services (hostels and nursing homes), are one of the fastest-growing areas of employment in the nonprofit community services sector. Overall, in 2006, the community services employed 268,400 people, overwhelmingly women, a figure which had risen 18 percent from

2001 (AIHW, 2007). This growth is forecast to escalate dramatically over the next three decades.

Despite pressures for increased social policy expenditure and investment, Australia has become one of the lowest welfare spenders in the advanced world (Adema and Ladaique, 2009), largely because of the particular model developed (Castles, 1983 and 2001). Welfare in the form of income security was and continues to be selective and highly targeted as opposed to universal. Other traditional means of enacting social citizenship (education and health) continue to be functionally located in and delivered by the Australian states as opposed to the Commonwealth, the political entity from which Australian citizenship takes its legal meaning.

As we have illustrated, in the Australian arrangements, nonprofit community services were almost completely disarticulated from the primary redistributive mechanisms (that is, redistribution from capital to labour via legislated centralised wage fixing) and occupied a marginal, fragmented, and politically immaterial role. Accordingly, community services were not considered to play a core role in the postwar Australian welfare state and in addition were considered of lesser importance than other institutional arenas for the promotion of Australian social citizenship rights.

This situation has changed. Local versions of very familiar economic and political developments, such as microeconomic reform, entrenched unemployment, and an increasingly targeted and residualised public welfare system, have disarticulated the traditional institutional arrangements for the delivery of welfare. What we are witnessing is the process of re-articulating a new set of arrangements that, paradoxically, shift nonprofit community services from the margins to the very centre of the new political settlement being enacted—a settlement which has seen the state prioritise the interests of capital over labour. Specifically, two of the three prongs holding up the 'Australian way'—tariff protection and centralised wage fixing—have been dismantled. In terms of welfare the paradox is that whereas nonprofit community services are brought to the centre, they are left standing alone on the platform of a welfare state largely stripped of its supporting redistributive foundations. Because the role of community services in the emerging politics of welfare is so stark in the Australian context, it provides an excellent arena for the identification and articulation of both the opportunities and hazards inherent in similar developments elsewhere.

THE ORGANISING RATIONALITY OF NEW PUBLIC MANAGEMENT

Accompanying these institutional developments in the revamped Australian welfare state has been another set of pressures. These arise from the ubiquitous application of the principles of NPM, carried through by an accompanying set of practices. Of particular note is the impact of what is now mature purchase of service contracting in virtually every subfield of the personal social services. Once, governments funded the nonprofit community sector with block grants, with very limited conditions attached and with quite crude evaluation of how money was spent and how services were delivered. Now, after twenty years of practice, governments have learned how to engage in procurement with the nonprofit sector in ways which seriously curtail the autonomy of contracted organisations, and which dictate in very specific terms what forms of intervention organisations shall undertake. Sometimes, the contractual relationship is established through legislative means, and in the process, the risks of delivering personal social services are transferred to non-state locations and to the employees who work in them.

In a new system introduced in 2007, for example, the Victorian Government legislated that the primary arena of intervention into families considered to be 'at risk' is to be undertaken by nonprofit family support services. In general terms, the statutory authority charged with child protection has responsibility for the assessment of cases notified to it. After investigation and when no application for a protection order is made, the case is transferred to a 'secondary child and family service' (Office for Children, 2005). In Victoria, 6 percent of notifications result in a protection order (Office for Children, 2005), so intervention by Child Protection (the responsible statutory body) in the bulk of cases is time-limited and episodic.

For most families experiencing significant difficulties, therapeutic intervention and family support are undertaken by the nonprofit community services sector. The Department (the statutory authority), through the provisions of funding contracts, has enjoined the nonprofit organisations to connect with one another in localised service delivery systems. One organisation is nominated as lead agency, which takes referrals from Child Protection, assesses their needs, and manages further referral for intervention to one of the other partner organisations. If there is no 'space' in the system, the lead agency or another contracted for the task has the role of 'managing' the case until intervention is able to commence. By definition, these are high-risk cases, yet, as they wait for assistance to lower that risk, the nonprofit organisation 'managing' these families inevitably faces what may well be an escalating risk of harm occurring to the notified children *because* there is no intervention. In this way, the political risks associated with 'failure' in child protection have shifted from the state to the nonprofit sector.

In this example (and there are many more), the model of intervention and the functioning of the nonprofit agencies are set by the contract. Furthermore, as a condition of funding, all agencies must conform to a uniform model of organisational management and must participate in 'quality assurance' processes. These processes are time intensive and extensive and model a particular mode of organisation which inevitably shapes all those organisations which participate. As was indicated above, the situation is made even more fraught in that government does not fully fund the services it buys. In the case of children's services, this means that agencies fund the shortfall themselves at the same time as they lose the discretion to spend their money on services and programmes of their own choosing.

In 2004, Spall and Zetlin reported on a large research project looking, in part, at the implications of purchase of service contracting on Australian nonprofit community service organisations providing disability services. They found that where contracting was vigorously pursued, organisations responded by becoming more entrepreneurial and developed business-like practices, strategies, and orientations. They also noted that the organisations still claimed a commitment to the traditional values of social justice. However, it was also found that entrepreneurial organisations were favourably disposed to commercialisation, partnering with the for-profit sector and the use of business management techniques. They suggest that these organisations might *'use decoupling to accommodate the contradictions between some beliefs and organisational systems and structures'* (Spall and Zetlin, 2004, 288). Spall and Zetlin also noted that one of the strategies that organisations used to manage income shortfalls was the increased casualisation of staff whereas previously, their commitments were to developing and maintaining a stable permanent workforce.

CONSTITUTING INSTITUTIONAL CHANGE

Earlier in this chapter we characterised the developments in the Australian welfare regime as institutional change. So too, we suggest, is the shift to entrepreneurial modes of operating. In doing so, we invoke a particular body of theory which provides a useful analytical framework for understanding the impact of the shifts on the organisations themselves. Drawing selectively on a set of concepts developed theoretically and refined empirically within the corpus of neoinstitutional theory (Powell and DiMaggio, 1991), we consider that the overall welfare regime brought into being through welfare reform functions as an institution. That is, it is a set of norms and expectations regulating the interaction of social actors—groups, agencies and individuals—in the promotion of 'welfare' (Bouma, 1998). Institutions are constituted by and reflected in fields, for example, the community services field. The developments in the Australian welfare state discussed above represent institutional change, the effect of which is to disrupt pre-existing field-level consensus by introducing new ideas and practices (Greenwood, Suddaby, and Hinings, 2002).

Neoinstitutional theory traditionally focuses on organisations (see Greenwood, Suddaby, and Hinings, 2002). Recently, neoinstitutional accounts have directed attention to institutional change processes that emphasise field-level variations in logics or cultural accounts (Aldrich 1999), which we call the organising rationality for the why and how of an organisation. The rationality accompanying the developments in state-community sector relations can be thought of as an institutional logic; a common meaning system that represents an array of material practices and symbolic constructs that constitute organising principles guiding activity within a field (Galvin, 2002). Institutional logics provide the rules of the game and shape what answers and solutions are both available and considered appropriate (Thornton and Ocasio, 1999).

The Weberian notion of 'value spheres' incorporated into neoinstitutional theory by Friedland and Alford (1991), which is nested within the overarching concept of the institutional logic or rationality of a field, is useful. They note that institutional fields can be pluralistic, with the result that multiple subrationalities can operate within them. Within the welfare field, traditional nonprofit community services promote a particular value sphere or substantive rationality—normally summarised as a commitment to social justice and fairness (Kalberg, 1980: Townley, 2002). They can be contrasted with the rationalities of the new institutional logic imported into the field by the developments in the welfare state and particularly through the application of NPM principles. Usually, such processes are characterised by both accommodation and resistance on the part of those organisations drawn in to the process. As we will demonstrate, both types of rationalities exist in nonprofit community service organisations and directly affect their employees.

Specifically, we suggest that the dominance of the ethic of care in the nonprofit community services sector has, in the past and to a certain extent still, authorised an approach to service delivery which emphasised the *care* part of care work, resulting in quite poor wages and conditions.

MARKET DYNAMICS AND PAID CARE WORK

Here we provide a brief overview of the main characteristics of employment in the community services sector before turning to examine how industrial institutions have constructed and remunerated paid care work within the context of a specific institutional order. Finally we consider how the marketisation of care work through the dynamics of NPM (or, we suggest in theoretical terms, the shift from one institutional order to another) has influenced the employment policies and practices of nonprofit organisations.

Overview of Sector Employment

The paid care workforce is highly gendered, with almost nine out of every ten care workers being female (Meagher and Healy, 2006), and as we discuss later, this gendered nature reinforces the institutional order of the field, a factor which has real material consequences for employees. Furthermore, it is a workforce which is ageing faster than the labour force as a whole (Meagher and Healy, 2005). Occupational groupings for care workers range from professionals (such as nurses and social workers) to intermediate service workers, (such as child care workers, personal care and nursing assistants). This latter group is the largest, making up almost two thirds of the total care workforce in community service industries. There is of course large variation between the different subsectors of community services and the different occupational groups employed in them. Nursing homes, for example, are far more likely to employ professional staff than are child care services, where more than 90 percent of workers are employed in an intermediate service work occupation (Meagher and Healy, 2006). In the aged care sector, meanwhile, there has been a shift toward the greater use of personal care workers and a reduced reliance on registered nurses over time, with personal care workers now making up 64 percent of workers in the sector compared to registered nurses, who make up just 17 percent of workers (Martin and King, 2008).

Well over half of all care workers work part-time, with female care workers much more likely than their male counterparts to work part-time hours (Meagher and Healy, 2006). A large proportion of those in the lower status occupations work very short hours. In 2006, almost a quarter of aged and disability care workers worked less than 20 hours a week (AIHW, 2009), with a fifth of community-based aged care workers working fewer than sixteen hours a week in community-based care (Martin and King, 2008). Indeed recent Australian Bureau of Statistics (ABS) data for the community services sector suggests a growing problem of female underemployment, larger than that for the total female workforce.[3] There is nevertheless a widespread belief (a feature of the institutional logic of the field) that this workforce *prefers* shorter and casual hours to accommodate their own familial caring activities (for instance, Dawe, Saunders, and Nguyen, 2008)

The casualisation of work in the sector is on the rise (ASU, 2007; Dawe et al., 2008) largely as a function of NPM, a powerful carrier of institutional change. In community-based aged care for example, 32 percent of community care workers were employed on a casual or contract basis in 2007 (Martin and King, 2008). Casual employment is, however, unevenly spread throughout the sector. Whereas residential aged care facilities are less likely to employ casuals than are community-based agencies, there has, however, been an increase in casual employment both for registered nurses and personal care workers in residential care, almost a quarter of whom were employed on this basis in 2007 (Martin and King, 2008).

Average wages in the community services sector are very low in comparison with those in other industries, and men earn more than women at any given level of qualification. This, we suggest, is clearly a function of the institutional order of the community services field which constructs care work as qualitatively different from other forms of work. Even *within* the community services sector, care workers earn substantially lower hourly rates of pay than non-care workers (Meagher and Healy, 2006). A recent profile of the wages in the community services sector by the Australian Fair Pay

Commission (AFPC) indicates that in 2006 women working in community services earned on average $20.40 per hour compared to $23.10 per hour in all industries (AFPC, 2008). Within community services there is considerable variation in hourly earnings, which is at least partly aligned with qualification level (Meagher and Healy, 2006). There is also a larger gender pay gap in community services than across all industries, which further reflects the gendering of occupations *within* community services (AFPC, 2008) as a highly influential feature of the institutional order of the field.

The Industrial Construction of Paid Care Work as 'Work'

The recognition of paid caring work as work is reflected in, and intertwined with, changes in the protection offered to employees via industrial regulation. These changes (ranging across all industries) have been a core part of the reconfiguration of the Australian welfare settlement—a process we suggested is the main carrier of institutional change in the community sector. At the same time as there has been an increase in female participation in the labour force there has been an erosion of the standard employment relationship (SER) over the last two decades with a growth of temporary and part-time work. The SER has been the bedrock of Australian labour regulation and is based on a concept of full-time permanent waged work, with industrial relations regulation and collective agreements addressing basic conditions such as working time and wages for such work (Campbell, 2008). This 'ideal worker' norm (Williams, 2000) has deep historical roots and in Australia can be traced back directly to the lingering influence of the Harvester decision outlined above. While the male breadwinner/female caregiver model assumed by Justice Higgins no longer reflects the increased participation of women in paid employment, nor indeed the growth of non-standard and part-time work, it remains a powerful 'imaginary' underpinning the devaluation of much of the paid work women undertake, particularly in the community sector.

Until the 1990s, many workers employed in the community services sector were excluded from Australian 'industrial citizenship,' including coverage by an industry award, minimum wage rates, and other employment conditions (Briggs, Meagher, and Healy, 2007). This anomaly reflects the extent to which the institutional order of the community sector characterised it as substantively *different* from other forms of work in other industries. Apart from those covered by occupation-specific awards such as nurses awards, or employed by local government or in 'health' services such as nursing homes and hostels, community services work has not historically been understood as 'work' to which industrial rights adhere. This is because:

> care work fits poorly within established conceptions of work and industry that underpin industrial institutions. These institutions employ wage-setting criteria that do not readily recognise the work community

services workers do. Especially the less visible dimensions of care work such as relationship building and use of self. (Briggs et al., 2007, 499).

Nevertheless, despite the resistance from government and from large nonprofit agencies funded by government to any industrial recognition of community services work that fell outside the award system, the fight for a Social and Community Services (SACS) Award was ultimately won in the New South Wales (NSW) jurisdiction in 1991. However, this was not before the very question of whether social work was an 'industry' (as opposed to a 'vocation') under the *Conciliation and Arbitration Act 1904* was decided in the affirmative by the High Court (Briggs et al., 2007). In the mid-1990s, the NSW SACS award was followed by the winning of similar awards in other States and territories.

Despite providing basic industrial protection for community service workers, these SACS awards significantly undervalued the paid care work they covered, possibly because the work was not considered to be real but more an extension of the (gendered) affective relationships existing within families and social networks. Indeed with the advent of enterprise bargaining in the early 1990s, the wages of the overwhelmingly award-reliant community services workers failed to keep pace with wage increases in many other industries. In a recent and revealing pay equity decision of the Queensland Industrial Relations Commission (QIRC), the factors contributing to the low wages and gendered undervaluation of paid care work in the nonprofit sector are clearly spelled out in an agreed statement of facts between the relevant union and employer associations (Queensland Industrial Relations Commission [QIRC], 2009). One of the main factors accepted by the parties is that government funding models directly contribute to the undervaluation of the work in the sector. In theoretical terms, the institutional order of the community sector legitimising a particular orientation to care work was carried not only by participants within the sector but also by significant others (for example, governments) on the boundaries of the field.

Four key reasons given in evidence before the QIRC for the cultural and gendered devaluation of care work concisely articulate the profound challenges in any industrial recognition of paid care work and indeed much of the Australian and international literature on this topic (for instance, England, 2005; Briggs et al., 2007; Meagher, 2007; Folbre, 2008). These reasons (neatly summarising the institutional logic of community services) were nominated in the QIRC decision as:

- Caring work is associated with the supposedly inherent caring skills of women;
- Both within the sector and the broader community, care work is seen as a vocation rather than an occupation;
- The evolution of the work from voluntarism and the continued widespread use of volunteers have complicated the assessment of the value of the work; and

- The nature of the client group can cause community services workers to compensate for shortfalls in funding by providing unpaid or underpaid work.

The QIRC provided for significant wage increases particularly for a number of professional occupations, such as crisis accommodation workers, to be phased in over two to three years. The QIRC decision was apparently influenced by the tacit agreement of the Queensland Government to meet the increased costs of wages in funding provided to the nonprofit agencies covered by the award in question. Such government recognition of increased wage costs incurred by wage movements in industry awards has, however, been uncommon in the community services sector. State governments asserted for many years that they were subsidising the 'good works' of charitable and other nonprofit organisations and in doing so implicitly defined care work in these organisations as different from similar work undertaken, for example, in statutory agencies. The effect of this is to reinforce the institutional order of the community sector wherein care work is not really work at all but something substantively different.

Indeed after the NSW SACS award came into existence, the NSW government initially refused to provide agencies with funding to cover the wages provided for in the award (Briggs et al., 2007). Inadequate government funding in turn underpins much of the resistance by nonprofit agencies to improved wages and conditions for paid care workers, a feature reflected in evidence before the QIRC and most recently in the submissions of nonprofit agencies to the Australian Industrial Relations Commission (AIRC) as part of a federal award modernisation process aimed at producing a single industrial award to cover most community services workers across Australia.

It is not only agency resistance to accepting the industrial citizenship of care workers that underpins poor wages and conditions but also, as noted in the QIRC decision, the deep ambivalence many community services workers have to pursing their industrial rights; a function we suggest which is also related to the institutional order of the field. In this case, one of the common 'rules of the game' is that caring is affective not instrumental and that people undertaking caring activity need 'special' dispositions. This ambivalence is reflected in the very low rate of union membership in the sector, which fell from 23 percent in 1994 to below 15 percent in 2007 (AFPC, 2008). As suggested above, there is a perception in many nonprofit agencies, shared by many care workers themselves, that 'money drives out love' and that care workers should be motivated not by the money they earn but by the good they do (Meagher, 2007). The content of paid care work thus shapes many workers' self-understandings in ways that may not reconcile with perceptions of industrial citizenship (Briggs et al., 2007). These self-understandings illustrate another means by which the institutional order of the field is produced and reproduced over time—in this case by workers as institutional agents. As we have demonstrated, the institutional order dominating the community services field is produced by a range of actors operating at different levels—regulators and funders; organisations themselves; and individual participants in those organisations. Enter New Public Management.

The Influence of NPM Processes on Employment Outcomes

In terms of employment in the community services sector, the focus of NPM on private sector management practices has seen the introduction of decentralised wage bargaining, individual employment contracts, performance-based pay, and downsizing (O'Donnell, Allan, and Peetz, 1999). Analysis of the Australian case suggests that when NPM reforms are introduced in the delivery of care services in the context of significant funding pressures, concerns about the quality of services and quality of employment emerge (Parker, Ryan, and Brown, 2000). As King puts it, outsourcing and tender requirements mean that organisations are contracted by and accountable to the state and federal governments (depending on the type of funding) for the amount, type, quality, and cost of their care services. The competition between agencies *'encourages them to become more focused on (or more distracted by) the efficient management of financial and human resources in order to meet huge demands on care services'* (King, 2007, 201). What often disappears from view in the implementation of this 'efficient management' is any focus on the rights or interests of paid care workers (or indeed of the people who use their services). Furthermore, in terms of the pre-existing institutional order of the field which valued the affective and voluntaristic dimensions of care, NPM has introduced a powerful wave of institutional change which swamped (and continues to swamp) the old institutional order of voluntaristic charity.

Whatever the impact of NPM, the link between inadequate government funding of outsourced care and the low wages and poor conditions in community services continues to be cited in almost every Australian study on the sector that touches on the issues of high turnover and the consequent need for the better attraction and retention of paid care workers (for example, Victorian Government, 2005; Productivity Commission, 2008; Australian Council of Social Service [ACOSS], 2009). Managers in nonprofit agencies report the problems of inadequate and conditional government funding on the quality of services, complaining about short staffing that is exacerbated by the low wages they can afford to pay care workers (AFPC, 2008). Despite this situation, which is intensified by the ageing of the population and the looming 'crisis of care,' improved wages and conditions simply do not appear on the broader policy agenda, suggesting that remnants of the pre-existing institutional order have melded with NPM-inspired processes of institutional change.

A recent study suggests that the impact of NPM in the Australian nonprofit sector has had profound consequences for employees' working conditions;

specifically low and inequitable pay rates, work intensification, increasing demands for documentation, and workplace violence (Baines, 2009). Workers' experiences reflect being caught between the competing rationality of a commitment to social justice (the dominant value sphere of the pre-existing institutional order) and the rationality of the lean work organisation characterising the agencies in which they work (the dominant value sphere of NPM-influenced institutional order). On the one hand, those interviewed felt positive about 'making changes, building, empowering, helping, trying new solutions, and, perhaps most importantly, working in ways that felt consistent with the values that initially drew them to the sector' (Baines, 2009, 8). On the other hand, they were frustrated by changes in the labour process that had increased the pace and volume of their work and by negative management responses to their requests for time to undertake advocacy or community development work, 'further undermining their capacity to work in tandem with their values' (Baines, 2009, 9).

The findings of this study are reflected in the QIRC decision, which found that government funding models in the nonprofit community services sector had directly contributed to the gendered undervaluation of care work, a situation which the Commission maintained would not be tolerated in predominantly male occupations or industries (QIRC, 2009). The QIRC also noted the consequences that follow the implementation of outsourcing in the sector. These consequences include difficulties in attracting and retaining staff when funding levels do not increase or when funding does not allow for increments within a salary level to be paid; the use of precarious employment arrangements when only short term or project funding is made available; staff not being remunerated in accordance with the classification level the organisation believes is appropriate for the work value of the position, or because the funding agency specifies the wage level an employee is to be paid; and provision is not made for the payment of overtime (QIRC, 2009).

The regulatory force of the marketisation of care has been in the recent past and continues to be intertwined with the normative force of gender and is as powerful in directly and indirectly structuring the wages and conditions of paid care work. Meanwhile, despite the campaigning of unions to improve the wages and conditions of care workers in the community services sector, real change seems unlikely given the lack of commitment of government at all levels to rethinking funding and service models, beyond those that depend on and assume the gendered undervaluation of paid care work. In theoretical terms, what we observe in this context is a partial remaking of the dominant institutional order of the field of community services which, while retaining a very particular orientation to care as a form of not-quite-work, is based ultimately in a form of voluntaristic devotion to the well-being of others. Currently, this is occurring within a context which demands further economies within funded community sector organisations and results in a continued undervaluation of caring work.

CONCLUSION

As we have illustrated, the poor pay and employment conditions of people working in the nonprofit community services sector are a unique combination of both past and recent history. The model of the mixed economy of welfare has ensured that the nonprofit sector is integral to the delivery of nearly all forms of personal social services. That same model was very much predicated on the role of charitable and voluntary endeavour in providing support and assistance to vulnerable people. In reality, the now defunct Australian wage earners' welfare state was highly gendered in that it revolved around the male labour force supporting women and children. It was also the main engine of redistribution from capital to labour and, unlike the British post–World War II welfare state, pushed personal social services to the margins.

Those conditions have changed as the pre-existing institutional order of the Australian welfare settlement enacted within a particular context of state-nonprofit relations in the delivery of community services has eroded. The 'Australian way' is defunct, and, for all intents and purposes, redistribution is now undertaken via service delivery in a number of state-delivered and state-funded domains such as health and education services. Joining them are community services. As we have also demonstrated, the sector, for a variety of historical reasons and because of the more recent depredations induced by NPM, has been unable to value itself and its employees as part of what is a large, and growing in terms of labour market importance, *industry*. Furthermore, we have suggested that part of the problem of developing such collective awareness is the long-standing refusal of Australian governments to increase expenditure in the sector, if only to the point of full costing, a refusal made possible by the strength of the prevailing institutional logic about what is care and what is work.

Finally, returning to a consideration of the implications of the impact of the Australian model of outsourcing on the future of the policy objectives underlying the externalisation of the delivery of public services on employment in the sector, we suggest that the future is troubled. This is particularly so in relation to sustainability. We know that the sector is large; we know that it is growing; we know that it has trouble attracting and retaining suitable staff. If we add into the mix the inevitable rise in demand for care work associated with the rapidly aging baby boomers, we suggest that the sector as it currently stands will not be able to cope. This, in turn, raises quite frightening concerns about the extent and quality of care that vulnerable older people in particular will receive in the very near future. Government responses to date largely involve invoking market solutions. The 'rationality' of the market, however, will never work well as a way of improving the quality of care precisely because it does not recognise the linkages between the quality of care and the quality of paid care work (Braithwaite, 2001).

NOTES

1. Australia is a federated political system wherein the Commonwealth of Australia is constituted by the State Governments of New South Wales, Victoria, Queensland, South Australia, Western Australia, and Tasmania as well as two territories, the Northern Territory and the Australian Capital Territory. The division of functions between the Commonwealth and the States is set out in the Australian Constitution. In general, the Commonwealth's role is provision of block and tied grants to the States, and the States regulate and fund the community sector.
2. A majority of nursing homes and long day care child care services are provided by the for-profit sector, whereas in-home care and care for people with disabilities are mainly provided by the nonprofit sector (Briggs et al., 2007, 517).
3. In May 2009, 16 percent of female community and personal services workers wanted and were available to work more hours than they currently do. This compares with 10 percent of female workers and 7 percent of male workers across all occupations (ABS, 2009).

BIBLIOGRAPHY

Adema, W., and Ladaique, M. (2009). How expensive is the welfare state? Gross and net indicators in the OECD: Social expenditure database (SOCX). *OECD Social, Employment, and Migration Working Papers*, No. 92. Paris: OECD Publishing.

Aldrich, H. (1999). *Organizations evolving*. Thousand Oaks, CA: Sage.

Australian Bureau of Statistics (ABS). (2009). *Australian labour market statistics*. Cat. No. 6105.0 July 2009.

Australian Council of Social Service (ACOSS). (2009). *Australian community sector survey: Report, 2009*, Vol. 1. National, ACOSS Paper 157. Sydney: Australian Council of Social Service.

Australian Fair Pay Commission (APFC). (2008). *Health and community services industry profile*. Research Report No. 2/09. Canberra: AFPC, Commonwealth of Australia.

Australian Institute of Health and Welfare (AIHW). (2009). *Health and community services labour force, 2006*. National Health Labour Force No. 42. Canberra: AIHW.

Australian Institute of Health and Welfare (AIHW). (2007). *Australia's welfare*. Canberra: AIHW.

Australian Services Union (ASU). (2007). *Building social inclusion in Australia: Priorities for the social and community services workforce*. Melbourne: ASU. Available at http://www.asu.asn.au/media/building-social-inclusion2007.pdf. Accessed 18 October 2009.

Baines, D. (2009). If we don't get back to where we were before: Working in the restructured nonprofit social services. *British Journal of Social Work*. Advance access published 29 January 2009, 1–18.

Bouma, G. (1998). Distinguishing institutions and organisations in social change. *Journal of Sociology*, 34, 233–245.

Braithwaite, J. (2001). Regulating nursing homes: The challenges of regulating care for older people in Australia. *British Medical Journal*, 323 (August), 443–446.

Briggs, C., Meagher, G., and Healy, K. (2007). Becoming an industry: The struggle of social and community service workers for award coverage, 1976–2001. *Journal of Industrial Relations*, 49 (4), 497–521.

Campbell, I. (2008). Australia: Institutional changes and workforce fragmentation. In S. Lee and F. Eyraud (eds.), *Globalization, flexibilization, and working conditions in Asia and the Pacific* (pp. 115–152). Oxford: Chandros Publishing.

Castles, F. G. (2001). A farewell to Australia's welfare state. *International Journal of Health Services.* 31 (3), 537–544.

Castles, F. G. (1983). *The working class and welfare.* Sydney: Allen and Unwin.

Dawe, S., Saunders, J., and Nguyen, N. (2008). *Vocational education and training and casual workers in the home and community care sector.* Adelaide: National Centre for Vocational Education Research.

England, P. (2005). Emerging theories of care work. *Annual Review of Sociology,* 31 (August), 381–399.

Folbre, N. (2008). Reforming care. *Politics and Society.* 36 (3), 373–387.

Friedland, R., and Alford, R. R. (1991). Bringing society back in: Symbols, practices, and institutional contradictions. In W. W. Powell, and P. J. DiMaggio, (eds.), *The new institutionalism in organisational analysis* (pp. 232–266). Chicago: University of Chicago Press.

Galvin, T. L. (2002). Examining institutional change: Evidence from the founding dynamics of U.S. health care interest associations. *Academy of Management Journal.* 45 (4), 673–696.

Greenwood, R., Suddaby, R., and Hinings, C. R. (2002). Theorising change: The role of professional associations in the transformation of institutional fields. *Academy of Management Journal,* 45 (1), 58–79.

Kalberg, S. (1980). Max Weber's types of rationality: Cornerstones for the analysis of rationalization processes in history. *American Journal of Sociology,* 85 (5), 1145–1179.

King, D. (2007). Rethinking the care market relationship in care provider organisations. *Australian Journal of Social Issues,* 42 (2), 199–212.

Martin, B., and King, D. (2008). *Who cares for older Australians? A picture of the residential and community based aged care workforce, 2007.* National Institute of Labour Studies, Adelaide: Flinders University. Available at http://nils.flinders.edu.au/assets/publications/NILS_Aged_Care_Final.pdf. Accessed 17 September 2009.

Meagher, G. (2007). The challenge of the care workforce: Recent trends and emerging problems. *Australian Journal of Social Issues,* 42 (2), 151–167.

Meagher, G., and Healy, K. (2006). *Who cares? Volume 2: Employment structures and incomes in Australia's care workforce.*, Paper No. 141. Sydney: Australian Council of Social Service.

Meagher, G., and Healy, K. (2005). *Who cares? Volume 1: A profile of care workers in Australia's community services industries.* Paper No. 140. Sydney: Australian Council of Social Service.

O'Donnell, M., Allan, C., and Peetz, D. (1999). *The new public management and workplace change in Australia.* Working Paper 126. Sydney: School of Economics, University of New South Wales.

Office for Children. (2005). *Protecting children: The next steps.* Melbourne:. Department of Human Services.

Parker, R., Ryan, N., and Brown, K. (2000). Drivers and outcomes of the new public management in three public sector agencies. *Journal of Contemporary Issues in Business and Government* 6 (2), 33–41.

Powell, W. W., and DiMaggio, P. J. (Eds.). (1991). *The new institutionalism in organisational analyses.* Chicago: University of Chicago Press.

Productivity Commission. (2008). *Trends in aged care.* Productivity Commission. Canberra: Commonwealth of Australia. Available at http://www.pc.gov.au/_data/assets/pdf_file/0004/83380/aged-care-trends.pdf. Accessed 21 September 2009.

Queensland Industrial Relations Commission (QIRC). (2009). *Queensland community services and crisis assistance award—State 2008*. Queensland Services Industrial Union of Employees and Queensland Chamber of Commerce and Industry Limited, Industrial Organisation of Employers, and Others (A/2008/5). Available at Accessed

Rickard, J. (1984). *H. B. Higgins. The rebel as judge*. Sydney: George Allen & Unwin.

Smyth, P., and Cass, B. (Eds.). (1998). *Contesting the Australian way: States, markets, and civil society*. Cambridge: Cambridge University Press.

Spall, P., and Zetlin, D. (2004). A sector in transition? A question of sustainability for community service organisations and the sector. *Australian Journal of Social Issues* 39 (3), 283–298.

Thornton, P. H., and Ocasio, W. (1999). Institutional logics and the historical contingency of power in organizations: Executive succession in the higher education publishing industry, 1958–1990. *The American Journal of Sociology*, 105 (3), 801.

Townley, B. (2002). The role of competing rationalities in institutional change. *Academy of Management Journal*, 45 (1), 163–179.

Victorian Government. (2005). *Disability services workforce study*. Melbourne: Department of Human Services.

Wearing, M. (1994). Disclaiming citizenship? Social rights, social justice, and welfare in the 1990s. In M. Wearing and R. Berreen (eds.), *Welfare and social policy in Australia: The distribution of advantage* (pp. 177–198). Sydney: Harcourt Brace.

Williams, J. (2000). *Unbending gender*. New York: Oxford University Press.

13 Contracting with Voluntary Service Agencies in the USA

Implications for Employment and Professionalisation

Steven Rathgeb Smith

In the United States, government contracting with voluntary agencies emerged in the 1960s as a central government strategy to address urgent social problems.[1] Indeed, government's primary response to a wide variety of social problems including emergency relief, AIDS, community living for the developmentally disabled and chronic mentally ill, job training for the disadvantaged, and foster care, has relied heavily upon government contracting. This reliance on contracting has in turn profoundly affected social policy, the governance and management of voluntary agencies receiving contracts, the staff and volunteers in these agencies, and the clients receiving services (Smith, 2010a; Smith and Lipsky, 1993).

This chapter examines the growth of contracting with voluntary agencies with a specific focus on social and health services and the impact on the staff and volunteers of voluntary agencies in these fields. The basic argument advanced by this chapter is that contracting tends to promote greater professionalisation within voluntary agencies but over time contracting also tends to place greater constraints on the discretion of professionals working in them. This has been abetted by changes in the structure of contracting that places greater emphasis on outcome evaluation, client choice, and competition. The first section of this chapter provides an overview of the development of contracting with voluntary agencies in the USA. The second provides a mapping of the current employment in USA voluntary agencies, and the third details the impact of contracting on employment, including its implications for agency management and public policy, the professionalisation of staff, and changes to employee discretion. The chapter concludes with a discussion of the future of employment in voluntary agencies given the trends in government contracting.

THE DEVELOPMENT OF CONTRACTING WITH VOLUNTARY ORGANISATIONS IN THE USA

Historical Overview

Contracting with voluntary agencies in the USA is actually a relatively recent development although government funding of such agencies has a long history. Indeed, public funding of voluntary social and health organisations dates to the earliest years of the American republic. For example, many hospitals and asylums from this period, such as McLean's Asylum near Boston and Massachusetts General Hospital, received significant public subsidies. In the mid to late 19ᵗʰ century, countless voluntary social service organisations were established, including Catholic Charities, Lutheran Social Services, Jewish Family Services, Goodwill Industries, the Salvation Army, and Volunteers of America. Many of these agencies received direct and indirect public subsidies from state and local government, although most voluntary social service agencies relied primarily upon private donations and fees to support their programmes. State and local government oversight tended to be minimal, and the federal government provided no subsidies whatsoever (Smith and Lipsky, 1993).

This pattern of modest public subsidies, informality in the government-agency relationship, and limited oversight by government of voluntary agency operations continued into the 20ᵗʰ century. The Depression did produce a big departure when the federal government was forced to provide emergency relief to millions of Americans, relying in part on voluntary agencies to provide aid with public funds. Nonetheless, this funding was temporary, so that, after World War II, the previous pattern of limited public funding of voluntary agencies, except in specific service niches such as child welfare, returned. Even into the 1950s, government funding of voluntary agencies was relatively informal; thus, government officials relied upon voluntary agencies to maintain accountability and to subsidise the cost of the service with private revenues, at least in part.

In short, formal contracting with voluntary agencies in the contemporary understanding did not exist. This situation changed dramatically in the 1960s with the advent of the 'War on Poverty' and a host of other federal social programmes. Many of these new federal initiatives established new social welfare organisations at the local level or depended upon existing social service agencies to add new programmes with government contracts. Notable examples include community action agencies, community mental health centres, child welfare agencies, job training programmes, Headstart, an early childhood education programme, and legal services for the disadvantaged. Federal funding to support these new programmes was given directly to local voluntary agencies in the form of contracts, or aid was channeled to state and local governments who then contracted with local voluntary agencies.

Many existing voluntary agencies were initially reluctant to accept government contracts, primarily because of concerns that government funding would undermine their mission and autonomy (Coughlin, 1965; Perlmutter, 1969). However, most agencies eventually accepted government contracts. This shift occurred for several reasons. First, some federal programmes employed matching funds so that a voluntary agency might be able to use a 25 percent donative match to obtain a 75 percent matching grant from the federal government. Thus at least initially, federal revenues allowed the expansion of existing services. Second, some of the early federal grant programmes had very loose accountability requirements so that voluntary agencies could accept the funds without onerous compliance requirements. Third, federal grants offered many agencies far more money than they could reasonably expect from private philanthropy and fees. Fourth, and relatedly, federal funding allowed voluntary agencies to reduce their dependence on private donations and fees, allowing agencies in some cases to increase their services to disadvantaged and very needy clients. And fifth, many federal programmes were structured as grants to state and local governments, who then contracted with voluntary agencies. Often, state and local government officials had established relationships with voluntary agencies such as Catholic Charities. With the advent of federal funding, government officials tended to continue these relationships and, at least initially, did not change the terms of the existing relatively informal agreements between the voluntary agency and government.

Significantly, government officials also needed to create new agencies in order to fulfill their programmatic objectives to meet the increased demand for service generated by the availability of substantial new federal money (Smith and Lipsky, 1993). These agencies such as community mental health centres frequently had grants and contracts directly with the federal governments.

Thus, federal social service spending soared in the 1960s and 1970s, primarily through contracts with voluntary agencies. The growth of contracting over time forced state and local governments to adapt and formalise their contracting procedures. Federal grant programmes included important programmatic regulations in relation to their standards and client eligibility. Furthermore, the sheer growth of contracting in social and related health services forced government agencies to rationalise a system that prior to the 1960s had been ad hoc and informal. Also, state and local government often had to establish contracting systems for entirely new agencies and services such as community mental health or job training.

Initially, state and local government established service contracts with elements of the earlier more informal system. For example, contracts typically did not have specific performance targets; instead, they simply requested information from agencies on their expenditures. In this sense, contracting was governed by the same line-item budget accountability that was characteristic of previous government-voluntary agency funding agreements. This type of accountability was also characteristic of the budget accountability for state and local departments.

In addition, contracts tended to be structured as cost-reimbursement contracts; thus, government would reimburse voluntary agencies for their costs based upon the contract. For instance, a child welfare agency with a $100,000 contract to care for foster children for one year would have to justify its costs in the contract submission. Once awarded, the state would divide the annual contract amount into regular allotments that were contingent on the satisfactory submission of the required paperwork including documentation on the services rendered.

On paper, the contract award process tended to be competitive. State and local governments issued Requests For Proposals (RFPs) inviting agencies to submit contract proposals. Once a contract was awarded, a provision for periodic re-bidding of the contract was sometimes part of the overall contracting procedures. In practice, though, agencies could depend upon keeping their contracts unless serious problems occurred.

Competition in the classic economic sense, then, did not typically exist in government contracting with voluntary agencies during this period. Many government administrators and line staff had close personal and professional relationships with the staff of voluntary agencies. Equally important, perhaps, government officials often faced a relative lack of agencies to offer services, especially during this buildup of federal (and state) funding of social programmes. For-profit human service agencies tended to be quite scarce, and many localities lacked a significant organisational infrastructure in social services and community-based health programmes. Indeed, except for the large urban areas, social services were dominated by the relative handful of voluntary agencies that had provided services for decades.

Thus, contracting for human services during this period tended to be predictable in the sense that contracts were rarely terminated and agencies could expect to be reimbursed for their costs, although delays in payments and haggling over reimbursement requests were common. In periods of government fiscal retrenchment, voluntary agencies might actually have their contracts cut or reduced, although the funding might eventually be restored. The overall predictability of the contracts was reinforced by the relatively low emphasis on outcomes and performance (except for the compliance with contract stipulations).

Diversification and Change in the Government— Voluntary Agency Relationship

The structure of contracting with voluntary agencies in social and health services started, however, to shift in the 1980s. Shortly after taking office, President Reagan won legislative approval for the consolidation of many federal grant programmes into block grants to state governments as well as substantial cutbacks in funding levels. Many voluntary service organisations especially community action and legal services agencies had their contracts sharply reduced very quickly (Gutowski and Koshel, 1982). As a result, the early to mid-1980s was a period of considerable turbulence for many voluntary agencies.

These federal cutbacks encouraged state and local governments as well as voluntary agencies to seek new sources of revenues. Many agencies increased their emphasis on private fundraising and donations. Yet another major change was refinancing of government contracts so that an agency would receive government funding from other sources than the declining federal programmes such as the Social Service Block Grant (SSBG). Consequently, child welfare agencies that previously received state dollars or SSBG funding for case management services for foster children would be reimbursed for these services through Medicaid for eligible clients. Eventually, eligibility for Medicaid was also broadened through new policies and legal decisions fueling an expansion of many community-based programs including home care and residential care (Government Accounting Office [GAO], 1981; 1984; 1995; Scarcella, Roseanna, Zielewski, and Geen, 2006).

In addition, new programmes at the federal level (such as the Ryan White Act for AIDS services) were also important sources of greater funding for contracting services to voluntary agencies. Furthermore, the welfare reform legislation of 1996 created a new programme, Temporary Aid for Needy Families (TANF), to replace the previous Aid for Families with Dependent Children (AFDC). Overall, the legislation produced a dramatic shift from a reliance on cash assistance for the poor to much greater use of services, especially contracted services with voluntary agencies, to help the poor and disadvantaged (Allard, 2009). Thus, government contracts with voluntary agencies for welfare-to-work, job training, counseling, child care, and transportation rose sharply in the years immediately after TANF implementation, even as some agency clients lost their benefits or faced new restrictions on cash assistance.

In recent years, the structure of contracting and government funding has also been changing. Increasingly, governments are utilising a mix of policy tools such as vouchers and tax-exempt bonds to support voluntary social and health agencies (Smith, 2010a; also, Salamon, 2002). For example, the Low Income Housing Tax Credit (LIHTC) was enacted in 1986 to promote the development of affordable housing. These tax credits are allocated to states on a formula basis and then awarded on a competitive basis to primarily voluntary housing agencies. Also, many tax credit awards are bundled with other funding sources and can include a formal partnership between a housing agency and other voluntary service agencies. Furthermore, the tax credits are typically combined with other public and private grants. Overall, the LIHTC programme has significantly boosted funding for voluntary housing agencies. Similarly, tax credits for individuals and families for the purchase of child care and community care services for dependent aged and disabled individuals has helped stimulate demand for more voluntary agency services.

Vouchers to support voluntary services have been on the rise as well. For example, in the 1960s and 1970s, most public funds for child care were distributed through formal contracts to voluntary organisations. Whereas voluntary agencies still receive contracts for child care, vouchers have become much more important, especially since the enactment of TANF.

Medicaid also figures prominently in this shift toward vouchers. Medicaid functions like a "quasi-voucher" because the eligibility for funding is tied to the client, and, increasingly, eligible clients are supposed to at least have input into the choice of their service providers. In practice, client choice is often quite restricted because clients must choose among providers who are willing and eligible to provide services. Also, government officials can directly and indirectly steer those eligible to specific providers.

One other notable policy tool of rising importance is a tax-exempt bond to support capital expenditures. (These bonds are issued by a municipal, county, or state government, and their interest payments are not subject to federal income tax, and in some cases, state or local income tax as well.) Large voluntary organisations such as hospitals and universities have used tax-exempt bond financing for their capital needs for decades. However, the use of tax-exempt bonds by voluntary service agencies providing social care is a relatively new development, reflecting rising service demand and the relative undercapitalisation of many agencies. Often, this bond financing is combined with other types of government support including contracts and tax-credits.

The implications of this more complicated and diversified funding for voluntary service agencies varies substantially. However, the alternatives to contracts such as vouchers tend to be less certain and predictable. For instance, vouchers are tied to users and not agencies; thus agencies have less control over their revenue. The LIHTC and tax-exempt bonds are usually one-time events that fund specific projects rather than ongoing funding for operations (as is typical of contracts). In addition, the shift to more diverse revenue streams increases the overall competitiveness of the funding environment. Tax credits and bond financing, for example, are woefully underfunded relative to the demand, creating intense competition among agencies for these funds. The growing role for vouchers means that agencies face pressures to actively market their services—and the quality of their programmes—to clients, their families, and the government administrators and professionals.

The growth in contracting with voluntary agencies (as well as for-profit agencies) has, meanwhile, encouraged government at all levels to push for greater levels of accountability. Many contracts are now 'performance based,' which typically means that voluntary agencies are not reimbursed unless they meet certain programmatic targets (Behn and Kant, 1999; Forsythe, 2001; Smith, 2010a; Smith, 2010b). Furthermore, state and local governments have imposed more rigorous financial management expectations and demanded more attention to outcomes. Some state governments have also conducted more frequent audits of their contract agencies and have increased their site inspections.

EMPLOYMENT AND AGENCY GROWTH

Contracting and the utilization of other policy tools—until the financial crisis hit in 2008—also fueled a growth of voluntary agencies, especially in social services and related community health services such as home health care and hospice care. Table 13.1 provides important detail on this growth from 1995 to 2005.

Table 13.1   Change in the Number of Reporting Voluntary Agencies in Social and
Related Health Services in USA by Category, 1995, 2000, 2005*

	Reporting Public Charities		
	1995	2000	2005
Human Services	63,528	81,043	100,436
Crime and legal related	3,818	4,956	6,044
Employment and job related	3,036	3,511	3,872
Food, agriculture, and nutrition	1,923	2,335	2,982
Housing and shelter	9,855	13,280	15,882
Public safety and disaster preparedness	2,191	3,455	5,068
Recreation and sports	11,904	17,439	24,519
Youth development	4515	5443	6501
Children and youth services	5,372	6,219	7,016
Family services	3,392	3,988	4,585
Residential and custodial care	4,654	5,032	5,388
Services promoting independence	5,920	6,766	7,813
Other human services	6,948	8,619	10,766
Health			
Treatment facilities––outpatient	1,654	2,020	2,343
Mental health	6,990	7,561	8,496

* Categories are as defined by the National Taxonomy of Exempt Entities
Source: National Centre for Charitable Statistics. Selected years.

This increase in the number of voluntary agencies has produced a steady
rise in employment in voluntary agencies in social and health services as
indicated in Table 13.2.

At the same time, as Table 13.2 also shows, employment growth in voluntary agencies has stagnated since 2002. Moreover, the employment in
for-profit service agencies rose significantly between 2002 and 2007. In
part, the growth of for-profit employment reflects the increase in government support for many community care services such as home care, where
for-profit firms may have advantages in terms of economies of scale and
access to capital. Increased government support and greater service demand
also helped encourage the expansion and establishment of many for-profit
child care agencies and community care programmes such as home care.

Importantly, the dependence on government funding among voluntary
agencies providing social and health care varies substantially. For services

Table 13.2 Employment Trends in Social Services, 1977–2007

	1977	*1997*	*2002*	*2007*
Type of service	*Employees*	*Employees*	*Employees*	*Employees*
Social Services				
Child day care**	189,918	627,711	751,733	851,624
Nonprofit	102,408	239,981	314,436	319,144
For-profit	87,510	387,730	437,297	532,480
Individual and family services*	182,947	762,779	907,796	1,147,521
Nonprofit	167,384	692,454	768,586	797,269
For-profit	15,563	70,325	139,210	350,252
Job training and vocational***	151,525	301,742	317,045	304,836
Nonprofit	138,368	269,738	283,655	272,850
For-profit	13,157	32,004	33,390	31,986
Residential care*	184,770	412,874	655,989	735,768
Nonprofit	135,144	240,732	483,985	539,803
For-profit	49,626	172,142	149,651	171,175
Miscellaneous social services [a]	144,762	143,281	145,929	164,633
Nonprofit	133,169	143,281	144,498	158,382
For-profit	11,593	n.a.	1,431	6,251
Subtotal, social services	853,922	2,248,387	3,034,499	3,495,143
Nonprofit	676,473	1,586,186	2,048,745	2,147,498
For-profit	177,449	662,201	985,754	1,347,645

* 2002 NAICS data not comparable to SIC data (cannot be estimated within 3% of SIC data).
** 2002 NAICS data almost comparable to SIC data (within 3% of sales or receipts from SIC).
*** 2002 NAICS data is comparable, or derivable, from SIC data.Source: U.S. Census Bureau. *Selected Years. Economic Census.*

such as community care for the disabled or workforce development, dependence upon government funding is very high, whereas in services fields such as emergency assistance, voluntary agencies rely upon a mix of public contracts and private donations (National Centre for Charitable Statistics [NCCS)], 2010). Given the importance of government contracts to voluntary agencies providing social and health services, the financial crisis and the problems with government revenues have led to severe cut-backs for many organizations, with staff layoffs and reductions in pro-gramme services.

CONTRACTING AND THE EFFECTS ON STAFF
AND VOLUNTEERS OF VOLUNTARY AGENCIES

Despite the uncertainty of government revenues, the resources gained by a voluntary agency through contracts can be quite welcome, given the challenges of raising private donations and earned income. But government contracting can have quite complex and profound effects on the staff and volunteers of voluntary agencies. In part, these effects are rooted in differences in organisational norms between government and voluntary agencies. Wilson (1967) observed that organisations are guided by five critical imperatives: equity, efficiency, responsiveness, fiscal integrity, and accountability. But voluntary agencies and government weigh these criteria differently. Voluntary service agencies are typically created by 'communities' of people interested in a particular problem or cause, such as community development, homelessness, or juvenile delinquency. Thus, the volunteers and staff of the nonprofit view the first priority as being responsive to this community (Smith and Lipsky, 1993). A community mental health centre may regard its primary responsibility as serving people with mental health problems in a defined geographic area. Or a halfway house for youth may regard its primary constituency as at-risk youth who have not been involved in serious criminal activity.

The primacy placed on responsiveness can lead to conflict with government because government places greater emphasis on equity as a guiding norm. Government officials face the challenge of justifying their allocation decisions given that the demand for government funding and services inevitably exceeds supply. Consequently, government officials are pressured to develop equitable and fair standards to guide their allocation decisions. These standards are especially evident in social services where government has increasingly strict standards of eligibility. For instance, government funded welfare-to-work programmes require that the contract agency only serve clients who are eligible under the TANF guidelines. Similarly, Medicaid funded programmes for the mentally ill have very strict eligibility requirements for who is eligible to be served as well as very specific expectations on reimbursable services (Smith, 2010a).

Over time, the government-nonprofit relationship can be regarded as a 'contracting regime' whereupon government and nonprofit agencies develop a common set of assumptions to guide their relationships. The regime concept suggests that two parties are mutually dependent upon each other so that each party cannot easily exit the relationship. However, an equally important aspect of regimes is that one party is typically much more powerful than the other. In the case of contracting regimes, government tends to be the more powerful partner and is in a position to dictate programmematic and financial expectations even in the face of opposition from the contract agencies (Smith and Lipsky, 1993; also, Considine, 2003; Considine and Lewis, 2003). For example, the state Department of Social Services and its contract workforce development agencies may develop specific norms about acceptable practice, referral policies, and reimbursement rates. These norms then guide the behaviour and strategic management of the state agencies and the providers. In this relationship, government is able to drive the evolution of these norms given their resources and political influence and the relative absence of alternative funding sources for their programmes.

PROFESSIONALISATION

Expectations by government for its contract agencies are an important contributing factor to the professionalisation of voluntary agency staff. This push for professionalisation has a number of components. First, government contracts increasingly reflect standards of professional practice in a particular service field such as mental health or drug treatment. Thus, in order to even be considered for the contract, a voluntary agency has to agree to adhere to accepted standards of professional practice even if the standards require the addition of new and different staff (or the training of existing staff). This shift is especially noticeable in voluntary organisations created through volunteer community initiatives, which view their primary responsibility as providing a service to a target group such as at-risk youth but without regard necessarily to external standards. Indeed, many voluntary organisations are founded as alternatives to existing and more traditional professional services.

Professionalisation also occurs because of the performance management regimes implemented by government (as well as private foundations). As noted, government increasingly expects detailed programmematic and administrative accountability of its contract agencies. In order to meet these expectations, voluntary agencies need to have qualified professionals who understand programme evaluation, IT systems, financial management, and strategic planning. For smaller community organisations, these professional expectations may require a complete revolution in the management of the organization, including the hiring of an executive director with different educational and professional qualifications and the investment of additional resources in the administrative infrastructure of the organisation.

The trend toward professionalisation is also evident in the increased hiring by voluntary agencies of professionals or the selection of board members with government administrative or programme experience. Today, many social and health agencies have executive directors who have previously held important government positions. Board members can now include prominent local leaders with credibility and legitimacy to influence government policy. Of course, individual agencies will vary in the extent to which they have staff with previous government experience; in general, the larger agencies and/or agencies with substantial dependence on government contracts are more likely to seek professionals with government experience.

Hiring staff with government experience is a very public acknowledgment that government contracting is a long-term relationship for many voluntary agencies. Government contracts fund many ongoing services such as child protective services, community programmes for the developmentally disabled and mentally ill, home care for the elderly, and welfare-to-work programmes. To be sure, the certainty of funding is often very unclear and unpredictable, and since the financial crisis, funding has been cut sometimes quite drastically for many agencies. Nonetheless, agencies tend to have long-term relationships with government and are expected to be able to weather the cyclical nature of government funding. As a result, voluntary agencies, if they are to be effective and sustainable, need to invest in their staff with the goal of building productive long-term relationships with government; staff with government experience can be of great assistance.

The movement of professionals back and forth between government and voluntary (and for-profit) service agencies also tends to promote a consensus on programmatic standards among government and voluntary agencies. Thus voluntary agency staff tend to structure the organisation in a way that will position them to obtain government contracts. Voluntary agency executives place emphasis on many of the same priorities and requirements as government contract administrators: sound financial management (including annual audits), attention to outcome evaluation (including the use of current programme evaluation models such as logic models, up-to-date tracking of clients and services, and a good reputation in the local community).

This impact of contracting is consistent with the predictions of institutional theorists including Powell and DiMaggio (1983), who suggested that organisations in a particular field (such as child welfare) are subject to powerful isomorphic tendencies that push organisations to become more similar. Voluntary agencies with government contracts tend to adopt similar internal practices in order to compete effectively for government contracts; moreover, they are in many cases required by the stipulations of the contract to abide by detailed financial and programmematic regulations (Considine, 2003). Isomorphic tendencies fit with the contracting regime idea whereupon government and voluntary service agencies develop norms and practices that guide their behavior. Shared professional standards are often part of this contracting regime. However, organisations with certain cultures or histories may resist these isomorphic tendencies, especially if government contracts are a relatively small part of their overall revenue or if they provide low-intensity services where government regulations are less intrusive and extensive (for instance, emergency assistance).

Professionalisation is further evident in the changing role of volunteers within voluntary agencies receiving government contracts. Volunteers can play many different roles including board members, support for fundraising campaigns, direct service with agency clients, and advocacy on behalf of the agency. Over time, professionalisation attendant to government contracts restructures the roles and responsibilities of volunteers. In regard to the board, contracting can pose serious challenges. The board of directors serve as the connecting link between the voluntary agency and the local community. This board role is especially critical if community-based service agencies are to effectively represent their communities and service users. Many board members of smaller and/or newer organisations tend to be unfamiliar with the intricacies of contracting. Consequently, board members can find it very difficult to exercise effective oversight over agency contracts. Thus, the board may be relegated to a position of supporting the executive's initiatives, especially as they pertain to government contracts, rather than the executive implementing the board's directives and policies. The danger for the organisation inherent in this power dynamic is that the board may encounter some unpleasant surprises. For example, the executive, in the pursuit of contract revenues, may obligate the agency to contracts that are underfunded or ill-advised. Board involvement in the agency may also wither as board members find that their governance roles are quite restricted. As board involvement declines, management mistakes or morale problems may go undetected until a crisis develops.

Other types of management problems may develop because of conflicts over agency mission. For example, the board of relatively young nonprofits may be made up of the founding members of the organisation who are deeply committed to a specific mission and vision. In some cases, the executive may try to steer the organisation in a direction that is quite different from the board's vision for the agency. The result may be conflict or protracted negotiations between the board and staff about the agency's future. Sometimes, the outcome is the resignation of some board members or the ousting of the executive as the board and staff try to define the agency's mission. Alternatively, the executive may be the driving force in agency governance until a crisis develops, such as inadequate cash flow, staff discontent, or lost contracts. In response, the board may exert greater control and oversight over agency operations, although the board often withdraws to its previous role as the crisis eases. In other cases, the board may be unable to find an appropriate executive director in the short term, so that the board retains an important role in day-to-day agency management and the overall agenda setting for the organisation and puts an interim executive director in place.

Despite the challenges of board governance in voluntary agencies with contracts, many boards have successfully addressed the organisational challenges of contracting in ways that strengthen board governance and productive board-staff relations. First, a board can recruit individuals with knowledge of contracting for board membership. Second, the board can become more engaged in advocacy on behalf of the agency with government officials—a process that can help provide members with valuable information on the agency's contracts and relevant government regulations. Third, the board can broaden its membership. Often this effort includes adding more professionals including lawyers, accountants, and high-tech entrepreneurs. The effect is to "professionalise" the board and to reduce the influence of members without professional qualifications and background. To be sure, this professionalisation does not necessarily need to occur. So for example, the board may choose to enlarge itself and retain significant community representation while adding new members with additional skills. Some organisations even require that any new members volunteer a significant amount of time in the agency prior to consideration for board membership (Saidel and Fletcher, 2005). Indeed, community participation in agency governance can be critical to effective management and governance (Smith, 2010b).

Another development is the changing backgrounds and qualifications of the executives of voluntary contract agencies. In social and health care, the norm for an agency executive until relatively recently was an individual who began a career as a clinician and gradually gained administrative experience. Today, executives are much more likely to have received formal training in management, particularly from schools of public administration, and less frequently from business (Hwang and Powell, 2009). More professional managers have in turn reinforced the professionalisation of other aspects of voluntary agency governance including the oversight and training of volunteers; the recruitment of board members; and the role of direct service staff.

The impact of professionalisation is also apparent in the changing roles of volunteers within voluntary agencies. At their inception, many voluntary service agencies are entirely volunteer organisations with volunteers or relatively low-paid staff. A good example would be a community organisation devoted to reducing teen delinquency. These volunteers might do advocacy to call attention to the problem as well as to direct service with at-risk youth. After these organisations receive government contracts, they have money to hire paid staff to provide more extensive services with more qualified personnel in place. Thus, the volunteer role tends to shift to support roles such as fundraising support and special events, board service, and outreach to the community. Exceptions to this general tendency are programmes such as emergency assistance where the direct service role of volunteers remains important.

Professional management has also brought a new approach to managing employees, including a shift to more flexible personnel policies reflecting in part greater attention to carefully managing costs and risk management (Herman, 2009; also, Young and Tippins, 2001). This rising importance of risk management reflects, in part, the process of organisational growth and development—greater organisational complexity, regardless of the revenue source, tends to drive changes in management (Carlson and Donahue, 2003). More professional management in concert with the turbulent contracting environment tends to encourage agencies to move to more contingent personnel policies. The hallmark of voluntary service agencies prior to the advent of competitive contracting was full-time employment, often with substantial benefits. Staff tended to stay at agencies for a very long time, especially within larger service agencies offering the opportunity of upward employment mobility. Whereas this emphasis on full-time employment remained during the initial wave of contract funding in the 60s and 70s, it is increasingly under siege. In response to the sometimes sharp cutbacks in funding, voluntary agencies, especially agencies providing more routine services such as home care, are relying to a much greater extent on part-time employees or contract employees who work on an "as needed" basis. Typically these workers do not have the same salary and benefit package as full time employees. Voluntary agencies in these service categories also can face intense pressure from for-profit agencies that tend to pay lower wages and benefits.

CONTRACTING AND EMPLOYEE DISCRETION

Many scholars have called attention to the importance of discretion in the delivery of public and voluntary services (Lipsky, 1980; Sosin, 2010; Brodkin, 1986; Hasenfeld, 2000). In general, discretion refers to the capacity of workers to act with autonomy toward clients, which usually means the ability to act independent from the demands and expectations of authorities (Jewell, 2007; Sosin, 2010). Furthermore, voluntary agencies may arguably offer workers and volunteers more autonomy than other forms of organisation. Public organisations are subject to bureaucratic rationality that places constraints on employees and requires them to be accountable to multiple stakeholders within and outside the organisation. For-profit organisations operate with a different type of accountability: efficiency and the profit motive. Moreover, workers are accountable to owners including, in the case of publicly traded companies, their stockholders. By contrast, voluntary organisations in their pure type are only accountable to their members or target group. A couple of examples illustrate the point. A self-help group of recovering alcoholics is likely to be an informal group of individuals with no external accountability to government or for-profit organisations, operating with a lack of hierarchy. Likewise, neighbourhood associations are typically started by neighbourhood residents concerned about the quality of life in their communities and also lack bureaucratic accountability or accountability to owners broadly defined.

Arguably, professionals and volunteers who are committed to a particular cause (for instance, neighborhood revitalisation or emergency assistance) or target group (for example, domestic violence victims or at-risk youth) are attracted to the nonprofit form because of the potential for a commitment to the client that is less constraining than other forms of organisation (Majone, 1984). Thus, paid employees and volunteers may have the opportunity for broad discretion in responding to client needs, subject to staff and resource restrictions. Self-help groups do not have to worry about eligibility standards, and the volunteers in a church soup kitchen may be able to respond to client need without regard to immigrant status or income levels.

Voluntary agencies and their representatives have often portrayed the lack of accountability to government or owners—or 'autonomy' as it is often dubbed—as a valued and important trait. In this view, voluntary agencies and their employees can make decisions in the best interests of their clients or foster social change, innovation, and reform. In the 1960s, some advocates invoked the importance of organisational autonomy to caution against accepting government funding and contracts, for fear that funding entanglements with government would compromise the mission of voluntary agencies (Coughlin, 1965). However, other scholars at the time also criticised the autonomy of voluntary social welfare agencies— and by implication the discretion of agency employees—because of their discriminatory and inequitable practices toward vulnerable and disadvantaged clients that resulted from their lack of broader accountability to the public (Cloward and Epstein, 1965; Kahn, 1962; Billingsley and Giovanni, 1972).

Despite the concerns of scholars such as Coughlin about the potential problems with contracting on agency autonomy and discretion, some scholars initially concluded that government funding did not substantially interfere with agency autonomy (Perlmutter, 1969; Kramer, 1982 and 1987). In this view, government and voluntary agencies were mutually dependent upon each other: voluntary agencies were dependent upon government for funding and government was dependent upon voluntary agencies to provide services. Consequently, neither side could take advantage of the other.

As previously stated, however, the recent period has seen the emergence of the contracting regime structure whereupon government is the more powerful partner in the relationship, with voluntary agencies receiving contracts. Indeed, the pressure to hold contractors to a higher standard of accountability is pushing government to implement increasingly stringent forms of monitoring and regulation over voluntary agencies. For example, performance contracting is quite common in many service fields such as mental health and child welfare (Behn and Kant, 1999; Smith, D., 2009; Smith, S. R., 2010b). Importantly, performance contracting can be conceptualised as a strategy to control the discretion of 'street-level' workers in voluntary agencies (see Lipsky, 1980). The implicit assumption of performance contracting is that a mismatch can exist between the priorities of government and the staff of voluntary agencies. Thus, government needs to provide financial incentives through the reimbursement process to focus on key government priorities such as placement with a permanent family (for instance, foster care) or the attainment of full-time employment (for example, welfare-to-work programmes).

From the government's perspective, then, discretion by workers in voluntary agencies is a potential problem because workers may be able to use their discretion to subvert the implementation of government policy priorities. However, the staff of voluntary agencies often contend that performance contracting is too narrowly targeted and can prevent workers from using their knowledge of clients and the local service system to offer the most effective service. Workforce development contracts offer a good example. The professional staff in a voluntary agency may believe that, in order for a person to be in a position to obtain and keep a full-time job, specific training and support services are required, including perhaps providing counseling for on-job skills. However, performance contracting typically neglects this more holistic approach to services and instead focuses on the job placement.

In essence, performance contracts are a standardised approach to service delivery, whereas the staff of voluntary agencies might ideally prefer to tailor services to individual needs. As Elmore (1979–80) noted, this more individual approach takes advantage of the local knowledge of street-level workers. Their decision-making discretion is shaped by the organisational culture and history, so that workers interpret the needs of their clients not only through the lens of their professional training but also through the mission and culture of the agency which tends to emphasise certain norms, beliefs, and practices (Sosin, 2010).

Performance contracts of course do not eliminate discretion and indeed can sometimes have inadvertent and unintended results that undermine the attainment of government goals. For instance, performance contracts can encourage voluntary agencies to practice 'creaming,' whereupon voluntary agencies choose clients with a high degree of probable success in meeting performance targets (Smith and Lipsky, 1993; Behn and Kant, 1999; Considine, 2003). Furthermore, many of the clashes between government and voluntary agencies and their representatives are rooted in disagreements on the proper level of discretion within voluntary agencies with contracts. For instance, government may try to control the process of service delivery and by implication agency output, by controlling the inputs such as client referrals and eligibility standards. Complaints from voluntary agencies about the burden of too many regulations often are a reaction to efforts to constrain the decision-making authority of voluntary agencies through regulation.

Innovation in contract design has sometimes tried to address this tension on discretion. The state of Oklahoma instituted a different payment system for contract agencies called the Milestones Reimbursement System, whereupon the state decided to reimburse contract agencies for outcomes and to allow agencies discretion on the method to reach these outcomes (Rosengrant, 1998; Frumkin, 2001). This system requires extensive collaboration between government and voluntary agencies on the appropriate outcomes and an agreement that government regulation will shift from controlling the process of service delivery to more focus on the outcomes. Many less formal, but similar contract reforms exist around the country.

The impact of heightened accountability expectations for the discretion of workers in voluntary agencies is also apparent in the professionalisation of volunteer management. One of the challenges of volunteer management is the wide variation in skills, aptitude, and motivation. But judicious matching of volunteers' skills with positions, careful screening and selection, and ongoing training and oversight are currently emphasised as a strategy to improve the quality of volunteering (McCurley, 2002). This shift can have positive benefits for clients because it can reduce the unpredictability and unevenness of volunteer services, especially in services requiring skilled individuals such as mentoring at-risk youth.

Reducing worker discretion is also evident in the enthusiasm for the implementation of new professional standards of care such as evidence-based practice. For example, the state of Oregon has mandated that an increasing percentage of the public dollars spent on contracted services (primarily with voluntary agencies) should be in support of agencies employing evidence-based practice (Oregon Department of Human Services, 2009). The main intention of the evidence based practice movement is to promote the integration of practice informed by research into the delivery of services in order to improve effectiveness. Key service decisions with clients would thus be guided by evidence-based practice norms, reducing the extent to which agency staff and volunteers could use their own judgment in programme implementation. Thus, drug treatment programmes would use the latest evidence based strategy to interview clients and assess their needs, creating more uniformity and, it is hoped, more positive outcomes for clients.

CONCLUDING THOUGHTS

Despite the fiscal crisis facing state and local government, voluntary agencies are likely to continue to be very prominent in contracting with government for key social and health services. Fiscal constraints will encourage government to seek ways to lower service costs, and contracting is perceived as a strategy to achieve this goal. The widespread attention to social innovation and entrepreneurship will keep voluntary agencies in the spotlight as agents of social reform and innovation. Indeed, the Obama administration has been able to raise $45 million from several foundations to help support the Social Innovation Fund (SIF) that will give grants to promising voluntary organisation programmes (Corporation for National and Community Service, 2010). Relatedly, the broad interest in voluntarism and community service ensures that government will continue to support voluntary agencies in order to promote civic engagement and community building.

But the financial crisis is squeezing many voluntary agencies, even as they are profiled for their contributions to the community. Thus, voluntary agencies are likely to continue to attract millions of young people for service and volunteering; but the paid staff of voluntary agencies will also face serious challenges including heightened expectations on accountability; pressure on wages and benefits from competition and insufficient funding levels; and organisational instability, especially among smaller organisations. And even after the current fiscal crisis abates, contract funding will very probably be insufficient to fully cover agency costs and meet the continued demand for an array of voluntary services, including community care for the disabled and aged, child care, workforce development, and substance abuse treatment.

Thus, voluntary agencies will need to adapt their management and organisational structure to emphasise flexibility, performance, and efficiency while retaining a commitment to equity, social justice, and community support and engagement. This effort will require an ongoing investment in training and education by voluntary agencies because sustainability and employee satisfaction will need an adequate infrastructure, an effective board of directors, trained professionals, and a solid revenue base. Given these trends, larger agencies will have an edge in attracting and retaining qualified employees. Smaller and newer voluntary agencies will need to think carefully about the potential for collaboration with other voluntary agencies or even merger with other agencies.

Overall, the staff and volunteers of voluntary agencies receiving government contracts are more important than ever in providing valued public services to the citizenry. In many areas of the country, voluntary agencies are the only organisations providing key services such as emergency assistance, community care, or workforce development. Workers in voluntary agencies are the new street-level bureaucrats (Lipsky, 1980), who play a central role in the access and utilisation of public services by the citizenry, especially social and health services. Indeed, government contracts with voluntary agencies are one of the principal vehicles by which the welfare state has expanded in the USA (Smith and Lipsky, 1993; Smith, 2010a; Allard, 2009). As such, the entire citizenry has an enduring interest in the quality, motivation, and effectiveness of the staff and volunteers of voluntary agencies. Government and voluntary agencies will need to make continuing and sustained investments in these paid and volunteer employees in the coming years in order to provide quality public services to the citizenry.

BIBLIOGRAPHY

Allard, S.W. (2009.) *Out of reach: Place, poverty, and the new American welfare state*. New Haven: Yale University Press.

Behn, R.D., and Peter A. K. (1999). Strategies for avoiding the pitfalls of performance contracting. *Public Productivity and Management Review*, 22, 4 (June), 470–489.

Billingsley, A., and, Giovannoni, J. D. (1972). Children *of the storm: Black children and American child welfare*. New York: Harcourt Brace.

Brodkin, E. (1986). *The false promise of welfare reform: Implementing quality control in welfare*. Philadelphia: Temple University Press.

Carlson, M., and Margaret M. (2003). *The executive director's survival guide: Thriving as a nonprofit leader*. San Francisco: John Wiley.

Cloward, R. A., and Epstein, I. (1965). Private social welfare's disengagement from the poor: The case of family adjustment agencies. In Mayer N. Zald (ed.), *Social welfare institutions: A sociological reader* (pp. 623–644). New York: John Wiley and Sons.

Considine, M. (2003). Governance and competition: The role of non-profit organisations in the delivery of public services. *Australian Journal of Political Science*, 38 (1), 63–77.

Considine, M., and Lewis, J. M. (2003). Bureaucracy, network, or enterprise? Comparing models of governance in Australia, Britain, the Netherlands, and New Zealand. *Public Administration Review*, 63 (2) (March/April), 131–140.

Corporation for National and Community Service. (2010). *Investing in innovative community solutions*. Available at http://www.nationalservice.gov/pdf/10_0527_sif_fact_sheet_final.pdf. Accessed 15 July 2010.

Coughlin, B. J. (1965). *Church and state in social welfare*. New York: Columbia University Press.

Elmore, R. F. (1979–1980). Backward mapping: Implementation research and policy decisions. *Political Science Quarterly*, 94 (4), 601–616.

Forsythe, D. .W. (Ed.). (2001). *Quicker, better, cheaper? Managing performance in American government*. Albany: The Rockefeller Institute Press.

Frumkin, P. (2001). *Managing for outcomes: Milestone contracting in Oklahoma*. PricewaterhouseCoopers Endowment for Business in Government. Available at http://www.businessofgovernment.org/sites/default/files/ContractinginOklahoma.pdf. Accessed 10 May 2010.

General Accounting Office (GAO). (1995). *Medicaid: Spending pressures drive states toward program reinvention*. Washington, D.C.: The U.S. Government Accountability Office (GAO). Available at GAO/HEHS-95-122. http://www.gao.gov/archive/1995/he95122.pdf. Accessed 10 May 2010.

General Accounting Office (GAO). (1984). *States use several strategies to cope with funding reductions under social services block grant*. HRD-84-68. Washington, D.C.: The U.S. Government Accountability Office (GAO). Available at http://archive.gao.gov/d6t1/124882.pdf. Accessed 10 May 2010.

General Accounting Office (GAO). (1981). *Intertitle transfers—A way for states to increase federal funding for social services*. HRD-81-116. Washington, D.C.: The U.S. Government Accountability Office (GAO).

Gutowski, M. F., and Koshel, J. J. (1982). Social services. In J. L. Palmer and I. V. Sawhill (eds.), *The Reagan experiment* (pp. 307–328). Washington, D.C.: The Urban Institute.

Hasenfeld, Y. (2000). Organizational forms as moral practices: The case of welfare departments. *Social Service Review*, 74 (3), 329–351.

Herman, M. L. (2009). Unmasking the discipline of risk management. *Risk Management Essentials*, 18 (3) (Fall), 1, 10–12. Available at ttp://www.nonprofitrisk.org/library/newsletter/091009.pdf. Accessed 1 May 2010.

Hwang, H., and Powell, W. W. (2009). The rationalization of charity: The influences of professionalism in the nonprofit sector. *Administrative Science Quarterly* 54 (2), 268–298.

Jewell, C. J. (2007). *Agents of the welfare state: How caseworkers respond to need in the United States, Germany, and Sweden*. New York: Palgrave MacMillan.

Kahn, A. J. (1962). The social scene and the planning of services for children. *Social Work*, 7 (3) (July), 3–14.

Kramer, R. M. (1987). Voluntary agencies and the personal social services. In Walter W. Powell (ed.), *The nonprofit sector: A research handbook* (pp. 240–257). .New Haven: Yale University Press.

Kramer, R. M. (1982). *Voluntary agencies in the welfare state*. Berkeley and Los Angeles: University of California Press.

Lipsky, M. (1980). *Street-level bureaucracy*. New York: Russell Sage.

Majone, G. (1984). Professionalism and nonprofit organisations. *Journal of Health Politics, Policy and Law*, 8 (4) (Winter), 639–659.

McCurley, S. (2002). Keeping the community involved: Recruiting and retaining volunteers. In Robert D. Herman and associates (eds.), *Jossey Bass handbook of nonprofit leadership and management*, 2nd ed. (pp. 587–622). San Francisco: Jossey-Bass.

National Centre for Charitable Statistics (NCCS). (2010). *Programme Service Revenue by NTEE*. Unpublished draft. 03–11–2010.

Oregon Department of Human Services. (2009). *Evidence Based Practices in Oregon: An Overview*. Available at http://www.oregon.gov/DHS/mentalhealth/ebp/main.shtml. Accessed 3 May 2010.

Perlmutter, F. (1969). The effect of public funds on voluntary sectarian agencies. *Journal of Jewish Communal Service*, 45(4) (Summer), 312–321.

Powell, W. W., and. DiMaggio, P. J. (1983). The iron cage revisited: Institutional isomorphism and collective rationality in organisational fields. *American Sociological Review* 48, 147–160.

Rosegrant, S. (1998). *Oklahoma's milestones reimbursement system: Paying for what you get*. Kennedy School of Government Case Programme, Case # 1477.0.

Saidel, J., and Fletcher, K. (2005). Governance futures case studies. *The* Nonprofit Quarterly, 10 (3) (Fall), 34–53.

Salamon, L. M. (Ed.). (2002). *The tools of government*. New York: Oxford University Press.

Scarcella, C. A., Roseanna, B., Zielewski, E. H., and Geen, R. (2006). *The cost of protecting vulnerable children, V: Understanding state variation in child welfare spending*. Washington, D.C.: The Urban Institute.

Smith, D. (2009). Making management count: A case for theory- and evidence-based public management. *Journal of Policy Analysis and Management*, 28 (1), 497–505.

Smith, S. R. (2010a). The political economy of contracting. In Y. Hasenfeld (ed.), *Human service organisations as complex organisations* (pp. 139–169). Thousand Oaks, CA: Sage.

Smith, S. R. (2010b). Nonprofits and public administration: Reconciling performance management and citizen engagement. *American Review of Public Administration* (March), 40, 129–152.

Smith, S. R., and Lipsky, M. (1993), *Nonprofits for hire: The welfare state in the age of contracting*. Cambridge: Harvard University Press.

Sosin, M. (2010). Discretion in human service organisations: Traditional and institutional perspectives. In Y. Hasenfeld (ed.), *Human service organisations as complex organisations* (pp. 381–404). Thousand Oaks, CA: Sage.

Wilson, J. Q. (1967). The bureaucracy problem. *The Public Interest*, Issue No. 6. pp. 3–9.

Young, P. C., and Tippins, S. C. (2001). *Managing business risk: An organisation-wide approach to risk management*. Washington, D.C.: American Management Association.

Part V

Conclusions

14 Public Service Delivery and the Voluntary Sector

Trends, Explanations, and Implications

Ian Cunningham and Philip James

INTRODUCTION

The purpose of this collection of papers has been to increase our understanding of employment issues in the nonprofit voluntary sector in the light of its relationship with state funding bodies. In doing so it has sought to address two key areas of interest:

1. How the process of outsourcing is impacting the internal and external labour markets of voluntary organisations; and
2. How employers, employees, and their representatives deal with the tensions and contradictions from outsourcing, including the effect on service quality.

These questions have been pursued in the preceding chapters by reference to three overarching foci: the policy and labour market contexts within which the expansion of the role of voluntary sector organisations in the delivery of public services has been occurring; the way in which the employment policies and practices of such organisations have come under challenge and have been reformed; and how the work experiences of those employed in the voluntary sector have been changing. These questions have further been explored through analyses that have focussed on UK developments, particularly in relation to the first two of these themes, and on those occurring in a number of other Western industrialised countries—Australia, Canada, Germany and the United States—that have undergone similar processes of outsourcing to the third sector.

In this chapter we draw together the key themes to emerge from preceding chapters, focusing, as promised in the introductory chapter, on points of similarity, difference, and contradiction in the developments that have occurred, and on the dynamics that underlie them. The chapter commences therefore with an examination of the central features of what has been happening with regard to the role of the voluntary sector in public service delivery, which serves to highlight how the changes taking place have involved a combination of dominant trends surrounded by 'within trend' variations relating to different areas of service provision and different policy, and funding, contexts. It, then, moves on to explore what light the volume's chapters shed on how the developments taking place can most usefully be theorised. Finally, a third section identifies key areas of future research, and a fourth makes some, brief, final concluding observations.

SIMILARITIES, DIFFERENCES, AND CONTRADICTIONS

Policy Trajectories and Outcomes

At the most straightforward level, what emerges from the contributions in this volume is a common trend internationally toward the subcontracting of the delivery of public services to voluntary sector organisations. This trend has encompassed not only an expansion in the role of voluntary sector organisations but a shift in how delivery of public services is funded, which has involved proportionally less reliance on the provision by the state of grant income and a greater focus on funding via contracts. What also emerges, at the more general level, is that this trend has been informed by an almost ubiquitous New Public Management agenda encompassing pressures for cost savings, efficiency and value for money, and the adoption of more 'business-like' approaches to management; albeit an agenda that, as the chapters by Baines and Greer and his colleagues demonstrate, has been embraced to varying degrees in different countries, and for that matter in regions within them, in part because of marked national temporal differences with regard to their adoption.

At the same time, it has become apparent that this essentially neoliberal process of reform has been legitimised by reference to wider non-market-based rationalities. These rationalities may arise via the advocacy of wider human rights discourses centred on the need to develop less rigid and oppressive services tailored more to the (self-identified) needs of clients, as noted by Baines in her chapter on Canada, or by references to a number of alleged virtues of voluntary organisations, such as their closeness to clients, independence, and innovativeness, as observed by Davies in his on the UK.

How far these wider processes of legitimisation are authentic, as opposed to merely being used as supportive ideological tools, remains an open question. There is no doubt, though, that they sit uneasily with some of the outcomes associated with NPM-inspired market-based reform. These outcomes encompass, among others, reduced levels of funding, a greater standardisation of work processes (see further below), and a tendency for smaller organisations to be marginalised in the contracting marketplaces that have emerged.

There is no question, however, that the role of voluntary organisations has expanded considerably within all the countries considered in this volume. This point is graphically illustrated by the fact that the majority of social care in the UK is now, as Davies notes, provided by such organisations, as well as by the large increase that has occurred in the number of staff employed by them, as detailed by Clark and Wilding in their, also UK-focussed, chapter. How far this expansion has served, though, to improve service outcomes is, as Davies further notes in his chapter, far from clear on the basis of existing evidence.

Indeed, at the level of the workplace, the chapters in this volume (both UK and overseas) reveal significant tensions between worker perceptions of what is needed to provide quality services and their everyday reality. In particular, as will be explored in more detail below, it seems that workers have, as an accompaniment of outsourcing, commonly experienced increasing workloads, closer monitoring and bureaucracy, understaffing, and stress brought on by the pressures from the external environment that, in their view, compromise the ability they have to provide quality services. This view, in turn, raises the issue of how far the commissioners of services to the voluntary sector actually share the same notions of quality services as those who are employed in it, and the related question, raised in the chapter by Smith, among others, of how far nonprofit providers are able to remain true to their missions with regard to the servicing of their vulnerable clients.

Worker Orientations and Commitment

A theme stressed in a number of chapters is that in the main, despite NPM-inspired pressures for changes in the culture of organisations to be more 'business-like,' working in the nonprofit sector demands a high commitment vocation and orientation to a particular mission or cause from its employees. Hurrell et al., for example, although acknowledging that the sector is increasingly seeking to recruit from the pool of graduate labour of *players* (Brown and Hesketh, 2004), also identify how the sector benefits from the recruitment of *purists* who come to the sector with a commitment to the values of specific organisations.

Although coming from different theoretical perspectives, the chapters by Baines, Cunningham, and McDonald and Charlesworth add to this point by highlighting the high level of commitment to a cause among employees joining the sector. In his chapter, for example, Cunningham presents a perspective on the psychological contract which is multifaceted and acknowledges traditional relational and transactional orientations to work, but also involves employees possessing a *voluntary sector ethos* that is based on prior orientations of altruism, commitment to the well-being of particular vulnerable groups, related political or ideological beliefs, and a desire to care. The chapters by Baines and McDonald and Charlesworth, meanwhile, complement this effort to theorise worker orientations in the sector by highlighting the presence, of a highly gendered, and elastic, form of worker commitment which is based on prior orientations among women flowing from those they apply to care in the home.

Despite this high level of commitment among employees in the non-profit sector, which it can be noted has been borne out by other studies (Baines, 2004; Nickson et al., 2008; Cunningham, 2008), evidence from the contributions in this book indicate that it does not constitute a bottomless well of goodwill. Rather, the tensions caused by pressures from outsourcing, increased competition, and NPM-inspired managerialism, and its accompanying emphasis on cost cutting and efficiencies, combine to place considerable strain on the commitment of employees. Evidence from the UK presented in the chapters by Cunningham, and Cunningham and James, for example, suggests that this is the case with regard to the downward pressure on terms and conditions of employment that exist, and the same is true with regard to that provided in the contributions from Canada and Australia.

Skill Trajectories

In terms of skill trajectories in the marketised care sector, the chapters reveal a complex picture with regard to the degree to which we are witnessing a general deskilling of work in voluntary organisations as government monitoring, tighter controls over the labour process, and cost savings begin to impact. Clark and Wilding, for example, report how the introduction, or up-rating, of quality standards has led to the emergence of high-level skills gaps in areas such as strategic management, the management of human resources, information technology, legal knowledge, and fund raising. In a similar vein, in their chapter Hurrell et al., as already noted, highlight how outsourcing from government is leading to an increasing demand for graduates in areas such as business support. Similarly, Parry and Kelliher show that government-inspired workforce standards and skills agendas have prompted substance misuse providers to place a greater focus on staff development, and Smith's contribution points to the way in which a process of professionalisation has been engendered in the USA as a result of the performance management regimes imposed by government funders.

On the other hand, the chapters from our Canadian and Australian contributers show that the skills apparent in the sector's core activity of care work can be undermined and degraded within a climate of outsourcing, marketisation, and NPM. Baines, for example, highlights how NPM usually leads to calls from outsourced agencies to provide more services with less financial resources. As a consequence, organisations remove care activities that are seen as wasteful and require employees to adopt practices that are closely monitored, highly routinised, and tightly scripted, thus reducing employee discretion and skill. She also draws attention to the role that computer-based technology plays in processes of work intensification, increased supervision, and routinisation.

In their chapter, McDonald and Charlesworth provide us with insights into why aspects of care work are devalued and deskilled. Key to this process, in their view, are the cultural and gendered forces at work. They argue that the highly gendered nature of care work provides an institutional logic where such work is associated with inherent natural caring traits among women, rather than with particular workplace skills and interventions that are developed over a period of time to deal with challenging situations. In this way the dominant institutional order portrays care as a form of 'not quite work,' so that limited value is placed on it.

On the surface, the findings from these chapters, as well as from that by Smith, suggest some degree of polarisation of skills where, on the one hand, there is a significant sector demand for employees with high-level management/graduate skills, while, on the other, cost cutting and efficiency savings encourage the de-skilling of front-line workers. It is, nevertheless, debatable whether we are seeing the emergence of a ubiquitous polarisation of skill in the sector. Other studies have, for example, revealed how workers on front-line services who work with people with challenging behaviour are allowed to exercise significant discretion and autonomy at work (Baines and Cunningham, 2009). The conclusion we can reach from these findings is therefore that the impact of outsourcing and the NPM agenda on skills in the voluntary sector is complex and variable and encompasses both positive and negative developments.

Pay and Conditions

From a UK perspective, Clark and Wilding in their chapter indicate that there is a degree of uncertainty as to whether there has been a uniformly unfavourable shift in employment conditions (including pay) in voluntary organisations compared to the public sector, while acknowledging that such a shift may have occurred in the social care area. On the basis of their Anglo-German comparison, meanwhile, Greer et al. argue, more generally, that a 'race to the bottom' among contractors is not an inevitable outcome of marketisation.

The evidence, overall from across this volume, nevertheless, is of a steady degradation, internationally, of pay and other employment conditions for those delivering front-line services as a result of the impact of cost-cutting and efficiency pressures. At the same time, within particular national contexts, the evidence further suggests that the impact on pay and conditions is variable, with some organisations riding out the storm more successfully than others.

In seeking to explain this variability Greer et al. highlight how labour market factors can be influential in this regard, but also how the stability of the funding regime is vital in securing stable terms and conditions. The validity of this last point, in turn, receives support from the chapter by Cunningham and James, where it is noted that cuts in the Supporting

People programme appear to have had a particularly significant impact on terms and conditions: findings in line with similar studies exploring the impact of variable relationships in public sector outsourcing (see Cunningham, 2008).

This does not, however, negate the impact of numerous examples outlined in this volume of cases where financial restrictions from funding bodies in the UK, and elsewhere, are leading to pressures on employment terms and conditions. These pressures have stemmed from a variety of sources, including a failure by funders to provide inflationary uplifts, changes in policy direction and priorities, and related funding cuts, and they are shown in many instances to have led to pay cuts for existing workers; failures to provide annual inflationary pay rises in line with comparable workers in the public sector; the removal of incremental points on pay scales; and the recruitment of new employees on inferior terms and conditions. Furthermore, as also noted in the chapters by Cunningham, and Cunningham and James, other key areas of employment conditions, such as travel and subsistence allowances and pensions provision, can also be undermined at the same time as demands for greater worker flexibility (such as working more unsocial hours) and work intensity occur.

It also emerges that such trends can serve to compound existing sources of labour market disadvantage. McDonald and Charlesworth in their Australian study, for example, in illustrating how competition between agencies brings about efficiency pressures on pay which exacerbate recruitment problems, highlight how these NPM-influenced institutional pressures interact with the aforementioned normative force of gender to support the undervaluation and poor wages and conditions of care work. In a similar vein, in her chapter, Baines draws attention to how the position of ethnic minorities can be disproportionately affected given their significance in the Canadian voluntary sector workforce, while Cunningham and James reveal that other groups of staff, such as older workers and the disabled, can be similarly affected by the climate of insecurity created by competition across the sector.

The Role of Employee Voice and Governmental Regulation

Insofar as the marketisation of public services involves an inherent tendency to worsen the employment conditions and experiences of those employed in the voluntary sector, the question arises as to how far mechanisms exist to place limits on this marketisation as a result of governmental regulation, whether in the form of laws or policy requirements or forms of worker representation.

As regards the first of these potential countervailing influences, one of the contradictory features, at least in the UK, with regard to the process of marketisation, is how government and service commissioners have sought to simultaneously protect service quality and enhance 'business like' management by laying down employment-related requirements on those providing contracted services. The previously mentioned agendas relating to workforce standards and skills provide one illustration of this. Another, explored by Parry and Kelliher in their study of human resource management among substance misuse providers, is the way in which service commissioners have acted to prompt voluntary organisations to upgrade their human resource policies and practices more generally. This outcome has also been reported in other studies (Cunningham, 2008) and suggests that a disjunction may well at times be occurring in the treatment of staff, whereby their substantive terms and conditions are worsening at a time when they are becoming the subject of more formal, consistent, and fair procedural employment regimes, such as in relation to the handling of disciplinary, grievance, performance management, and absence issues.

Turning to the issue of legal regulation, in European Union member states transfers of staff from public to voluntary sector organisations as a result of outsourcing are covered by legal protections relating to their existing terms and conditions of employment. Three of the chapters, those by Cunningham, Greer et al., and Short, shed light on the effectiveness of these protections. In each case the analyses provided suggest that they are of relatively limited value.

In his chapter, for example, Short notes that employers often act to circumvent the requirements of the Transfer of Undertakings (Protection of Employment) Regulations. Similarly, the chapters by Cunningham and Greer et al. highlight that the role of these regulations, and their German equivalent, in protecting employees upon the transfer of their employment to another employer is patchy. Thus, in the former case, it was shown that although the impact of TUPE was apparent in shaping management's thinking in terms of being cautious with regard to changing the terms and conditions of employees transferred into their organisation as a consequence of EU procurement regulations, their provisions did not rule out such moves in the future as re-tendering became a more established feature of market conditions in the sector. Meanwhile, in the latter, Greer et al. raise concerns over the future of employee terms and conditions in the employment services of Germany once the time-limited protection concerning transfers is finished.

In his chapter, Short also sheds light, more generally, on the capacity, both current and potential, of unions to offer protection to the terms and conditions of voluntary sector workers, focusing particularly on the UK union for which he works, UNISON. In doing so, he reports that only around 25 percent of workers in the sector are union members, and that unions face major challenges in changing this situation against the background of hostility to union recognition among employers, the presence of small and fragmented workplaces, unsocial hours working, and a lack of member activism. He also, however, concludes that his union is now well placed to better address these challenges as a result of the adoption of a number of 'new ways of working.'

Other chapters to some extent echo this optimistic view by pointing to a degree of success in the UK and beyond in relation to union activity in the sector. A case in point is that by Baines, who reports how unions have become vehicles for participation and voice in the face of the curtailment of traditional opportunities for shared decision-making in the sector. Despite these illustrations of positive trade union activity, however, the overall picture to emerge from the chapters is that the prospects for protection of worker terms and conditions through collectivism are currently fragmented and therefore limited.

THEORISING RECENT DEVELOPMENTS

It is clear from the contributions to this volume, as well as other work reported elsewhere, that the study of employment issues within voluntary organisations in the era of contracting requires a multitheoretical approach. Indeed, the authors of them can be seen to have utilised a range of theoretical resources, including the construct of the 'market bureaucracy,' neo-institutional theory, feminist literature, interorganisational analytical frameworks, the concept of the psychological contract, and industrial relations and labour process perspectives. Given this, it seems appropriate to make some observations regarding the value of these diverse theoretical tools as a means of aiding the design of future research.

As Davies (in this volume) and others (see Cunningham and James, 2009) have noted, the concept of the 'market bureaucracy' (Considine, 1996) is of value in evaluating outcomes between the state and voluntary sector in industrialised economies because it provides a construct that enables them to be compared against a heuristic characterisation. That is a characterisation under which competition is placed at the centre of relations between purchasers and providers of services, and contracts between them are increasingly arms length, based on price and marked by the imposition of highly detailed and transparent, job or task specifications and requirements regarding performance standards and continuous improvement. Moreover, in being shown to also be of value descriptively, this characterisation serves to negate the assumption that outsourcing of services to independent providers represents the emergence of some postbureaucratic ideal.

This said, the market bureaucracy concept is stronger as a descriptive and analytical tool than as an explanatory one. One key resource utilised by a number of the contributers in this latter, explanatory, arena is that of neo-institutional theory. The chapter by Greer et al., for example, uses it to explain the pressures for institutional convergence across national boundaries arising from the NPM agenda and the way that these are producing common outcomes in the UK and Germany against the background of funding regimes that focus on costs and bureaucratic targets. Meanwhile, the chapter by McDonald and Charlesworth uses such theory to explore how in the Australian context an older institutional order of social justice has combined with the new dominant sphere of NPM to depress pay rates for a predominantly female workforce. Differently again, and operating at the level of the workplace rather than the nation, Parry and Kelliher reveal how institutional pressures inspired by NPM have been hugely influential in shaping human resource policies and practice in areas such as recruitment and training, while Smith similarly draws attention to the way in which such pressures have served more narrowly, to engender a process of professionalisation within voluntary agencies.

However, not withstanding its value to the analyses referred to above, institutional theory does have its limitations. Institutional pressures represent only one level of interaction that shapes relations between purchasers and providers (Marchington and Vincent, 2004; Vincent, 2005, for summaries). Another is the *interpersonal* one that encompasses the activities and influence across purchasers and suppliers of organisational actors labeled 'boundary spanning agents' (Marchington and Vincent, 2004). Papers in this volume, for example, emphasise how *organisational relations,* or the degree of (resource) dependency between organisations, are variable and salient in determining employment outcomes in nonprofit organisations.

Institutional theory also suffers from an inability to explain the exact way normative pressures from the NPM agenda impact on the day-to-day working practices and conditions of employees in the voluntary sector, nor how workers react to or resist such pressures. This is where other theoretical approaches can help. In particular, in order to gain a fuller understanding, several contributors in this volume shift the focus of analysis to management's efforts to cut costs and make efficiencies at the level of the labour process through exploring the incidence of work intensification and deskilling as a way to cope with the pressures of NPM.

An evaluation of worker resistance can also begin by utilising the labour process perspective, as Baines illustrates in her chapter through an examination of how workers resist management efforts through refusing to engage fully with processes which effectively undervalue traditional approaches to care. Several chapters, such as that by Short, also highlight, more generally, the value of exploring how the institutions of industrial relations through trade unions provide a useful focal point for studying the possibilities for resistance and protection of worker rights.

In attempting to understand the complex nature of worker orientations in the sector, Cunningham makes productive use of the concept of the psychological contract (albeit with some amendments) as a tool for exploring how workers react to changes to terms and conditions of employment or to the mission of their organisations as a consequence of the impact of purchaser-provider relations. Baines and McDonald and Charlesworth choose instead to more directly explore the influence of gender on worker orientations in nonprofit voluntary organisations and how these are linked, in a predominantly feminised workforce, to feminine notions of caring and self-sacrifice. This line of analysis raises the question as to whether the notion of a *voluntary sector ethos* should be developed to more directly embrace such traits as a means of providing a better understanding of employee orientations in the sector.

A CONTINUING RESEARCH AGENDA

All this said, the various contributions to the volume have served also to highlight a number of issues relating to the impact of outsourcing on employment relations in nonprofit organisations worthy of further investigation. To begin, it is clear that further study is needed in relation to the impact of particular funding regimes and streams. In particular, it would be useful to ascertain the social, political, and economic processes in policy decisions that appear to place greater value (monetary and otherwise) on certain care services as opposed to others, and their implications for terms and conditions of employment.

As has been seen from earlier chapters, the impact of outsourcing on pay and other conditions of employment appears to have been somewhat variable and to depend in part on the nature of the surrounding funding regimes. Against the background of significant public sector cuts internationally, there still, though, seems a need to gain a better understanding, ideally through longitudinal research, of how far processes of undermining pay and conditions in a market bureaucracy, such as the one in social care, are ubiquitous and hence will ultimately cause even the strongest and wealthiest voluntary organisations to embark on a race to the bottom over pay.

Another significant area of future investigation in the UK context and beyond is in relation to the impact of outsourcing on skills among the voluntary sector workforce. This could take a number of routes including exploring whether particular types of services lend themselves to processes of deskilling; examining the degree to which personalisation is leading to an up-skilling among front-line workers, and how far it counters forces for deskilling; and investigating to what extent the skills sets required of male and female care workers differ and, insofar as they do, the implications that these differences have for their work and the value placed on it.

Further work on the issue of employee voice also seems to be needed. A number of contributions to this volume have pointed to a threat to worker commitment within the voluntary sector flowing from the unrelenting pressures from the marketisation of social services. At the same time, evidence has also been presented of a fragmented collective response from the union movement, largely because of a lack of tradition of unionisation in the sector. The role that individual and collective voice does, and could, play in protecting such commitment, and thereby the quality of services, consequently seems an issue meriting greater and more detailed attention.

Indeed, there are several avenues of research in the specific area of service quality that could usefully be pursued. The chapter by Davies illustrates that the links between voluntary sector provision, outsourcing, and quality of service is at best unproved. Further research could therefore usefully be undertaken on these linkages. Such research could begin by attempting to establish what the different parties to the purchaser-provider relationship understand by the term 'quality' in service provision, and, where there are differences, how these are resolved, if at all. This could be followed by investigations into how workforce issues such as staffing numbers, skills, and qualifications and working hours are factored into assessments of quality by purchasers during any outsourcing or re-tendering process.

While it is clear that one of the benefits of this volume is the international comparisons we have been able to draw upon, these have only given us glimpses of the convergence and divergence in trends relating to the employment outcomes of outsourcing public services to voluntary organisations across developed industrial economies. Moreover, only one of these comparisons (Greer et al.) is a dedicated international comparison. This leads us to suggest a need for more dedicated international research, perhaps including countries such as New Zealand, which has gone down the road of significant outsourcing of its social care provision, as well as European ones. In the latter case it would, in particular, be useful to explore in more detail the extent to which EU employment protection legislation through TUPE provides sufficient protection for the terms and conditions of employees who have been transferred to another employer after re-tendering exercises.

Moreover, there are other areas of the sector that have largely gone unresearched. The new coalition government in the UK has heralded a new policy of allowing parents, private companies, and voluntary organisations to establish their own schools. Again, in the latter case, the implications for the employment of teachers etc by voluntary organisations that take up this option will deserve serious scrutiny. There are also issues worthy of further sector-based employment research surrounding the increasing use of faith-based organisations in providing social services; the employment implications of voluntary organisations securing public service contracts through consortia; and the employment issues arising from mergers of voluntary organisations. Moreover, this volume has arguably confined itself to the institutional fields of social care and employment services. Yet the voluntary sector populates a range of other activities where issues relating paid employment are no less significant. For instance, we have limited understanding of how overseas aid voluntary organisations manage their staff and the degree to which they face the same challenges in managing expatriates compared to private sector multinationals. In addition, there is limited understanding regarding employment relations in environmental organisations.

CONCLUSION

As a relatively new focus of study in the area of employment relations, the voluntary sector presents a rich and varied field of research upon which to utilise a wide variety of conceptual and theoretical tools. In the context of the outsourcing of public services to voluntary organisations, this volume has addressed a number of important and central issues within this field, including staff recruitment, trends in pay and conditions, worker orientations, skill trajectories, the redesign of work tasks and processes, and the role of gender in shaping various aspects of employment relationships in the sector, as well as the more general issue of how the dynamics of purchaser-provider relations impact such dimensions of employment. It has also done so drawing on, relatively uniquely, both domestic and internationally orientated contributions.

As the foregoing discussion has highlighted, however, there is much scope for further research to be undertaken in relation to the specific issues explored in the present volume and others that have not. It is also clear that, against the backdrop of the growing trend internationally to transfer the delivery of public services to the voluntary sector, there is much scope for such research to have a strong policy orientation given the implications that this process of transference has for both those delivering services and those receiving them. In particular, in the light of how this transfer of provision seems to commonly involve an 'escape' from collective voice mechanisms that are typically found in public sector employment, as well as a reduction in the work experiences of those delivering services, important, and related, questions meriting closer attention include how this transfer of provision affects the quality of services that are subsequently provided, and what can be done to ensure that these impacts are not negative.

Indeed, there also seems a need in the light of such analyses to engage with the ideological and policy underpinnings of the current trend internationally to outsource the delivery of public services and the factors that are serving, more generally, to differentially shape how it is approached and operationalised within particular national and subnational settings. For greater understanding in these regards would do much to shed better light on such matters as whether the outcomes of outsourcing vary within different policy contexts and whether some such contexts can be viewed as yielding better delivery outcomes than others.

It is to be hoped that, having read this volume, academic readers will be motivated to address this need for further, policy-orientated, research, and that policymaker and practitioner readers will be similarly prompted to reflect on the wisdom of their current policies and practices and to amend them in the light of the evidence and arguments provided by this volume's contributors. Certainly, the editors feel that their endeavours in compiling the volume will have been rewarded if it serves to engender such motivation and reflection.

BIBLIOGRAPHY

Baines, D. (2004). Caring for nothing. Work organization and unwaged labour in social services. *Work, Employment, and Society*, 18 (2), 267–295.

Baines, D., and Cunningham, I. (2009). *White knuckle care work—Working on the edge with the most excluded.* Paper presented at the 27th Annual Labour Process Conference, Edinburgh, April 6–8.

Brown, P., and Hesketh, A. (2004). *The mismanagement of talent; Employability, and jobs in the knowledge economy.* Oxford: Oxford University Press.

Considine, M. (1996). Market bureaucracy? Exploring the contending rationalities of contemporary administrative regimes. *Labour and Industry*, 7 (1), 1–28.

Cunningham, I. (2008). *Employment relations in the voluntary sector.* London: Routledge.

Cunningham, I., and James, P. (2009). The outsourcing of social care in Britain: What does it mean for the voluntary sector workers? *Work, Employment, and Society*, 23, (2), 363–375.

Marchington, M., and Vincent, S. (2004). Analysing the influence of institutional, organizational, and interpersonal forces shaping inter-organisational relations. *Journal of Management Studies*, 41 (6), 1029–1056.

Nickson, D., Warhurst, C., Dutton, E., and Hurrell, S. (2008). A job to believe in: Recruitment in the Scottish voluntary sector. *Human Resource Management Journal*, 18 (1), 20–35.

Vincent, S. (2005) .Really dealing: A critical perspective on inter-organizational exchange networks. *Work, Employment, and Society*, 19 (1), 47–65.

Contributors

Donna Baines, Associate Professor, Social Work and Labour Studies, McMaster University.

Eleanor Burt, Senior Lecturer in Voluntary Sector Policy and Management, School of Management, University of St. Andrews.

Sara Charlesworth, Principal Research Fellow, Centre for Applied Social Research, RMIT University.

Jenny Clark, Research Manager, National Council for Voluntary Organisations.

Ian Cunningham, Reader in Employment Relations, Department of Human Resource Management, University of Stathclyde.

Steve Davies, Senior Research Fellow, School of Social Sciences, Cardiff University.

Ian Greenwood, Lecturer in Industrial Relations and Human Resource Management, Leeds University Business School.

Ian Greer, Senior Research Fellow in Comparative Employment Relations, Leeds University Business School.

Scott A. Hurrell, Lecturer on Work and Employment Studies, Stirling Management School, University of Stirling.

Philip James, Professor of Employment Relations, Oxford Brookes University.

Clare Kelliher, Reader in Work and Organisation, School of Management, Cranfield University.

Catherine McDonald, Professor of Social Work and Head, Academic Group (Social Work, Social Science, Community Studies, Youth Work and the Centre for Applied Social Research) School of Global Studies, Social Science and Planning, RMIT University.

Dennis Nickson, Professor of Service Work and Head of Department, Department of Human Resource Management, University of Stathclyde.

Emma Parry, Principal Research Fellow, School of Management, Cranfield University.

Dora Scholarios, Professor of Work Psychology, Department of Human Resource Management, University of Strathclyde.

Mike Short, National Officer, Community and Voluntary Sector, UNISON.

Steven Rathgeb Smith, Professor of Public Policy, Waldemar A. Nielsen Chair in Philanthropy, Public Policy Institute, Georgetown University, Washington, D.C.

Mark Stuart, Professor of Human Resource Management and Employment Relations, Leeds University Business School.

Chris Warhurst, Professor of Work and Organisational Studies, the University of Sydney.

Karl Wilding, Head of Research, National Council for Voluntary Organisations.

Index

Redundancy, 8, 123; precautionary
redundancy notices, 56
Restructuring; avoidance of TUPE
obligations, 56; impact on staff
participation, 178–79; market
orientated, 9, 21, 124, 164,
169–74; pay systems, 56; state—
voluntary sector relationship, 32
Re-tendering, 139–41; impact on
employee psychological contracts and commitment, 142–
150
Ridley, N; public service provision, 20

S

Scottish Council for Voluntary Organisations, 24, 89, 93; full-cost
recovery, 92
Select Committees; Health Select Committee, 30: Public Administration Select Committee, 24, 26,
27, 30, 31
Service commissioners; behaviour
change; cost concerns, 126, 133;
employment standards, 230–31;
full cost recovery, 133
Service quality, 9; employee concerns,
144, 148, 227; full-cost recovery, 125, 133; future research,
234–35; impact of job insecurity,
130; impact of marketisation,
21, 26, 50, 57, 123, 133, 196,
198, 230–231, 234; psychological contract, 9; recruiting personnel from other sectors, 163;
retendering, 129, 136, 139–140,
150; union campaigns, 69, 179,
234; vouchers, 207; workforce
skills, 47, 176, 220
Skills, 4, 5–6, 37, 228–29; board members of nonprofits, 108, 214;
competency framework, 114,
115; deskilling, 128, 173, 176;
dilution, 129; employer needs and
responses, 48, 82, 85, 91; full-
cost recovery, 93, 99, 133; gaps,
47–48; gender, 169, 194; government guidance, 82; graduate skill
shortages, 88, 89–90, 91, 95, 96,
100; NHS framework, 56, 69;
polarisation, 229; public service
delivery. 46, 47; regulation, 7,
80–81; resourcing training and
development, 48, 82; shortages, 6,

46–48, 89; skills-based assessed,
115, 117; Skills for Health, 76;
Skills Third Sector, 69; social
care, 49; soft skills, 48; substance
misuse, 76; union campaigning,
161, 179; union learning, 68;
volunteers, 112, 218
Small workplaces/enterprises, 5;
consortia and merger, 29, 219;
employment share, 42; expertise
of board members, 213; impact
of competitive tendering, 27, 29,
66, 164, 165, 219, 226; information technology, 177; pay policies, 130; redeployment policies,
129; resource dependency, 159;
services to the unemployed, 159;
skills gaps, 47–48; skills shortages, 47; training, 42–43, 69;
staff recruitment, 114–16, 212;
support for, 165; union membership, recognition and recruitment drives, 6, 54, 59, 61, 67,
69, 165, 231; volunteer deploy-
ment, 107; works councils, 161
Social care; Canada, 9; contribution
of voluntary sector, 5, 17, 21,
227; employment condition and
insecurity, 128–30, 133, 229;
graduate recruitment and shortages (*see* Skills); outsourcing, 16,
73, 124–25, 126, 133; outsourcing social care in USA, 207; pay
trends, 45, 101; private sector
provision, 17, 26; qualifications
accreditation, 76; recruitment
problems (*see* Skills) retendering,
27, 142–49; skills shortages (*see*
Skills); union organisation and
recruitment, 62, 180; voluntary
sector workforce levels, 43, 125
Social movement unionism, 179, 180
Staff turnover, 132, 147, 160; Australia,
196
Substance misuse, 74; employer HR
policies, 76–84, 231; regulation
of sector 75–76; worker qualification standards, 76, 228

T

Temporary workers, 6, 42, 156, 175, 193
Trade unions, 41, 231–32; influence, 6,
42, 164, 166, 174–75, 178–79,
197; membership, 55; member